Through the Gate

Ted Watson

Through the Gate

The true story of Warrant Officer
Edwin Watson, Légion d'honneur
No.630 Squadron
RAF Bomber Command
World War Two

by

Kenneth Ballantyne

First Published in Great Britain in 2018
by Laundry Cottage Books
Admaston, Shropshire, England
TF5 0AD

Tel: 01952 – 223931

Email: mingulay187@gmail.com

ISBN 978-0-9550601-9-9

Proofreading & editing by
Sue Browning Editing and Proofreading

By the same author & published in
Great Britain by Laundry Cottage Books:

Another Dawn Another Dusk
ISBN 978-0-9550601-3-7

All the Things You Are
ISBN 978-0-9550601-4-4

First Wave
ISBN 978-0-9550601-3-7

Holding the Line
ISBN 978-0-9550601-8-2

Through the Gate
ISBN 978-0-9550601-9-9

The Journey
[Title no longer available]

Other titles published in Great Britain
by Laundry Cottage Books:

'J' for Johnnie
John Trotman, DFC*, Légion d'honneur
ISBN 978-0-9550601-7-5

The D-Day Dodger
Albert F Darlington
ISBN 978-0-9550601-2-0

Bibliography

A Higher Call; Adam Makos; Atlantic Books 2013

Bomber Command 1936-1968:
  An Operational & Historical Record; Ken Delve;
  Pen & Sword Aviation, 2005

Bomber County Aviation Resource

Bomber History - The Canal Raids; Malcolm Brooke

Coastal Dawn -
  Blenheims in Action from the Phoney War
  through the Battle of Britain; Andrew D Bird;
  Grub Street, 2012

Cockfield Fell Heritage Walk - *This is Durham*

International Monetary Fund GDP [PPP] per Capita Index 2016

Meteorological Office Digital Library & Archive

North-East Diary 1939-1945; Roy Ripley & Brian Pears

Raffles Hotel - Brief Chronology

The Bomber Command War Diaries;
  Martin Middlebrook & Chris Everitt;
  Midland Publishing Limited, [my edition] 1995

The Luftwaffe Album:
  Bomber & Fighter Aircraft of the German Air Force
  1933-1945 - Joachim Dressel & Manfred Griehl,
  translated by MJ Shields, FIInfSc, MITL;
  Arms & Armour Press, 1997

The World Carrot Museum [ref. Woolton Pie 1941]

United Nations Human Development Index 2016

West Bromwich Local History Society -
  West Bromwich at War 1939-45

Wikipedia - Cockfield, County Durham

www.rafbombercommand.com

www.rafww2butler.wordpress.com [Aircraft Q failed to return]

www.steamindex.com – [ref. George & Jeremiah Dixon]

Acknowledgements

My greatest thanks, of course, go to Ted Watson who has shared his memories, experiences, photographs, log book, wartime diary and inner feelings with me during the creation of this account. He has also spent many hours both with pen and paper and with me, recalling the events, places and people which have brought his story to life in such a vivid way.

A very big thank you is also due to Ted's daughter, Julie, who despite a busy life at work and home has acted variously as facilitator, her father's PA, post mistress, and together with her husband David, kind and generous host for our many visits.

The impressive main picture on the front cover is reproduced by the very kind permission of the artist, Alex Hamilton GAvA. The painting is called *Foxtrot Finals*, a copy of which I happily own. I also have a copy of another of Alex's paintings, *Strike in the Aegean*, which, like many of his paintings, depicts an actual event during the war. Alex's website showing his stunning paintings can be found at www.alexhamilton.net and is well worth a visit.

My thanks to Louise Bush of the Lincolnshire Aviation Heritage Centre for permission to use the image of the museum's very finely restored watch tower on the back cover, a building with which Ted is particularly familiar.

I am grateful to Howard Parker who has kindly allowed me to recount his childhood experience of being trapped in a flooded cellar during the West Bromwich blitz, and of his brother's service with No.161 (Special Duties) Squadron at RAF Tempsford.

To all those people, many anonymous, who have generously uploaded information to the Internet which, piece by piece, helped to shape, cross-reference and contextualise some of the details in this book. My particular thanks are due to the authors of two outstanding pieces of work and I am very grateful to each of them. Malcolm Brooke for kindly permitting me to rely on his work on the Dortmund-Ems Canal raids at www.bomberhistory.co.uk which provides an invaluable commentary upon each raid and its effect. My account of the defensive strategy and gun emplacement arraignment is taken from Malcolm's work and I have thus been able to cross-reference Ted's experiences of attacking the canal with the raid's impact. Brian Pears and the late Roy Ripley for creating the North-East Diary 1939-45 and for uploading it to the internet at www.ne-diary.genuki.uk for everyone to enjoy. It is a substantial body of work which provides a fascinating insight upon the daily events along the coast of north-east England and the borders of Scotland. It is thanks to Brian and Roy's work that I have been able to cross-reference much of Ted's own early memories, and from their work have sourced the stories of Squadron Leader Douglas Farquhar, DFC, and the incident involving Oberleutnant zur See Friedrich Koch.

As always, my thanks are due to Martin Middlebrook and Chris Everitt for their seminal work, *The Bomber Command War Diaries*. It is the indispensible reference book about Bomber Command during the Second World War and few authors of the subject would, or could, be without it.

Photographs are reproduced with the kind permission of the respective owners, or from my own collection or are in the public domain.

I am again indebted to Sue Browning of Sue Browning, Editing and Proofreading for once more kindly correcting my literary waywardness and grammatical inexactitudes, and for guiding the flow of this story through the pitfalls of writing. Where I have dabbled with the manuscript after she returned it to me, I take full responsibility for any resulting errors.

Last but never least, my wife Elaine has steadfastly supported me through the years of writing this latest book, read the many drafts, and sensitively suggested alterations and improvements. Without that support the manuscript would not have seen the light of day.

Kenneth Ballantyne

The Author

Born to Army officer parents at Gibraltar Military Hospital in 1949, Kenneth Ballantyne was educated at schools across Europe, Scotland and England. His father, a career soldier with the Royal Artillery, had served throughout the Second World War, as had his mother, who trained as a nurse at the outbreak of hostilities and then joined the First Aid Nursing Yeomanry before later serving with the Women's Royal Army Corps in post-war years.

Part of Kenneth's early years were spent living and playing amongst the bomb craters left in the German Ruhr by RAF Bomber Command. When he was seven, his parents took him and his brother Iain to the Reichswald Forest War Cemetery to educate them about the true price that had been paid for their lives and freedom, an experience which became an indelible memory.

After several years as a police officer, Kenneth graduated and then practised law as a solicitor before retiring to combine his love of writing with his interest in history and the personal experiences of those who fought in the World Wars, an interest which had grown out of his formative years in Service life and that visit to the Reichswald Forest. A member of the Bomber Command Association, the Shropshire Aircrew Association, the Metheringham Airfield Museum and Friends of RAF Skellingthorpe, he now spends much of his time collecting and recording the true stories and experiences of the men and women who served on the Home Front and in the Armed Services during the two World Wars as an important historical project for an enduring legacy.

Kenneth established Laundry Cottage Books in 2005 in order to put his first book into print, and several other titles have followed. He has also helped veterans write their own accounts, some of which have been published by Laundry Cottage Books.

Dedication

To the lasting memory of Enid Watson

- and -

For Julie, Stewart, David, Stephanie and James

- and -

To all who served on No.630 Squadron
RAF Bomber Command
in the air and on the ground
during World War Two

Contents

Through the Gate

Introduction

When the British government reluctantly and very belatedly issued the richly deserved Arctic Star on 19th December 2012, it was a golden opportunity to redress the balance, rectify the injustice and recognise the debt owed to all those men and women who had served so unstintingly with RAF Bomber Command by also issuing them with a campaign Star. It is difficult to avoid the conclusion that the government still believes that the deaths of 55,573 aircrew as well as the many men and women killed on RAF aerodromes are not worth a medal.

Gongs, honours and titles are readily handed to sports people, pop artists, actors, the business community, political 'friends' et al., many of whom have already been richly rewarded for following their chosen careers. But nowhere is there a medal for the truly brave, for the people who really are heroes and deserve to be called so, those of RAF Bomber Command who served in the air and on the ground with such dedication and distinction during World War Two. Few who fought in that war did so as a chosen career; for the vast majority it was thrust upon them, disrupting their future and for too many denying them of any future at all.

'Out, damned spot! Out, I say!' As Lady Macbeth sought to wash the blood of King Duncan from her hands, so have successive prime ministers from Winston Churchill onward, sought to wash the blood of German cities from theirs. The men and women of Bomber Command, doomed youth, who had no passing bells, did not wield the dagger but have been accused of the responsibility and have suffered the unjustified censure for the decision of others.

A whole generation fought against Nazi fascist rule to uphold the principle that genuine democracy is preferable to dictatorship in all its guises, including elective dictatorship. The salutary lesson that Adolf Hitler came to power through the ballot box is still a powerful one for all democratic nations. It was only after securing power that he dispensed with freedom. Today, there are clear parallels with the 1930s and many challenges to our way of life remain, some of which are not only deeply insidious but are also too often conveniently ignored or steadfastly denied to exist.

The great sadness for the German people is that they were seduced by Hitler's rhetoric. Most Germans were not Nazi Party members and many were strongly opposed to it, although overt opposition or expressed criticism would only lead to the Dachau concentration camp, opened in the mid-1930s. The general populace of Germany did not want war but they did want their national pride returned. Along with a requirement to pay immense reparation, Germany had been stripped of its air force, its empire, and much besides by the Treaty of Versailles. The country was plunged into a deep depression long before the 1929 financial crash caught the rest of the world. Versailles was the revenge of a victorious public and had intentionally emasculated Germany. Hitler tapped into the natural desire of a nation to restore its pride.

In 1935 he called the bluff of Versailles and re-formed the German Air Force, the Luftwaffe. At first, he used the cover of Lufthansa, Europe's largest civil airline, to train his pilots and navigators, and to test the flying times of routes across the continent such as Berlin to London, ready for future bombing raids. By 1938, the swastika was openly displayed; appeasement had emboldened. However, Nazi party members in the Luftwaffe were few and far between. German law forbade military personnel joining the Party once they had enlisted or been conscripted.

The relentless aerial battles in the skies over occupied Europe and the Mediterranean was for the most part, fought between the decent young men of the RAF doing their duty and the decent young men of the Luftwaffe doing theirs. Neither wanted war but both were compelled by duty, conscience, necessity or force to fight. The cost was horrific for both sides. Of the Luftwaffe's 28,000 fighter pilots who saw combat during the war, only 1,200 survived. The story of 1st Leutnant Franz Stigler stands as an example to all. He learned morality in combat from Leutnant Gustav Roedel, his outstanding commander in the Western desert, "*You follow the rules of war for you, not your enemy. You fight by rules to keep your humanity.*" That was the essential difference between the Nazis and the rest of Germany; the Nazis had no humanity.

In 2013, I received a telephone call from Julie Blake kindly ordering a copy of my then latest title, *First Wave*. The book was, as had been all my other titles which she bought, destined for her father, an RAF Bomber Command veteran of thirty-seven missions during World War Two. During the conversation Julie remarked that I really ought to meet her father.

The arrangements were made and Elaine and I travelled to County Durham. What I found in Ted Watson was a man who had not only kept his records and photographs from before the war, his wartime diary, and his operational log book but was also a delightful and unassuming man who was simply a pleasure to be with and to listen to.

From the age of eleven, when children went outside to play, made their own entertainment and had friends in the real world, scouting was his great passion. The movement has adapted to that changing world and remains as popular as ever, with more than 20,000 young people waiting to join, held back only by a shortage of scout leaders.

The pinnacle of Ted's scouting life came in 1943 when he was given the rare distinction of being appointed King's Scout. It came at almost the precise moment that he started his RAF aircrew training, a task he had volunteered for even though he was in a reserved occupation.

As I got to know Ted better or, more truthfully, as he got to know me, the deeper he dug into his emotional memories, some of which were clearly still painful. What emerged at the end was a compelling story of commitment, loyalty, service, courage and sensitivity. It is a story which carries the reader with it as the principal witness to Ted Watson's life.

Kenneth Ballantyne
Laundry Cottage
8th January 2018

King's Scout Edwin Watson 1943

Through the Gate

Chapter One

"Nature study will show you how full of beautiful and wonderful things God has made the world for you to enjoy. Be contented with what you have got and make the best of it. Look on the bright side of things instead of the gloomy one."

From Lt-General Lord Baden-Powell's last message to scouts [1940]

It was a lazy wind that blew off Cockfield Fell that early evening, cutting through my clothes like a hot knife in butter. My face and knees were stung by flying crystals of ice that, masquerading as rain, danced and cavorted in a wild conspiracy with the wind. If I didn't get a move on, I would get a soaking as well as being chilled to the bone before I reached the 1st Cockfield Boy Scout Group Headquarters for our weekly meeting.

I didn't possess a coat and I had saved hard to help my parents buy my uniform. I put my head down and lengthened my stride along the narrow country lane leading from home to Cockfield village. There were no cat's eyes, no central white lines, no footpath, almost no road signs and even less traffic. On a pleasant day, it was an enjoyable two miles or so to walk, but this evening it was simply the route that lay between me and my destination.

School had finished as usual at 4.30pm; I had gone home, got changed into my scout uniform, had my tea and set off in what dismal daylight remained in the sky. The rain made no effort to ease and I quickened my pace. After about ten minutes, a Rolls Royce glided past me with a gentle shwoosh of its tyres on the wet road, its engine silent against the wind. Even in the pale light and the rain, the coachwork of its body panels gleamed.

I knew whose car it was; everybody in the area knew it. There were not too many cars on the roads of northeast England in the middle of the worst depression the world had ever seen and even fewer were Rolls Royces. It belonged to Lord Barnard, who lived at the splendid Raby Castle. The car slowed and then stopped some fifty or sixty yards ahead of me. The chauffeur lowered his window and beckoned me. I ran up to the car and as I reached it, Lord Barnard pushed open the rear door.

"Are you going to the troop meeting tonight, Ted?"

"Yes, sir, I am," I replied.

"You don't want to walk in this weather. Jump in and I'll give you a lift. I'm going through Cockfield to my meeting in Durham."

I couldn't believe my luck and greeted his invitation with joy and enthusiasm. With the rain getting heavier, to be given a lift in any car was a treat; to be given a lift in a Rolls Royce was a real thrill, but for an eleven-year-old to be given a lift by Lord Barnard was a huge privilege and said a great deal about the man.

Christopher William Vane was the 10th Baron Barnard. He had served as a major in the Westmorland and Cumberland Yeomanry during the Great War, in which he had twice been wounded and had been awarded the Military Cross. He had fairly recently, in 1930, been invested as a Commander of the Order of St Michael and St George. The Order, which is in the personal gift of the monarch, ranked as the sixth highest honour in Britain at the time of his investiture; today it ranks fourth. However, what was of greater importance and significance to me on that day was that I was being given a lift by the Scout Association Commissioner for County Durham.

He was not at all aloof and we chatted easily for the few minutes it took to travel the remaining distance to the village. The Rolls whispered to a stop outside the building just as Leslie Young, our scout master arrived, together with my friends Jack Rand, who was the Troop Leader, and Joseph Teasdale. The car had barely stopped as the chauffeur slipped from behind the steering wheel and opened the back door for Lord Barnard to climb out. Leslie and my two friends immediately saluted the County Commissioner but, as I jumped out of the car a second or two later, I could have knocked them all over with a feather. The Commissioner returned our salutes and left us to our duties and business. As a result of this chance meeting with Lord Barnard, he offered to pick me up each month thereafter outside the Sun Inn at the junction of Esperley Lane with the main road when he travelled to Durham City Scout Headquarters for his Commissioners' meeting.

During his time as County Commissioner, he was a great scouting inspiration to me and to dozens of other young lads involved in the scout movement, including such simple kindnesses as offering to take two or three of us to the HQ in Durham from time to time. We greatly appreciated these visits as we would not have been able to go otherwise.

Although the Great War and its aftermath had spawned the beginnings of a shift in the structure of British society, it would be thirty years and another war before the true impact was felt. In the meantime, the rural population remained fairly settled in communities which were established and cohesive providing an essential network of mutual support. People knew each other and would stop and speak, even if only in convivial greeting.

My parents, Edgar and Grace Watson, lived in Rose Cottage near the village of Cockfield, County Durham. My mother had five sisters, Alice, Amy, Meggie, Mary and Annie. Thursday 8th January 1925 saw the barometer slowly falling over the whole of the British Isles as a deepening area of low pressure moved in and brought unseasonably mild conditions on a south-westerly wind. Darkening clouds, heavy with the threat of rain, scudded by overhead.

As the dull light of the late afternoon began to fade, my mother knew it was almost time. She wrapped her shawl tightly around her shoulders, closed the front door of Rose Cottage and set out across the field footpaths to my grandparents' farm some two miles away and about a quarter of a mile off the main road. A few hours later, whilst the wind outside moaned its way across the land and rattled the farmhouse windows, I was born. Over the next few years, I was followed by my sister Grace, and brothers Eric, Maurice, Howard and Frank, all of whom were born at home.

The world into which I had arrived would be unrecognisable today. When I was growing up, we were immensely proud of Britain and of what the people of these small islands had achieved over many centuries. It is now unfashionable to feel that pride for reasons that are many and complex. The funeral of King Edward VII in May 1910 saw the last great gathering in Britain of royal households from around the world. In addition to political leaders, forty-nine royal heads of state, including nine reigning European kings, attended, although many would lose their thrones and some their lives within the next few years. Fortune smiled on the House of Saxe-Coburg & Gotha, though. On 17th July 1917, George V changed the name to Windsor, and with the British Empire at its maximum extent, the monarchy survived. The King reigned over one in four of the world's population and the Empire embraced a quarter of the earth's land mass. It was indeed true that the sun never set on the British Empire, the largest and probably the greatest that the world has ever seen.

The drinking water supply to my grandparents' farm was a well, which necessitated the task of drawing the water up every morning. It is only when we have to carry water that we realise how much we use, as every camper soon finds out. A dairy farm uses a great deal in connection with the animals as well as the domestic use of the family, and so garnering water from different sources was a major task, and carrying it had to be undertaken each day, often several times. On one occasion, though, the job had a particularly bitter twist for my grandfather when, as he leaned over the wall of the well, his fob watch slipped out of his pocket, and, complete with silver chain, plunged down into the well, never to be seen again. In the end, my grandparents had to leave the farm as it gradually and quite literally fell down around them, undermined by the steady collapse of the ancient workings which lay beneath it.

My home at Rose Cottage was in Esperley Lane and was about two miles from Cockfield. There was a farm about a quarter of a mile away with the next one some mile and a half distant. The cottage was two up, two down and already over a hundred years old. It had no electricity, a single cold tap for running water, and an outside privy toilet. What heating we had came from the coal-fired kitchen range. There was no refuse collection service for us, not that very much got thrown away, and with no plastic, the main medium for packaging was glass. The jars and bottles for which we had no further use were buried in a dip in one of our fields, as was the custom, there waiting to become the collectible items of the future.

The cottage came with a smallholding of fifteen acres set in six long, narrow fields running beside the main road, a relic from the medieval ridge-and-furrow land usage. We grew a hay crop and turnips to give winter feed for our cow as well as summer grazing. The land also produced some oats, barley and arable crops for sale. We kept two pigs and about thirty hens, which were divided between three coops. The milk from the cow was cooled and then filtered through an Alva-Laval separator. My mother made butter from the cream that was produced by agitating it until the thick liquid formed into lumps and became sticky. Next, she squeezed the whey from it so that it made a solid mass. Then using two wooden butter pats, she tapped and patted the whole lot into butter; rather like playing table tennis on her own.

Every week Mother would bake bread, pies, pasties, tarts, and sometimes cakes in the big bread oven at the side of the range, all to feed her hungry growing family. The cottage also had a large kitchen garden in which my dad grew all the vegetables and fruit that we needed to eat. Other delights such as nuts, berries and mushrooms we picked wild from the hedgerows and fields.

However, whilst our animals kept us supplied with milk, butter, eggs and winter pork in all its forms, the smallholding was not large enough to support the family. Consequently, my father needed another income, which he obtained from his work as a wagon-way man. His job, which covered three local mines, was to install and maintain the coal-transporting wagon ways which were powered by steam engines. This work included the tunnel under the main road, the bridges, and the screens; all part of moving coal to the main railway station.

One of my uncles kept the Sun Inn, which had a small commercial garage attached to it; both businesses still trade today. My aunt and uncle were almost our closest neighbours and I often spent time there. My cousin Larry from the Sun was about the same age as me, but when he was fourteen he developed a carbuncle. The doctor thought that the underlying infection was most likely to be *streptococcus pyrogenes*, which in the days before antibiotics was very often fatal. Poor hygiene, such as not hand washing after going to the lavatory is, even today, one of the most common sources of this infection, although in the late 1930s Larry could also have contracted it from drinking raw milk or eating an infected egg. Despite the doctor's efforts and my aunt's ministrations, Larry's condition deteriorated rapidly as he developed sepsis. He died a few days later.

All of my infant and early teenage years were spent living in and around the small village of Cockfield, which nestles on the eastern slopes of the Pennines. Its name is linked to Cockfield in Suffolk. In the early 13th century, Sir Robert de Cockfield, or more likely de Cokefeld, a Suffolk knight who was judge and sheriff for Henry III in this part of the north, decided to reclaim the ancient manor and estates of the area around the modern-day village. He named it Beaurepayr, meaning 'beautiful place'. However, his English tenants were not too partial to the French language and very quickly substituted his own name for the village and the nearby fell. It may well be that this was when the French 'de Cokefeld' became anglicised to Cockfield.

Maintaining its early medieval origins, this was never a stereotypical northern mining village, and a stranger strolling through its environs could be excused for believing that he or she was in the Cotswolds, the Yorkshire Dales or anywhere south of Bristol. Front Street, the main route through the village, is not lined by back-to-back mining cottages but by detached double-fronted stone-built villas. Such terraces as there are, are substantial and spacious. The crowning glory of Cockfield is the expansive, tree-lined village green in the centre, which continues in both directions along Front Street as exceptionally wide, neatly kept treed verges.

As the coal on the Fell ran out in the 19th century, so the south-west Durham coalfield opened up and the population of the village expanded significantly. Nevertheless, it has always retained and maintained its rural heritage. The coal seams in the area and across the Fell run comparatively shallow and it was some of these workings which would, centuries later, cause the downfall of my grandparents' farm.

The village nestles 750 feet up the Pennines and lies in the shadow of Cockfield Fell, which slopes down to the Gaunless River and valley. The Fell is regarded by English Heritage as '*one of the most important early industrial landscapes in Britain*'. It has four Iron Age settlement enclosures, early coal mines which date back to at least 1303 when the Bishop of Durham granted mining licences, a railway from the 1830s, even earlier tramways, and medieval agricultural field patterns. At almost 350 hectares, Cockfield Fell is England's most extensive Scheduled Ancient Monument, described as '*an incomparable association of field monuments relating to the Iron Age settlement history and industrial evolution of a northern English county*'.

The enduring influence of the Roman occupation is evident in the number of roads that run, or would have originally run, in a straight line between two points. It is thought that one of the main reasons why the area has been so well preserved is that, unusually for a lowland fell, it was never subject to enclosure during the 18th and 19th centuries. Instead, in 1869 the Fell became a regulated pasture, managed by the Fell Reevers, giving local stockholders the right to graze their animals on the Fell upon payment of an annual rent.

The beautiful trees and wide grass verges of Front Street in Cockfield

23

Cockfield was always a well-served community and when I was growing up it had three churches, two schools, both of which I attended, and a church hall. For a fairly small village, Cockfield does nevertheless occupy a remarkably notable place in history, being the birthplace and home of Quaker brothers George and Jeremiah Dixon. George was a chemist, mathematician, engraver, engineer, geologist, and, like his father, a coal mine owner. He helped to pioneer the use of coal gas for heating and lighting and was indirectly instrumental in the early moves for Edward Pease's future Stockton to Darlington railway. Through his various business interests, and the mines in particular, he was a major employer in the district.

There can be few people who have not either sung 'Dixie', the anthem of the Confederacy side in the American Civil War, or at least heard the words to the song, '*Oh, I wish I was in the land of cotton, Old times there are not forgotten. Look away, look away, look away Dixie Land!*' The origins of Dixie can be traced all the way back to Cockfield and one of its sons. Educated at John Kipling's School in Barnard Castle, Jeremiah Dixon was a bright scholar. Whilst he was still quite young, he had the good fortune to meet three highly influential people; mathematician William Emerson, scientific instrument maker John Bird, and Thomas Wright, a natural philosopher.

In 1760, the Royal Society appointed Charles Mason to go to Sumatra to observe the transit of Venus and selected Jeremiah to assist him. Three years later, the two men were instructed by George III to sail to America and settle the long-running dispute between Thomas Penn and Frederick Calvert over the exact line of the boundary dividing the two colonies of Pennsylvania and Maryland on the eastern seaboard. Their work was completed in 1767 and the settled boundary became known as the Mason-Dixon Line, although colloquially it was increasingly referred to as the Dixie Line or more simply, Dixie.

When the War of Independence followed in 1775, the Dixie Line remained in place and became an important symbol of the tensions over slavery which would lead to the American Civil War eighty years later. From Virginia in the north to Texas in the south, all the eleven south-eastern states below the Dixie Line formed the

Confederacy with the purpose of breaking away from the Union and retaining slavery. The song 'Dixie', generally accepted as written by Daniel Decatur Emmett, emerged in the 1850s and was quickly and readily adopted in 1861 as the *de facto* anthem of the Confederacy. Thus a direct line can be drawn between the American Civil War and my home village of Cockfield.

The other side in the war had its famous anthem too. Julia Ward Howe sat up through the night to write the words of 'The Battle Hymn of the Republic' and set it to William Steffe's 1856 Methodist hymn tune, 'Say, Brothers, Will You Meet Us'. It is one of the most recognisable hymn tunes ever sung. Over the years, this rousing tune has had various sets of words put to it, some officially, others not quite so. In addition to the original Methodist hymn, there was the poem, 'John Brown's Body', which became a firm favourite and indeed was the catalyst for Ward Howe being asked to write the alternative set of words to Steffe's music. In the Second World War, the tune played host to an airborne version entitled 'Our Sergeant-Major Jumped from Twenty Thousand Feet', the climax of that little ditty being that somebody had tied a reef knot in the CSM's parachute cord, preventing it from opening when he bailed out of the aircraft!

When I was five years old, it was time for me to start at the village Church of England Infants' School. Each morning I would walk the two miles from home up the hill to the school near the top end of Front Street, and then I would walk back again in the evening. There was no public transport for me and since we did not own a motor car, walking was the only option. Not that I really gave it any thought; walking or cycling to wherever they wanted to go was what most people did then. Even if we had had a motor car, my father would have no more thought about taking me to school in it than he would have believed that in his lifetime he would see a man walk on the moon.

In order to give the children time to walk back to their homes again for lunch, the break was one and a half hours. Another of my uncles, Albert, owned Hall Farm, which was at the other end of the village and so every lunchtime, together with my cousins Alan and Grace, I walked back down Front Street to the farm where, as was customary, we sat in the kitchen to eat. Sometimes,

I ate my sandwiches or, especially in the winter, if there was a cooked meal on the range, I would share that. When my sister Grace started school, she came down to the farm for lunch with us too.

As we got older, Alan and I often tried to make it a quick lunch so that we could go outside and help break in the foals, getting them used to the halter or being tethered, before we had to go back to school for the afternoon lessons. By now we were considered old enough to be taught how to kill and pluck the poultry and geese on the farm, which were then sold to the villagers for their festivities, and so nine weeks before Christmas I learned this most fundamental country skill.

There was no free school milk in these days, even though local authorities had the power to provide it. All over Britain, councillors were afraid that providing free school milk for young children might put a ha'penny or, Heaven forbid, a whole penny on the rates, and that would never do! I was very lucky because we had milk at home and I usually had some more at lunchtime at the farm, but many children were not so fortunate. Rickets sufferers were a common sight and had a greater number of civic leaders adopted a more enlightened attitude, a whole generation of children would have been given a much better start in life, especially in the towns and cities.

In 1930, not only was Cockfield without school milk but it was also without an electricity supply and so the buildings, including the schools, were lit by paraffin lamps, with coal fires for heating. The trouble with coal fires is that they are lovely and warm when you stand next to them, but ten feet away the room is stone cold. Since our teacher usually managed to stand in front of the fire, there was precious little heat left to escape into the room to warm the children. Consequently, in winter time most of our lessons were received in the perishing cold which radiated off the solid walls of the old stone building. We sat at our desks whilst our noses dripped, our fingers and toes became numb, and each breath we took created a small plume of condensation which puffed out of our mouths like thirty-one little kettles bubbling on the stove.

The electric power supply didn't reach the village until 1936, but not everyone was connected straight away. Then, like now, the utilities were privately owned companies and the connection charges were substantial and so Hall Farm did not enjoy the delights of electricity until after the Second World War. Undeterred, my Uncle Albert continued to milk the herd by hand during the intervening years until the connection opened up the opportunity for milking machine equipment to be installed and he saw some real benefit from his investment beyond a simple light bulb.

In June 1919, John Alcock and Glaswegian Arthur Whitten (Teddie) Brown had become the first men to fly non-stop across the Atlantic. A few weeks later, the airship R-34 had flown from East Fortune in Scotland to New York and then back again. The future of long-distance travel for fee-paying passengers seemed to lie with airships, and in 1923 Ramsay MacDonald's Labour government commissioned two craft under the Imperial Airship Scheme, the purpose of which was to assess their future viability for transporting mail and passengers throughout the British Empire. The immense 777-foot-long R-101 was at the time the largest flying craft in the world. It was built at Cardington in Bedfordshire by the Air Ministry team whilst the slightly smaller R-100, at a mere 709 feet, was built by a subsidiary of Vickers at Howden in Yorkshire.

In the knowledge that only one would survive, the two teams competed with each other to see which could build the best airship, and thus they did not share important technical or developmental information. Vickers, however, had two gifted young engineers on their team, both destined to become household names. The first was the head of the design team, Barnes Wallis, who would, *inter alia*, in 1935 design the geodesic fuselage structure for the Vickers Wellesley and Wellington bombers, and later during the war, the famous 'bouncing bomb' for the Dam Busters raid. The other engineer was his assistant and the chief technical calculator on the programme, Nevil Shute Norway, the best-selling author.

The two airships took six years to build, and at some time during the summer of 1930 during her test programme, there was an advertisement in a local paper for people to go and see the R101 as she flew along the east coast. Although I was only five at the time, I vividly remember my parents taking me to see this immense craft float by in the sky, not very far above our heads. A few weeks later disaster struck the R101 when on 5th October it crashed in northern France at 2.07am on its way to Karachi, killing all but six of the fifty-four passengers and crew on board. Airship production in Britain was brought to an abrupt halt; the R-100 was scrapped and all further development effort was put towards the aeroplane.

Although life was hard in the pre-war days and we had very little money, the 1920s and 1930s were lovely decades to grow up in. There was so much that was new but we didn't have the consumer pressures that exist today; the American invasion hadn't yet occurred. As well as clearly remembering seeing the R101, I can also remember the first time I saw an aeroplane flying overhead. This might seem strange now when aeroplanes are so much a part of everyday life, but in the 1930s they were still a novelty, especially to a young lad from the north-east.

It was Monday 8th July 1935; I remember it simply because it was exactly six months after my tenth birthday. I was haymaking with my uncle and Larry at the Sun on that beautiful warm, dry day. As it did for most of the village boys, haymaking took priority over school lest the weather broke. The grass had been scythed a week or so beforehand and turned several times; now that it was dry, the job was to get it under cover. The constant ineluctable clamour of traffic, car radios and mobile telephones that is so much a part life today was still many years and a world war away. That day, the only noise that drifted across the field was the soft, lazy call of the wood pigeons from the shade of the trees. As we worked steadily, throwing the hay onto the cart with pitchforks, I became aware of another sound gradually intruding into the scene. It was the spluttering chugging of an engine, but a very different note from that of the occasional motorcycle which passed along the road; this was a much heavier sound.

I looked in the direction of the noise and realised that it was coming from the sky. After a few moments, against the clear azure blue, I picked out a distant black shape. I called to Larry and pointed at the approaching biplane, no more than two or three hundred feet high and flying straight towards us. Excitedly, I

28

dropped my pitchfork and waved with both arms to the pilot, who, as his aeroplane roared overhead, waggled its wings in reply to my greeting. I had glimpsed the future. I knew that whatever else I did, at some point in my life, I wanted to do that. I wanted to be up there looking down at the myriad scenes which would unfold and roll by beneath me as I passed over the countryside.

It impressed me much more than the airship had done, because here I could see the pilot; I could imagine it being me; it was something I could perhaps do. I realised what it must be like to be a bird, to soar and glide over the land; freed from gravity, freed from boundaries, free to wander the skies. I watched it fly over the village and on towards the coast until finally it was lost to my view. A word from my uncle brought me back to reality, but the image of seeing that aeroplane has stayed with me ever since and was an experience that would shape my whole life.

That same year, the 1st Cockfield Boy Scouts held their week-long summer camp on the larger of the two village farms, and since some of my school friends who were a little older than me were already scouts, I went along to see what went on. I was intrigued by all the activities, the friendship and the fun that they had and decided that as soon as I turned eleven the following January, I would join, which I duly did, and became a Tenderfoot. In later years, my three brothers would follow me into the troop. Scouting would become the great passion of my teenage years, would occupy much of my free time, extend into my RAF service, and would inspire me throughout my life.

In these pre-war days, at a time before every family owned a television, and iPhones, iPods, iPads and Xboxes were no more than science fiction fantasy, Lord Baden-Powell's scouting movement had become an immensely popular pastime for boys and girls alike. At the beginning of the year following his 1907 summer camp for boys on Brownsea Island in Poole Harbour, Dorset, Baden-Powell formally founded the scout movement. It quickly attracted boys, and by the end of the year over 60,000 had become scouts in Britain. There is no absolute certainty about the identity of the first scout group, but the strongest claim lies with the 1st Glasgow Scout Group, which was formed from the Glasgow Battalion of the Army Cadet Corps on 16th January 1908 and holds the very first registration certificate dated the 26th of the month, just two days after the formal commencement date of the movement. No other group holds documentation which pre-dates the 1st Glasgow.

Concerned that girls were excluded from the scouts, two years later Baden-Powell founded the Girl Guide movement, the first troop of which was most definitely the 1st Pinkneys Green Guides in Berkshire. The troop still exists today.

In the summer of 1936 the Northern Counties Scout Jamboree was held in Lord Barnard's grounds at Raby Park, which was very handy for us since it was only three miles from Cockfield. It was my first major summer camp and I still recall the wonderful time I had. There were several hundred scouts gathered there, all the tents were neatly pitched in rows and we were very excited when during the event Lord Baden-Powell came to see us.

The 1st Cockfield Scouts had a trek cart which was six feet long and three feet wide mounted on a frame with two four-foot steel-rimmed wheels. During the summer months, we would load up this cart with all our kit and pull it to Raby Park, where Lord Barnard had generously allowed us to camp as often as we wanted.

County Durham was very lucky to have such an enthusiastically supportive Commissioner and also one who owned a large estate which he made available to the scouts all year round. Raby Park was a superb venue and particularly convenient for the 1st Cockfield because it was so very local. The grounds were partly forested and partly open parkland, with a large lake, all of which enabled scouts from our various troops to learn and practise many of the skills we needed for our badges.

It was at one of these regular weekend camps in 1939 that I asked Lord Barnard whether he thought I could become a King's Scout. He was very encouraging and replied, "Why not! I will have to be your examiner so have a go at it."

The rank of King's Scout, now Queen's Scout, is the highest position a boy scout can reach in the movement. It was devised at Balmoral Castle in October 1909 between King Edward VII and

Robert Baden-Powell, who it was that announced the decision the following month as, "*A new badge with the rank of King's Scout has been approved for those Scouts who prove themselves able and willing to serve the King, should their service at any time be required by him.*" In order to qualify, a boy had first to become a First Class Scout, which required him to pass ten tests, and then pass another four from a list of seven, of which one had to be the Pathfinder Badge. Thus, with the County Commissioner's encouragement, I decided to try to achieve the rare distinction of being appointed to the prestigious rank of King's Scout.

In the early autumn of 1938, not long after I had turned thirteen, my family faced a disaster. The day had started pleasantly enough, but by the afternoon the wind had strengthened to a gale that whipped off the Fell and brought the rain down in horizontal stair rods. In no time at all everything was ringing wet, including a group of ramblers who had been walking the country lanes. Desperate to get out of the weather, they took shelter in our large hay barn until the worst of the squall had passed over and then went on their way. Half an hour later, as the result of a carelessly discarded cigarette end, the barn was a mass of flames and with it burned our carefully and laboriously gathered hay crop which was to be the winter feed for our animals. It spelled the end of the farm for us and meant that we had to leave Rose Cottage.

It was undoubtedly a domestic calamity which could and should have been avoided, but it's an ill wind that blows no good. By then we were a larger family and really needed more space than the cottage gave us. A few months beforehand, the Newcastle Housing Association had purchased a narrow field adjacent to the Staindrop Road on the edge of Cockfield village and built six pairs of semi-detached houses. They were the epitome of modernity with hot and cold running water, three bedrooms, coal fires, large gardens, an inside bathroom and lavatory, and electricity. It seems strange now when electricity is taken so much for granted, to recall the excitement that we all felt at the prospect of electricity in our home. To be able to simply flick a switch in the middle of the night and see the way to the lavatory was luxury indeed.

No.2 Staindrop Road in Cockfield village

At Rose Cottage, if the same trip became an absolute necessity, it entailed having to light a paraffin lamp, get half-dressed and then turn out in the freezing cold or pouring rain, or both, to walk through the darkness to the privy at the bottom of the garden. My mother was even more delighted than the rest of us at the prospect of living in one of these lovely clean, new, modern houses after the years of hardship in the cottage. Thus it was that I moved from the countryside and came to live within the village bounds of Cockfield at No.2 Staindrop Road, and which for my last year at school, if nothing else, saved me a four-mile walk every day and a good soaking in bad weather.

New Year's Day 1939 fell on a Sunday. Not being a leap year, it was thus a common year starting and ending on a Sunday; it would not do this again until 1950. Since my birthday is 8th January, it always falls on the same day of the week as New Year's Day, and so in 1939 it was a Sunday that I turned fourteen and started to think about leaving my elementary school at the end of that summer term. At the time, only the top pupil from each school in the area was chosen to go to the Grammar in Bishop Auckland; it wasn't me. Nevertheless, I had excelled in geometry at school and was very good at drawing.

The headmaster, Mr Nutter, was very friendly with one of the company directors of Wilson's Forge in Bishop Auckland, and recommended me for a possible apprenticeship in the drawing office there. Now that I was about to leave school, it was very important that I obtained a job to help towards my keep at home, especially as Dad no longer had the farm income. The chance of an apprenticeship was an ideal opportunity. The arrangements were made for me to attend an interview and since the suggestion had come from the headmaster in the first place, I was sure that he would have given me a good reference.

I was very nervous as I sat in the director's office answering his questions but was delighted when I was offered the post. Although starting somewhere below the bottom rung on the ladder, the apprenticeship gave me experience in the different engineering departments of the works. As part of my training I began three years of night classes at Bishop Auckland Grammar School to study for my Junior 1 and 2, and then Senior 1 examinations to qualify for a permanent post in the drawing office.

For the time being I had to catch the country bus service each morning for the eight miles journey into Bishop Auckland in order to be at Wilson's before seven-thirty, but I resolved that I would save up and buy a bicycle as soon as possible to make travelling more convenient.

The village entrance on Staindrop Road

My sister, Grace

Chapter Two

"Lord how many are my foes?
How many those that in arms against me rise!
Many are they that are of my life distrustfully thus say
No help for him in God there lies."
Psalm III – John Milton [9th August 1653]

During the last few years of childhood whilst still at school, I was only vaguely aware that my parents and the other adults in my life were becoming increasingly concerned about a man called Hitler. When at fourteen I entered the world of work in 1939, the talk around me was of little else than the increasing prospect of another war with Germany and I very quickly came to understand the threat that the Nazis posed. My father had been too young to go to the Great War, but I did have two uncles who went. They both came back, although one of them was badly shell-shocked and never really worked afterwards. As the summer wore on, Neville Chamberlain's 'Peace for our Time' was exposed for the unrequited agreement Hitler had always intended it to be and the mood amongst the workforce at Wilson's grew increasingly pessimistic.

In January, the government had issued a National Service recruitment guide which contained a handwritten message from the Prime Minister: *"The desire of all of us is to live at peace with our neighbours, but to secure peace we must be strong. The country needs your service and you are anxious to play your part. This guide will point the way. I ask you to read it carefully and decide how you can best help."* It was a forty-eight page booklet designed to encourage men and women to volunteer for the Civil Defence services; the police, First Aid and nursing, a local fire service [there was no National Fire Service at this time] or air-raid precaution work [ARP]. For some, it was the opportunity they had been waiting for, but most just put the booklet in a drawer.

At the same time, the Government's Schedule of Reserved Occupations which listed those jobs, trades and professions which, because of their importance to the war effort, exempted the holder from military service, was published. A copy of the schedule was put up on the notice board at work and I scanned the listed occupations. With a sinking heart, I realised that my engineering apprenticeship placed me fairly and squarely in the reserved status and that if there was to be a war, I was destined to spend it at Wilson's.

Since my first sight of an aeroplane on that July day in 1935, I had wanted to fly. Aircraft had become steadily more commonplace until by the summer of 1939 the sky seemed full. I became quite expert at recognising the different makes: Blenheims, Battles, Hampdens, and Wellingtons; Sunderlands, Ansons, Whitleys, and Wellesleys, and of course the three that every schoolboy knew, Tiger Moths, Hurricanes and Spitfires.

One of the great advantages which electricity had brought us was that we were able to buy a wireless set. Dad had been able to acquire a 1935 Mullard MA3 in almost perfect condition. It sat on a table in our kitchen and became the focus of attention each evening when the BBC National Programme News was read by one of the regular team of announcers such as Alvar Lidell, Frank Phillips, John Snagge, Bruce Belfrage, Stuart Hibberd or, later, Yorkshireman Wilfred Pickles. It wasn't until 1940, though, that we knew any of their names, when the BBC started to identify its announcers in order to distinguish the broadcasts from German propaganda.

Even for a fourteen-year-old, it was not difficult to realise that the international situation in Europe was serious. In March 1938, Austria had been annexed by the Nazis, and a year later the Czechoslovak territories of Bohemia and Moravia were occupied. Hitler's desire was the reunification of Germany with East Prussia, but Poland stood in the way. In late August, the Germans closed their border with Poland and put an armed cordon around Danzig, which had been declared a Free City in the Treaty of Versailles. The cordon effectively shut the country off from the Baltic, its only coastline.

By the spring of 1939, the inevitability of war with Germany became increasingly difficult to deny. Much as it had done in 1914, Britain placed an over-reliance on diplomacy when dealing with a régime intent upon conflict. Chamberlain, with the support of most of his Cabinet, continued to vacillate and remained resolutely opposed to putting the country on any sort of war footing. Fortunately, there were some around the Cabinet table as well as others outside the government who did not share Chamberlain's faith in Hitler's word. In spite of the Prime Minister, who continued to pursue a policy of appeasement towards the German Chancellor, almost to the point of obsession, Britain did painfully, and all too slowly, continue to prepare for war.

As usual, Britain lagged far behind other European nations when it came to any form of National Service; six months away from war, we still didn't have it. As late as 27th April, the Secretary of State for War, Leslie Hore-Belisha, who in 1934 had given us pedestrian crossings with Belisha beacons, finally persuaded the Cabinet to introduce a limited form of conscription. On 26th May, Parliament passed the Military Training Act, which introduced conscription for men aged twenty and twenty-one, requiring them to do six months' military training, at the end of which they would become active reservists. It proved to be wholly inadequate. There was only one intake, that of Saturday 3rd June, before the outbreak of war overtook events, whereupon the Act was superseded by the National Service [Armed Forces] Act 1939, which extended conscription to all men between eighteen and forty-one.

Amidst all this international uncertainty, the world of commerce, innovation and aviation continued to develop, and on 8th July, Pan American Airways inaugurated the world's first heavier-than-air trans-Atlantic passenger service with its Boeing 314 flying boat, the *Yankee Clipper,* between New York and Britain. In January 1942, Winston Churchill would become the first head of government to make a trans-Atlantic crossing by aeroplane in Boeing 314A *Berwick.*

Recognising that war was the most likely outcome of the European crisis, the government sought to involve women as it had twenty-five years earlier by re-forming the various women's services. The ATS on 9th September 1938, the WRNS on 12th April 1939, followed in early June by the Women's Land Army, and finally on 28th June, the WAAF brought women into the heart of the war machine like never before. Throughout July and August, Civil

Defence workers, stretcher bearers and First Aid parties were hastily enrolled, and the public air-raid shelter scheme, which had been started during the Munich crisis, continued with a greater sense of urgency. Anderson shelters, which were first issued to householders in the south-east of England in February, continued to be distributed throughout the country.

The Anderson shelter was designed in 1938 by William Patterson and Oscar Carl Kerrison. It was named after Sir John Anderson, the Lord Privy Seal at the time, who had responsibility for preparing air-raid precautions. They were mainly issued to householders in the cities and larger towns as these areas were considered to be at high risk of bombing attacks. They were free to everyone with a garden and whose annual income was less than £250, otherwise they cost £7. They measured 4 feet 6 inches wide, 6 feet 6 inches long and 6 feet high and were delivered in kit form together with an instruction sheet and a rat-tailed spanner all ready for self-assembly. The main part of the shelter was made up of six corrugated iron sheets which bolted together to form the sides and arched roof. The ends, one with a door, were then added. The whole structure was set into a hole in the ground some three to four feet deep. The soil from the hole was then piled against the sides and onto the top, providing people with another area to plant with vegetables or flowers. The entire structure was designed to withstand a modest blast and protect the occupants from flying glass, shrapnel, roof tiles, bricks and much else in the event of a bomb explosion, but not a direct hit.

The quiet rural village of Cockfield was not thought to be a prime Luftwaffe target and so no-one there received an Anderson shelter. However, by late August we had all been issued with our own gas mask, that ubiquitous symbol of the Home Front, which had to be carried in its rectangular cardboard box at all times when out and about.

On 24th August, the Prime Minister recalled Parliament early as news of the Molotov-Ribbentrop Pact creating a neutrality agreement between Russia and Germany leaked out. The next day, Neville Chamberlain gave Edward Rydz-Śmigly, the Marshal of Poland, an 'ironclad guarantee' of assistance should Germany attack his country. Undeterred, German troops moved out of

Austria and into Slovakia, taking up positions on the Polish border. In Britain, the government issued the Emergency Defence Regulations and all reservists were called up, at last putting Britain on a full war footing. The last day of the month saw the final preparations for Operation Pied Piper, the evacuation of more than three million children, pregnant and nursing mothers, and disabled people from major towns and cities.

The weather that summer had been lovely and lasted throughout July and August, although on Tuesday 29th the Midlands experienced a three-hour thunderstorm which caused flooding and serious damage to many homes. Unwelcome in the best of times, for those affected families it was little short of catastrophic just days before the war started. Twenty-seven-year-old *Daily Telegraph* journalist Clare Hollingworth had been with the paper less than a week when her first assignment was to Poland to report on worsening tensions in Europe. By chance, she was on the Polish border that day and, thanks to a puff of wind which blew some camouflage netting aside, saw German tanks facing Poland and ready to invade. She filed her story and it became the scoop of the century.

Three days later, the tanks rolled in. The cities of Katowice, Teschen and Krakow were bombed before dawn with incendiaries and high explosives, and in the afternoon, the Luftwaffe attacked the civilian suburbs of Poland's capital, Warsaw. In Britain, the Prime Minister, in conjunction with the French government, sent Hitler an ultimatum: withdraw from Poland or war will follow.

At a meeting of the Privy Council, the King signed the order for the general mobilisation of all of our armed services, and full conscription began. This huge influx of troops created an accommodation problem and inevitably some troops, particularly army personnel, were billeted with private landlords. However, in order to prevent profiteering, the Army Council set the levels at which landlords could charge their Service lodgers; 8d for breakfast and 5d for supper, and for those requiring full stabling for a horse, two shillings and thruppence per day. Not for the first time did the army take greater care of its horses than it did its troops.

Throughout the sultry, still day, Operation Pied Piper occupied the nation's railway system as hundreds of thousands of children were moved out of the cities to safer areas at addresses which for the most part were kept secret from their parents. Teachers accompanied schoolchildren but only nursing mothers were allowed to go. Children were billeted with families they had never met before; it was pot luck on both sides. For some, it was a wonderful adventure placed in the bosom of a caring, loving family; an experience which would change their lives forever, and in some cases, lead to them choosing never to return to the city. For others it was a living Hell, a miserable existence which could not be over soon enough, an opinion shared by many unwilling foster parents!

September 1st also saw the introduction of three significant changes for the British population. Firstly, the blackout began. Each householder throughout the country became responsible for ensuring that between sunset and sunrise no light escaped from any of their doors or windows, and that all outside lights were extinguished. It was later reduced to half an hour after sunset to half an hour before sunrise. Next, the government took control of the railways, and finally, the BBC merged its National and Regional Programmes on the wireless to form the BBC Home Service, which, until the name was abandoned in 1967 in favour of the anonymous-sounding Radio 4, became a national institution famed and revered across the world.

All the next day, the nation held its collective breath whilst continuing the preparations for war. Operation Pied Piper carried on apace; blackout preparations, the filling of sandbags, and the call-up of conscripts all continued unabated, as too did the tide of volunteers outside recruitment offices. Anyone flying as aircrew with the various Commands did so as a volunteer and thus proportionately, throughout the war the RAF attracted the greatest number of non-conscripted personnel.

The hot sunny weather also continued, but on the day that the air-raid system became operational, as darkness fell, most of the country was gripped by violent thunderstorms; a clear and unambiguous portent of what was to come. That night, the words of former Foreign Secretary Sir Edward Grey on 3rd August 1914 must have been in the minds of so many people who had lived through the last war, "*The lamps are going out all over Europe, we shall not see them lit again in our lifetime.*"

For those beyond a certain age, Sunday 3rd September 1939 is a date that will never be forgotten. Like many others that morning, we had been to church earlier than usual and returned home for the sole purpose of listening to the wireless. At 10.00, our whole family gathered around the Mullard to listen to Alvar Lidell read the following announcement: "*This is London. The following official communiqué has been issued from 10, Downing Street. 'On September 1st, His Majesty's Ambassador in Berlin was instructed to inform the German Government, that unless they were prepared to give His Majesty's Government in the United Kingdom satisfactory assurances that the German Government had suspended all aggressive action against Poland and were prepared promptly to withdraw their forces from Polish territory, His Majesty's Government in the United Kingdom would, without hesitation, fulfil their obligation to Poland.*

At 9 am this morning, His Majesty's Ambassador in Berlin informed the German Government that unless, not later than 11 am British Summer Time today, September 3rd, satisfactory assurances to the above effect had been given by the German Government and had reached His Majesty's Government in London, a state of war would exist between the two countries as from that hour. His Majesty's Government are now awaiting the receipt of any reply that may be made by the German Government.' The Prime Minister will broadcast to the nation at 11.15. That is the end of the announcement. Please stand by for a few moments."

My mother got up and put the kettle on and, like the rest of the nation, we waited, aware that we were almost certainly just an hour away from war; that we had just one more hour of peace, that today would shape the destiny of millions of people. The kettle boiled. Its steam puffed gaily from the spout. Mother made the tea. Grace fetched the cups and saucers. She placed them on the table with the milk jug and sugar bowl. The certainty of domestic activity filled the passing moments.

The clock on the mantelpiece ticked inexorably towards the appointed hour. The BBC gave us a talk on 'How to make the most of tinned foods'. Every fifteen minutes, Alvar Lidell reminded us that the Prime Minister would address the nation at 11.15. In between, a suitable choice of light orchestral music filtered quietly from the wireless set. It was all very calm. It was typically British.

We drank our tea; we said very little; we waited. Shortly after 11 o'clock, my father once more turned up the volume on the Mullard and we prepared ourselves for the Prime Minister. People have become familiar with the first part of that historic and momentous statement, but Chamberlain actually addressed the nation more fully than the few words usually quoted. Alvar Lidell prepared us, *"This is London. You will now hear a statement by the Prime Minister."*

"I am speaking to you from the Cabinet Room of 10, Downing Street. This morning the British Ambassador in Berlin, handed the German Government a final note, stating that unless we heard from them by 11o'clock that they were prepared at once to withdraw their troops from Poland, a state of war would exist between us. I have to tell you now that no such undertaking has been received, and that consequently this Country is at war with Germany.

You can imagine what a bitter blow it is to me that all my long struggle to win peace has failed. Yet I cannot believe that there is anything more or anything different that I could have done and that would have been more successful.

Up to the very last it would have been quite possible to have arranged a peaceful and honourable settlement between Germany and Poland, but Hitler would not have it. He had evidently made up his mind to attack Poland whatever happened, and although he now says he put forward reasonable proposals which were rejected by the Poles, that is not a true statement. The proposals were never shown to the Poles, nor to us, although they were announced in a German broadcast on Thursday night, Hitler did not wait to hear comments on them, but ordered his troops to cross the Polish frontier the next morning. His action shows convincingly that there is no chance of expecting that this man will ever give up his practice of using force to gain his will. He can only be stopped by force, and we and France are today, in fulfilment of our obligations, going to the aid of Poland, who is so bravely resisting this wicked and unprovoked attack on her people. We have a clear conscience. We have done all that any country could do to establish peace. The situation in which no word given by Germany's ruler could be trusted and no people or country could feel itself safe has become intolerable. And now that we have resolved to finish it, I know that you will all play your part with calmness and courage.

At such a moment as this the assurances of support that we have received from the Empire are a source of profound encouragement to us.

When I have finished speaking, certain detailed announcements will be made on behalf of the Government; give these your close attention. The Government have made plans under which it will be possible to carry on the work of the nation in the days of stress and strain that may be ahead. But these plans need your help. You may be taking your part in the fighting services or as a volunteer in one of the branches of Civil Defence. If so you will report for duty in accordance with the instructions you have received. You may be engaged in work essential to the prosecution of war for the maintenance of the life of the people – in factories, in transport, in public utility concerns, or in the supply of other necessities of life. If so, it is of vital importance that you should carry on with your jobs.

Now may God bless you all and may He defend the right, for it is evil things that we shall be fighting against – brute force, bad faith, injustice, oppression and persecution – and against them I am certain that the right will prevail."

Alvar Lidell then continued, *"That is the end of the Prime Minister's statement. Please stand by for the important Government announcements which, as the Prime Minister has said, will follow almost immediately. That is the end of the announcement."* The BBC then broadcast a few minutes of church bells ringing before the promised details were announced.

"This is London. The Government have given instructions for the following important announcements. Closing of places of entertainment: all cinemas, theatres and other places of entertainment are to be closed immediately until further notice. In the light of experience, it may be possible to allow the re-opening of such places in some areas. They are being closed because if they were hit by a bomb, large numbers would be killed or injured. Sports gatherings and all gatherings for purposes of entertainment and amusement, whether outdoor or indoor, which involve large numbers congregating together, are prohibited until further notice. This refers especially to gatherings for purposes of entertainment, but people

43

are earnestly requested not to crowd together unnecessarily in any circumstances. Churches and other places of public worship will not be closed.

Air raid warnings: as from now, no hooter or siren may be sounded except on the instructions of the police. In the event of threatened air raids, warnings will be given in urban areas by means of sirens or hooters which will be sounded in some places by short intermittent blasts and in other places by a warbling note changing every few seconds. The warning may also be given by short blasts on police whistles. When you hear any of these sounds, take shelter. Do not leave your shelter until you hear the 'Raiders' Passed' signal which will be given by continuously sounding the sirens or hooters for a period of two minutes on the same note. If poison gas has been used, you will be warned by means of hand rattles. If you hear hand rattles, do not leave your shelter until the poison gas has been cleared away. Hand bells will be used to tell you when there is no longer any danger from poison gas.

Schools: all day schools in evacuation and neutral areas in England, Wales and Scotland are to be closed for lessons for at least a week from today. In reception areas, schools should be re-opened as soon as arrangements for the education of the children evacuated to the locality can be completed. The precise date of re-opening schools in reception areas will be decided by the authorities of the schools.

General: keep off the streets as much as possible; to expose yourself unnecessarily adds to your danger. Carry your gas mask with you always. Make sure that you and every member of your household, especially children able to run about, have on them their names and address clearly written. Do this, either on an envelope or something like a luggage label, not on an odd piece of paper which might get lost. Sew the label onto your children's clothes where they cannot pull it off. The London tube railways are required for traffic purposes and tube stations are not available as air raid shelters.

Now here is an announcement to unemployed persons: if you are already claiming benefit or allowances do not attend at the Ministry of Labour local offices until your next pay day. If you become unemployed and want to claim benefit or allowances you should attend at the Ministry of Labour local office. To avoid congestion, claims will be taken from 9 o'clock in alphabetical order surnames beginning with 'A' to 'H' in the morning, the rest in the afternoon. That is the end of these announcements."

The BBC then played a recording of 'God Save the King'.

So there we had it. It was war after all. Despite Chamberlain's unstinting, if misplaced, efforts to secure peace, it was not to be; the Nazis wanted a war and only total capitulation by every European nation would prevent it. Whilst the Prime Minister had been speaking, the War Telegram had been sent and the plans to deal with the start of hostilities took effect.

At 12.01, sixty-one minutes after the government's deadline had expired, the first RAF aircraft took off against the enemy. Bristol Blenheim N6215 reconnaissance aircraft from No.139 Squadron, piloted by Flying Officer Andrew McPherson with his crew of Commander Thompson, RN and Corporal V Arrowsmith, photographed many ships to the north of Wilhelmshaven and became the first British aircraft to cross the German coast during World War Two. The aircraft returned home safely at 16.50, and the Squadron Operations Record Book, Form 541, noted the following historic entry, *"Duty successful. 75 photos taken of German Fleet. The first RAF aircraft to cross the German frontier."*

The first ship to be sunk in the war came as early as 19.40 hours that same day when the *U-30* commanded by Kapitänleutnant Fritz-Julius Lemp torpedoed the civilian liner *Athenia* en route from Glasgow to Montreal. The German High Command considered a court martial for Lemp but finally decided on a cover-up and ordered the U-boat commander to alter his craft's log book. The truth finally emerged and it was condemned as a war crime in 1946 at the Nuremberg trials when Großadmiral Dönitz disclosed the details and Lemp's primary responsibility.

In 1939, Germany had been fearful that the American casualties on board *Athenia* would bring the United States into the war. Hitler need not have worried. Later that day, President Roosevelt followed the example of his predecessor Woodrow Wilson during the Great War and advocated American neutrality. Within forty-eight hours, Congress had officially declared the United States a neutral country in much the same way as Wilson had expressed it in 1914, *"...the true spirit of neutrality, which is the spirit of impartiality and fairness and friendliness to all concerned."* As for Lemp, he would later play an unwilling role in one of the war's greatest pivotal events.

On that first night of hostilities, Linton-on-Ouse sent ten of its Whitworth Whitley bombers, three from No.51 and seven from No.58 Squadron to Germany and dropped nearly five and a half million propaganda leaflets over nine cities around the Ruhr. Although all the crews landed safely, for Flying Officer O'Neill and his crew in K8969, it was in a French cabbage field near the River Marne.

The following day Flight Lieutenant Kenneth Doran led a daylight attack by ten Blenheims of Nos.110 and 107 Squadrons against the German pocket battleship *Admiral Sheer* and the cruiser *Emden* in the Schilling Roads of Wilhelmshaven harbour. The cloud base was at only 500 feet and Doran had no choice but to lead his attack on the *Admiral Sheer* in a shallow dive coming over the ship at no more than mast-head height. At least three bombs from the attacking aircraft struck the pocket battleship but they all failed to explode. Caught completely by surprise, the German gunners reacted quickly and shot down five of the Blenheims from the attacking force, causing the first casualties of the war.

No.107 Squadron also has the unhappy distinction that two of its members, navigator Sgt George Booth and air gunner AC1 Lawrence Slattery, became the first British prisoners of war when they were captured on 4th September 1939 after their Blenheim IV N6240 was shot down on the Wilhelmshaven raid. Their pilot, Sgt Albert Prince, didn't survive. Fifteen prison camps, more than five years' captivity and promotion to Flight Lieutenant and Sergeant awaited Booth and Slattery before they returned home.

Both Flying Officer McPherson and Flight Lieutenant Doran were awarded the Distinguished Flying Cross for their respective actions during these two days and their awards appeared in the *London Gazette* on 10th October. They were the recipients of the first gallantry awards to British forces in the war. Bomber Command would continue to prosecute the war on almost every day until the night of 2nd/3rd May 1945.

Now having to make up for lost and wasted time, on Monday 4th September the government through the Ministry of Labour and National Service began compulsory registration for all men of eligible age. To ensure that people knew what to do, posters, press notices and BBC bulletins announced that men born between the specified dates were to report to their local Ministry of Labour office to register on the date stated. The first such date was 21st October and was for men born between 2nd October 1917 and 1st October 1919. This procedure was carried on at regular intervals throughout the war.

It was the politicians who wielded the power and gave the orders to our commanders in the field. At times they gave the impression that they saw the war being prosecuted according to a defined set of rules to which both sides would abide. The RAF was permitted to attack only Kriegsmarine targets. No land-based targets were to be bombed because factories, even munitions factories, were private property! The Operational Order for the attack on the *Admiral Sheer* stated, "The greatest care is to be taken not to injure the civilian population. The intention is to destroy the German fleet. There is no alternative target." With the exception of the Vickers Wellington, the Air Ministry failed to grasp the inadequacies of its own bomber force and the immense defensive power of Germany's warships.

However, after the severe losses suffered in the *Admiral Sheer* attack, no more sorties were ordered for Bomber Command until 20th September. From then, for the next nine days, the only flights which were undertaken over German territory were either reconnaissance or propaganda leaflet drops, referred to by the crews as bumfleteer missions.

These lonely and dangerous daylight photographic reconnaissance sorties to garner information were carried out by Blenheims of No.2 Group and continued into late November. Some of the information and photographs which they brought back would be used later in the war, but the missions proved to be costly in both men and machines. Nevertheless, despite the instructions from politicians, on 3rd December, a No.115 Squadron Wellington managed to drop the first bomb of the war to fall on German soil. It was part of a force of twenty-four aircraft which attacked German warships off Heligoland. After its bombing run over the ships, the crew realised that one of their bombs had failed to drop; they had a hang-up. Before long, though, Messerschmitt Me109 and Me110 fighters arrived and in the ensuing mêlée of twisting, turning aircraft, the bomb became loose and dropped out through the still-open bomb-bay doors and exploded on the German island of Heligoland.

With an ominous feeling of déjà vu, the 158,000-strong British Expeditionary Force [BEF] had sailed for France on 10th September, but unlike their fathers in 1914, contact with the enemy did not follow straightaway. After the Polish campaign, the Germans paused for breath and to take stock; winter was coming. The BEF dug in along the Franco-Belgian border and waited. With so little obvious activity in Europe, the autumn became known to the British as 'the phoney war', to the Germans as *das Sitzkrieg* and to the French as *le drôle de guerre*.

However, for the RAF, the Royal Navy, and the Merchant Navy there was no phoney war. The first Royal Navy losses of the war came on 10th September when the submarine HMS *Oxley* was sunk, though not by the enemy but by HMS *Triton*. The true facts of the incident were kept from the public and were not made known until the 1950s. No blame was attached to the crew of *Triton*. A week later, the aircraft carrier HMS *Courageous* was sunk in the Western Approaches by two torpedoes fired from the *U-29* commanded by Kapitänleutnant Otto Schuhart.

In France, the 20th September saw No.88 Squadron Fairey Battle rear gunner, Sgt F Letchard open the score for the RAF with its first victory. The Battles of the Advanced Air Striking Force [the AASF] were on patrol near Aachen when they were attacked by Messerschmitt Bf 109s, one of which fell victim to Letchard's Lewis gun.

For most of this country, and England in particular, life simply went on as usual. The Luftwaffe didn't come and terrorise English towns and cities, the much feared gas attacks didn't materialise and people didn't panic. The sun kept shining and the fine weather we had enjoyed that year turned the unusually warm and dry September into an Indian summer, even in the north-east.

As the month turned, the weather became noticeably colder and whilst the western half of the British Isles enjoyed exceptionally high levels of sunshine, we in the eastern half were, for the most part, stuck under a blanket of cloud during the day with clearing skies at night. However, on the 3rd those clear skies opened a window to one of nature's true wonders when we were treated to an outstanding display of the Northern Lights, the Aurora Borealis, which was clearly visible from Cockfield, and which is actually further north than the Mull of Galloway, the most southerly point of Scotland. At Duntulm, on the Isle of Skye, Mr Seton Gordon described the display, *'the whole of the heavens from horizon to horizon seemed to be in motion and alive, and the light of the moon failed to diminish the grandeur of this spectacle.'*

Then the news broke that on the night of 13th/14th HMS *Royal Oak* had sunk whilst in Scapa Flow. It transpired that Kapitänleutnant Gunther Prien had managed to thread *U-47* through the eye of the needle and slip between the blockships guarding Kirk Sound to enter the very heart of the Royal Navy's Home Fleet anchorage. He torpedoed the battleship and then escaped by the same route despite an eight to ten knot tide race against him though the sound. By the time the British public were told of the disaster, the *U-47* was safely back at its base in Kiel and the triumphant crew, all of whom had volunteered for the mission, were on their way to Berlin to be congratulated by Hitler. Prien was awarded the Knight's Cross.

The mission was undoubtedly a remarkable piece of seamanship, but we should never have allowed it to happen because it was a carbon copy of the mission by the crew of the *U-18* on 23rd November 1914. On that occasion, Kapitänleutnant Heinrich von Hennig had manoeuvred his craft into the Flow and, hoping to sink a battleship, saw through his periscope only a handful of destroyers at anchor. Deciding not to risk his submarine for a destroyer, he turned to retreat from the Flow. However, whilst doing so the periscope was spotted by a lookout aboard the minesweeper HMS *Garry*. Assisted by the trawler *Dorothy Grey*, the *Garry* rammed the *U-18* and forced her to the surface where Hennig was obliged to surrender. After the incident, the defences of Scapa Flow were quickly strengthened but, as Prien ably demonstrated, not nearly enough.

Monday 16th brought what became known as the Battle of the River Forth, although the famous rail bridge was never a target. That day, several waves of Junkers Ju88 fighter bombers attacked the Royal Navy anchorage at South Queensferry, by Edinburgh. Two of the attackers were shot down by Spitfires of Nos.602 and 603 Squadrons and crashed into the Firth of Forth. A third, badly damaged by ground based ack-ack and trailing smoke from one engine, limped back across the North Sea and crashed in the Netherlands.

Undeterred, the Luftwaffe returned on 28th. This time, Heinkel 5449 from Stabsketté/KG26, call sign 1H+JA, piloted by Unteroffizier Kurt Lehmkuhl, had the misfortune to come across the Spitfire of Flight Lieutenant Archie McKellar, No.602 [City of Glasgow] Squadron at 6,000 feet. The Heinkel had already been hit by accurate ack-ack fire and McKellar sealed its fate. Lehmkuhl used all his experience but he could not shake off his attacker. The Spitfire's .303 bullets struck the Heinkel numerous times along its length, hitting the flight engineer and the radio operator, who were also the crew gunners, disabling the engines, smashing almost all the cockpit instruments, and wounding the pilot. Despite his injuries, Lehmkuhl skilfully glided his aircraft down and made a forced landing in the difficult terrain of the Lammermuir Hills near the small village of Humbie, south of Edinburgh. Lehmkuhl realised that escape was out of the question and surrendered, together with his navigator Rolf Niehoff, to Humbie's local policeman, who I think was Hugh Harris and was first to arrive at the crash scene.

This was the first German aeroplane to be brought down onto British soil and was adopted by the villagers, becoming forever known as the 'Humbie Heinkel'. The RAF was particularly pleased because it now had an almost intact Heinkel 111A bomber to examine. However, notwithstanding the completeness of the aeroplane, the technicians still missed the prize that was on board, the secret German radio beam navigational bombing aid, codenamed *Knickebein*. It would be another twelve months before the system was finally discovered in another captured aircraft.

The residents of Humbie were fascinated to see the Heinkel and turned out en masse to view it and, before the RAF had chance to cart it away, to retrieve some small memento of its appearance near their village. To this day, there is hardly a household in Humbie which does not own a piece of that Heinkel.

The Humbie Heinkel – 28th October 1939 [public domain]

From the very outset of the war, the north-east coast had been the focus of intense enemy action. Cargo ships in particular were early targets and the RAF were kept very busy intercepting and trying to destroy the attacking aircraft as they came across the North Sea. German mine-laying activities, their U-boats and the Luftwaffe inflicted a heavy loss on merchant ships which still plied the east-coast route. Not many days went by without one of the many coasters, often quite old coal burners, being sunk. The very personal battle of the men of the Merchant Navy against the sea and the enemy continued relentlessly throughout the war and their great courage is all too often overlooked.

*[top] Hawker Hurricanes of an unknown squadron during the Battle of
Britain and Supermarine Spitfires of No.65 Squadron also during the
Battle of Britain*

Chapter Three

"Gracious Lord, oh bomb the Germans.
Spare their women for Thy Sake,
And if that is not too easy
We will pardon Thy Mistake.
But, gracious Lord, what'er shall be,
Don't let anyone bomb me."
In Westminster Abbey [A Lady's Prayer] –
John Betjeman [1940]

The days began to shorten and the longer nights brought a reminder of the changing season. Nevertheless, the lovely Indian summer which we had enjoyed that autumn still echoed in the mild November; but in the first half of December the temperatures really began to tumble, bringing a noticeable chill to the air. Then, the second half of the month heralded hard frosts and fog at night, courtesy of an established anticyclone. The days were generally bright and clear but with no warmth in the sun, the frost barely lifted.

In France, the 9th December had brought the news of the first British soldier to die in the war. Corporal Thomas Priday, 1st Battalion Kings Shropshire Light Infantry, was leading a patrol near the Maginot Line on the Franco-German border when he stepped on a mine, not a German one, but a French one in an unmarked minefield!

The freezing weather stayed all over Christmas and the New Year. On Sunday 31st December, together with my brothers and sister Grace, I took a shortcut through The Fallows and joined our parents just as they were going into Cockfield's 800-year-old St. Mary's church for the midnight service. A few hours later, across the land, church bells echoed from a hundred ancient belfries to mark the dawning of 1940, but even as they rang out their greeting, few could have imagined just how momentously eventful, challenging, and defining the year would be.

On the 6th January, the wind turned to the south and it became a little milder again, but it was only a temporary relief because by the 10th a large European anticyclone lay across Britain, bringing deep, penetrating frosts. Then the snow came in on a northerly air stream. By the middle of the month, daytime temperatures no longer rose above freezing and it just kept getting colder. On the night of the 23rd, Rhayader in midWales recorded a low of -23.3°C, a record for England and Wales that would stand until 1982, when on the night of 10th January, at Harper Adams Agricultural College in Shropshire, the weather station mercury fell to a staggering -26.1°C.

January 1940 proved to be the coldest month in Britain since February 1895; the Thames froze over for eight miles between Teddington and Sunbury, ice covered stretches of the Mersey, the Humber and the Severn, and even the sea froze at Bognor Regis, Folkestone and Southampton. The Grand Union Canal was completely iced-over for its entire length between Birmingham and London. But it was the snow and icestorm that virtually paralysed the country. In the early hours of Friday 26th, it started to snow heavily across eastern Britain.

Public transport to and from Cockfield had long since ceased to run and since riding my bicycle in those conditions was impossible, on that Friday morning I set out in the darkness to walk the eight miles to Wilson's. The wind gradually strengthened from the south-east and blew the already heavy snowfall into deeper drifts, making my progress all the harder and slower. When I eventually arrived at work after my four-hour trudge, it was to find that the offices and the factory had been closed for the weekend. This was a most rare event and an indication of how bad the weather was. The office manager was there to tell me that because I had turned in, I would not be deducted my wages for Friday and Saturday morning. With that consolation, there was nothing for it but turn around and walk back home again; at least now with the wind at my back.

The storm carried on all weekend as the wind whipped up the fallen snow and piled it ever higher; Cockfield became completely cut off. Falling onto the frozen ground, the snow soon built up to more than two feet deep with drifts of six and eight feet at intervals along the unimpeded track of the wind. Before long, the weight of snow and ice brought down the power lines and the electricity went off. We kept the coal fire burning night and day as our only source of heat and cooking; it was like being back in Rose Cottage. Uncle Albert did his best to keep the roads in the village passable by hitching his snowplough to a team of horses, but we were completely cut off for several days, which prevented him getting the milk out to Bishop Auckland and onto the milk train.

Whilst we were trapped by the snow, the south of England was hit by the worst ice storm on record. This rare event of super-cooled raindrops that instantly freeze upon contact with the ground caused widespread damage. Cirencester experienced forty hours of continuous freezing rain as tree branches, telegraph poles, power lines and roofs snapped and collapsed under the weight. Even the birds were unable to fly, paralysed by the frozen rain on their feathers.

The following Monday morning brought no relief as the strong east wind continued to blow relentlessly. For a week after the snowstorm, much of Britain was at a standstill. Slowly, though, things began to move and people could return to work, but the lack of electricity remained a problem for many factories and offices for some time to come. There was at least some small comfort for the local roadmen who had been on the brew for some time when they were given temporary work helping to clear the roads to the various villages. It was 20th February before a mild south-westerly blew in from the tropics and brought a real thaw. With it, came the inevitable floods as all the snow and ice quickly melted away in the warm air.

We had not been alone in suffering these appalling conditions and no matter how hard it was for us, it was a great deal worse for the lads of the BEF in France, who were living under canvas and, expecting a German attack at any time, were trying to keep themselves and their equipment ready for action in the sub-zero temperatures. The biting cold and deep snow spread all across Europe and was one reason why the war seemed to have stalled. It later transpired that the morale of our troops had been badly affected by this long hard winter.

All in all, it had been a pretty terrible start to the war for Britain. It was a good job that we did not know that things would become a great deal worse before they started to get better.

As soon as the wind and snowstorm abated, the ground was cleared and our fighters were patrolling the coast again. On Saturday 3rd February, Flt Lt PW Townsend flying his No.43 Squadron Hawker Hurricane shot down a Heinkel 111H. The aircraft made a forced landing at Bannial Flat Farm, two miles north of Whitby. It was the first German aeroplane to crash on English soil in the war.

In an incident reminiscent of a scene from an Ealing comedy, three weeks later on 22nd February, No.602 Squadron under the command of Sqn Ldr Douglas Farquhar, DFC, was scrambled from its base at RAF Drem in East Lothian. At 12.30 that afternoon, Farquhar shot down a Heinkel 111P. With smoke pouring from his aircraft's port engine, the Luftwaffe pilot, Feldwebel Sprigarth, managed to make a forced landing on a rather remote field in the hills near St. Abbs Head, Berwickshire, and thus save the lives of his crew. Farquhar had followed the Heinkel down and, seeing that it had landed safely and largely intact, decided to carry out a manoeuvre which was a common practice during the Great War by pilots of the comparatively pedestrian aircraft of that conflict but not so easy in a modern Spitfire; he resolved to land beside the 111P and prevent the crew from destroying it.

As four of the five-man crew tumbled out of the Heinkel, they saw the Spitfire come over the brow of the hill flying very low, heading straight towards them. They initially feared they were to be machine-gunned, but the Spitfire pilot's intentions soon became evident when the fighter's undercarriage appeared. The German airmen then watched in amused disbelief as the Spitfire touched down on the field, raced on past them down the hill, cart-wheeled into a bog and finally came to rest upside down with its tail in the air.

The Luftwaffe men looked to their priorities, the first of which was to drag the injured rear gunner from his turret and make him comfortable on the grass before setting fire to their aeroplane.

Then they ran down the hill to rescue the RAF airman who had brought about their demise. They found the unfortunate squadron leader hanging upside down from the cockpit of his hapless Spitfire, suspended by his harness. With some considerable effort they managed to release Farquhar but then realised with horror that they had left their gunner lying too close to the now fiercely burning Heinkel and so everyone, including Farquhar, ran back up the hill to pull the injured airman away from the flames. They had just succeeded in doing so, were catching their breath and passing the cigarettes round, when a police officer and some local volunteers appeared at the top of the hill behind them. With police whistle blowing, the posse ran down to the burning Heinkel, surrounded the group of airmen, and promptly arrested everyone, including Squadron Leader Farquhar.

The Spitfire pilot's pleas of 'innocence' and insistence that he was on their side fell upon deaf ears until he suddenly remembered that earlier in the day he had stuffed the morning's post into the pocket of his tunic; it included his latest income tax demand, still in its OHMS envelope. Only then was he begrudgingly given the benefit of the doubt and released. There can be few people who have been truly grateful to have received a demand from the Inland Revenue! A few days later, the whole incident was mentioned in Parliament when Feldwebel Sprigarth was singled out for particular praise and thanks for his part in Farquhar's rescue.

As the weather eased its icy grip on Europe in the early spring, so the war gathered pace. Bomber Command's efforts were still principally targeted at the powerful ships of the Kriegsmarine, but with the mounting losses of aircraft and crews, daylight raids became unsustainable. On 12th April, the order came that Wellingtons and Hampdens would henceforth be used only for night operations.

Neutral Norway was of great strategic value to Germany, which needed its iron ore and access to its ports, both during the winter months when the Baltic was frozen and as a means to breach the British blockade. Britain also valued Norway, specifically as a route to aid the Finns, who had been attacked by the Soviets, and to deny it to Germany. Hitler got there first. His invasion of Norway started on 3rd April. In a coordinated operation, at 05.15

on 9th, the Wehrmacht crossed the border into Denmark. Three hours and twenty-eight minutes later, this small, largely unarmed and wholly unprepared country was forced to capitulate. Open resistance would have been pointless and futile, leaving the country razed and hundreds needlessly dead.

In the early days of Germany's Norwegian campaign, the Royal Navy had much success, including the sinking of the light cruiser *Königsberg* by aircraft of the RNAS, the first occasion during wartime that a major warship had been sunk by an aircraft. Nevertheless, the German landings were successful, aided by a delay in the mobilisation of the defending forces.

The first British troops landed at Namsos and Harstad on the 14th, followed by further landings at various points in northern, southern and central Norway, with the retaking of Narvik and Trondheim as primary objectives. Whilst at this stage the Norwegian government was not too particular about Britain's violation of its neutrality, we had been intending to do so for some time; it's just that the Wehrmacht beat us to it. Had the campaign gone well for the British, the Chamberlain government might have got away with the political consequences but, with isolated exceptions, the entire operation was a complete disaster, notwithstanding the great courage of those who took part.

The Germans, who were now the de facto defenders, had been able to develop establish lines of supply and communications, pour in reinforcements, and secure air and firepower supremacy. With shorter supply lines and a better prepared plan, the Germans were able to retain the initiative, and the task facing the British troops was an almost impossible one. That is not to say that the enemy were not made to fight hard to hold on to Norway, and they certainly suffered significant losses at the hands of the Royal Navy, but their superior equipment and air power was overwhelming on the land and very quickly proved to be decisive.

News of the impending disaster reached the British parliament, which debated the situation on Tuesday 7th and Wednesday 8th May 1940. Chamberlain opened the debate, followed by Clement Attlee for Labour and Sir Archibald Sinclair for the Liberals. But this was to be no ordinary House of Commons navel-gazing rumination, British and world history would turn upon its outcome. That this was the moment for Parliament to lead, to stand up and be counted, to justify its existence as a democratic institution, to hold the government to account, was clear from the outset.

There were many important and influential contributions to the debate, including from Great War Prime Minister David Lloyd George, the only solicitor to have occupied No.10 Downing Street, who lambasted the government for failing to recognise the threat Hitler posed when it had been repeatedly warned of that threat, for its dismissive attitude to Churchill's predictions of war, and for its tardiness over rearming during the 1930s when it had time to do so. But none were more devastating than two which came from the government's own benches. The first came from Sir Roger Keyes, a retired Admiral of the Fleet and the Member for Portsmouth North. He laid bare the ineptitude of the operation's planning and conduct, and the resultant impossibility of the task which had faced our troops in Norway.

The second has gone into history as one of the most influential and ruthless speeches ever delivered in the House of Commons, and it came from Leo Amery, a former Conservative Cabinet Minister and the Member for Birmingham South. He likened the campaign to the experience of a friend who had gone lion hunting in Africa and had taken the train to where he expected to find a man-eating lion the next day, ready to be hunted down and shot. However, as he slept that night, the man-eater was already out hunting. He found Amery's friend asleep and ate him. The parallels in the story were clear to all.

But his scathing and withering attack upon the government for its ineptitude was as nothing compared with his final vitriol, dressed in parliamentary language, which he saved for the government front bench. *"Somehow or other we must get into the Government men who can match our enemies in fighting spirit, in daring, in resolution and in thirst for victory.... We are fighting today for our life, for our liberty, for our all; we cannot go on being led as we are."* And then he delivered the *coup de grâce* of his speech. Having quoted Oliver Cromwell a few moments earlier, he once more leaned upon Cromwell and borrowed his words to the Long Parliament. He directed them at the Cabinet, and Chamberlain in particular, and in so doing, Amery invoked all the power of that historic dissolution, "*This is what Cromwell said to the Long Parliament when he thought that it was no longer fit to conduct the affairs of the nation: 'You have sat too long here for any good that you have been doing. Depart, I say, and let us have done with you. In the name of God, go.'*"

The debate concluded in a vote of confidence in the government, which although Chamberlain won, the scale of revolt by Conservatives was so great that his resignation became inevitable. Then, on that Friday morning, 10th May, Germany invaded the Netherlands and Belgium, the Royal Navy and Royal Marines invaded Iceland in order to deny Germany a north Atlantic base on our back doorstep, and during the night, Whitleys of Bomber Command made the first assault on the German mainland when they attacked communication targets.

With the war in Europe coming closer to our shores, a national government was needed, but Labour would not serve under Chamberlain or the Foreign Secretary, Lord Halifax. In truth, Halifax didn't want the job because he did not believe that he could properly lead such a government from his seat in the House of Lords. That evening, Neville Chamberlain resigned as Prime Minister but remained leader of the Conservative Party. King George VI sent for Winston Churchill and invited him to form a government. Three days later, Churchill addressed the Commons and promised the country nothing but 'blood, toil, tears and sweat'.

Before the war, the first news bulletin of the day from the BBC was broadcast at 6pm so as not to compete with newspapers. However, by now, the government felt it was more important to keep people informed and the BBC introduced a daily schedule of ten regular news broadcasts. Of these, the nine o'clock bulletin remained the main broadcast of the day and, if I was not at scouts or at night school, I would sit and listen to it with my father before I went to bed.

German forces swept across the Low Countries and into France from the north whilst simultaneously coming through Luxembourg and the Ardennes. For the commanders of the invading army, the plan was reminiscent of Schlieffen's ideas for conquering France a generation earlier. The names on the map and the land over which their forces now poured were certainly familiar to those who had been on the Western Front battlefields of the Great War. Indeed, this familiarity was uppermost in the minds of German commanders because they did not want to see their plans frustrated by the stalemate of trench warfare as had happened from 1914. But times had changed and, more importantly, technology had changed. Tanks and air power would prevent any return to extended trench fighting.

For the Fairey Battle and Blenheim squadrons of the AASF desperately trying to stem the flow of German troops and armaments, there was indeed nothing but blood, toil, tears and sweat. The obsolescent Battle and the lightly armed Blenheim were no match for the Bf109 fighters and their experienced pilots. Even by Bomber Command standards, the attrition of the crews was unprecedented and unsustainable. On 10th May, twenty-three of the thirty-two Battles which attacked German columns advancing through Luxembourg were shot down. The next day eight Battles took off to attack the columns again; only one returned.

On the 12th, seven of the nine Blenheims which attacked a German column advancing along the Maastricht to Tongres road were shot down by Bf109 fighters. Later that day, Flying Officer Donald Garland of No.12 Squadron, together with his navigator Sergeant Thomas Gray, were the first RAF recipients of the Victoria Cross during the war when their attack on the Albert Canal bridges at Maastricht led to their posthumous awards. Their gunner on the Lewis was LAC Reynolds. Flying Officer Garland had led a flight of five Battles of which only one returned.

By dusk that Sunday the AASF had only seventy-two serviceable aircraft from the 135 it had started with on Friday morning. The losses continued beyond being unsustainable; the AASF almost ceased to exist. The near suicidal daytime attacks against heavily defended targets had been so costly in crews and aircraft that the AOC-in-C Air Marshal Arthur Barratt ordered an end to the use of Battles and Blenheims in daylight raids. It is said that on the 14th, when told that forty of the seventy-one aircraft which had taken off that day were lost, he put his head in his hands and cried. We seemed to have already forgotten so many of the lessons from the Great War.

Fairey Battles of No.63 Squadron in 1938

Those crews who had survived were physically, mentally and emotionally exhausted. Many vomited violently in the last moments of delay before they climbed aboard their aircraft, consumed by fear that almost certain death awaited them; yet they still got in. The unremitting courage of these early Bomber Command airmen has passed largely unrecognised, but it remains amongst the highest order.

On Tuesday 14th May, the Luftwaffe razed Rotterdam, destroying 20,000 buildings and killing almost a thousand civilians, even though the country was on the verge of surrender. This needless act was the catalyst for Bomber Command's unrestricted attacks on German industrial targets later in the war. There could no longer be any pretence that this would be a war of military targets only and the embargo on attacking targets in Germany was lifted. The following night, ninety-nine aircraft attacked oil and rail targets in the Ruhr. Over the next six weeks, the news got steadily worse; the BEF were forced back to a small pocket around Dunkirk, France surrendered and we stood alone staring at invasion and defeat.

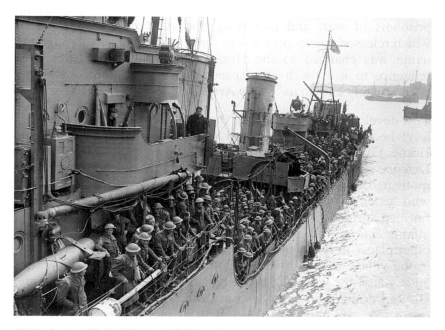

Troops evacuated from Dunkirk on a destroyer about to berth at Dover, 31st May 1940 Operation Dynamo [IWM Crown public domain]

One of our most distinguished and well-known 'local lads' was Sir Anthony Eden, appointed by Churchill as Secretary of State for War. On the same day that Rotterdam was attacked, Eden called for the formation of a local volunteer defence force made up of men aged between 17 and 65 and not, or not yet, eligible for military service. It was aimed mainly at less densely populated areas such as small towns and villages. Men volunteered in droves. Within twenty-four hours, 250,000 men had signed up; six weeks later at the end of June, more than one and a half million men had registered at police stations, far more than the administration of the scheme could cope with.

The primary function of the force, which had no uniforms or weapons at the start, was to observe anything unusual in their locality and then report it to the Regular forces. Known as the

Local Defence Volunteer Force, it soon became a source of considerable humour and was christened the Look, Duck and Vanish brigade. Nevertheless, there is no doubt that it did a great deal of valuable work, such as manning roadblocks, guarding prisoners of war, and protecting important installations, all of which released conscripted troops for front-line duties. In July, the name was changed to the Home Guard following Churchill's reference to it as such in a speech, and forever after it became affectionately known as 'Dad's Army'.

This development also brought the war to me on a very personal level because scouts were used as runners and cyclists for the Home Guard and for other organisations in the Civil Home Defence chain. We were physically fit, responsible teenagers, well motivated, trustworthy, accountable, disciplined and available; who better to fulfil this vital role? Almost as soon as Eden had finished speaking, Cockfield LDV was formed and a room in the infants' school was commandeered as its headquarters. Like many other places in rural Britain at this time, there were no telephones in the village and so it was essential to have a system of runners and cyclists for when the bombing started and the invasion came. Up and down the country, scouts and ARP dispatch riders were organised to be on hand to deliver messages wherever and whenever needed. Cockfield LDV quickly enlisted the 1st Scouts as runners, and my first job, should the invasion come, would be to run to Staindrop, about two miles away, and notify the LDV there, before running back to our HQ with any message in reply.

At the height of the invasion threat all through the summer of 1940, the scout troop was kept on a state of constant alert. When I was on the duty stand-by rota, as a senior scout I didn't even go home after work. When finally there was a chance to sleep, it was on a mattress with a blanket for cover on the floor of my old infants' school so that we were on hand to be ready at a moment's notice. We were kept in this general state of readiness for about eighteen months until the real threat of invasion had passed. By then, the village had been connected to the telephone system and the job of the scouts as runners was largely redundant. There was much excitement when the GPO installed two bright red public telephone boxes, each with its black Bakelite handset and shiny chrome push buttons 'A' and 'B'.

In the early hours of Saturday 25th May, not long after the sirens sounded, a much louder series of thuds rolled over the fells. Middlesbrough had just become the first British city to be bombed. By now I was used to seeing aircraft in the Durham skies. Aerodromes were opening up all over Britain and the north-east was no exception. Whilst Lincolnshire justly became known as 'Bomber County' because of the high number of Bomber Command airfields that would ultimately be built there, the north-east was home to many fighter, training and bomber stations, which all added to the increasing number of aircraft. After the Middlesbrough attack there were many more aeroplanes to watch throughout the summer months as the Luftwaffe stepped up its raids along the east coast and used our skies as a route to the west.

The Cockfield scout troop were kept busy in various ways, including helping the local council to take down all the signposts in the area so that if we were invaded, the enemy could not rely on our lovely informative finger posts and finials to tell them where they were and which way and how far it was to where they wanted to go. Across Britain, all scouts were constantly involved in many different Civil Defence activities. Another job we had was to collect bottles, jars, and any other sort of glassware that we could, all to be recycled.

It was vital for Britain, as an island nation at war, to grow as much food as we could and to import as little as possible, and the Women's Land Army and Women's Timber Corps were immensely important in this aim. Each late summer and autumn throughout the war, scouts went out into the countryside to help this great effort of self-sufficiency by collecting hips from the hedgerows to be made into vitamin C-rich rose hip syrup, which was then processed into various foods. It was also given to children as the thick, red, sickly-sweet syrup that a whole generation remembers with fondness, although dentists were not so keen about its impact on teeth. We also collected hazel nuts, brambles, elderberries and a range of other fruits from the hedgerows, as this was all good nourishment during the years when almost everything was rationed, in short supply or simply unavailable.

One thing that was not in short supply was invasion rumour. After the defeat of France and the withdrawal of our BEF troops, everybody knew that the moment had now come; that the invasion of our islands was the next phase of the war. However, if there really was an invasion underway, then the population needed to know. At the same time, German propaganda and false broadcasts designed to instil fear and panic needed to be avoided. Consequently, on 13th June, the government ordered that the normal ringing of church bells should be stopped until further notice; they were to be rung only in the event of an invasion taking place, and that would be the signal to the wider population.

In the early months of the war, the BBC Home Service broadcast mainly news bulletins interspersed with Sandy MacPherson at the organ. However, by the spring of 1940, people were thoroughly fed up with this diet and wrote to the BBC to say that they would rather face the German guns than have to listen to one more Sandy MacPherson tune. As a result, on the 23rd June the Home Service broadcast the first programme of what would become a wireless institution for the next twenty-seven years, *Music While You Work*. It started as two half-hour programmes, one in the morning and the other in the afternoon on weekdays, intended to help factory production by entertaining the workers.

The music was deliberately chosen to have a steady rhythm and pleasant melody and was broadcast uninterrupted into factories with the aim of keeping workers happy and thus aiding production. Introduced by Eric Coates' theme tune 'Calling All Workers', it was a great success for many years, not only in factories but with the public at large. It proved so successful that the following year the BBC added *Workers' Playtime* to the schedule. Broadcast at lunchtime three days a week from a factory canteen 'somewhere in Britain', it was a half-hour live show which enjoyed immense popularity and, like *Music While You Work*, would ultimately run long after the war had ended.

Chapter Four

"The Ruhr will not be subjected to a single bomb. If an enemy bomber reaches the Ruhr, my name is not Hermann Göring: you can call me Meier!"

Reichsmarschall Hermann Göring in a speech to the Luftwaffe, 9th August 1939

Prime Minister Winston Churchill's statement to the House of Commons at 15.49 on 18th June 1940 has become one of the most memorable speeches of all time and particularly the last paragraph of it, *"What General Weygand called the Battle of France is over. I expect that the Battle of Britain is about to begin…The whole fury and might of the enemy must very soon be turned on us. Hitler knows that he will have to break us in this island or lose the war…Let us therefore brace ourselves to our duty and so bear ourselves that if the British Commonwealth and Empire lasts for a thousand years men will still say, 'This was their finest hour'."* And so it was.

The speech laid bare just how precarious our position had become. On 30th June, German troops landed on the Channel Islands; it had been a thousand years since enemy forces had camped on British soil, and now in the summer of 1940 the imminent probability of invasion stared us in the face. People were on edge; invasion was on everyone's lips and we were kept in a permanent state of readiness. There was a significant increase in aerial activity along the north-east coast, with mounting attacks on its coastal towns and cities, and I spent many nights snatching sleep on the floor of the infants' school in between running messages.

The end of June brought a daylight raid by a single Heinkel 111 on the Saltend oil depot in Hull. One of the storage tanks was set on fire and the courage of the on-site staff in their efforts to save the whole depot from being destroyed resulted in the award of five George Medals, among the first of the war. The crew of the Heinkel, however, might rather have been elsewhere. Originally ordered to bomb the chemical works at Middlesbrough, they deliberated whether to press ahead with the attack or move to their secondary target at Hull. Unaware that they were being tracked by the defences of fighter control, they vacillated between the two targets until, short of oxygen, the pilot opted for Hull.

Accurate ack-ack fire over Hull, which was destined to become Britain's most bombed city, damaged the aircraft's instrument panel, but otherwise the crew escaped unscathed until caught by Spitfires of No.616 Squadron. In the first pass, the rest of the damaged instrument panel was shattered; next, a volley of bullets studded the port wing. The pilot just had time to see the engine cough and splutter to a stop before the next volley struck his aircraft from below, severed the hydraulic pipes and caused the undercarriage to release and drop down; then the flaps fell off into the sea. The final attack shot the starboard ailerons away and cut the fuel pipe to the remaining engine, which coughed once and stopped. The Luftwaffe crew were watching their aircraft being shot away from around them piece by piece.

Now the North Sea waited. The pilot carefully guided his doomed aircraft down to the calm waters with little hope of anything but disaster. The wheels of the trailing undercarriage struck the water, tipped the Heinkel over and the sea rushed in. The pilot and a more senior Kriegsmarine officer who was flying with the crew, Oberleutnant zur See Friedrich Koch, were largely unharmed and, after some difficulty, managed to release and inflate their dinghy before helping the rest of the crew into it. The wireless operator, though, was very badly injured, having been shot in the eye, the head, the chest and the arm. The mechanic was wounded in the buttocks and one leg. A patrolling Sunderland flying boat saw the men's distress flares and signalled to HMS *Black Swan,* which took them on board at 17.00. The men were subsequently transferred and taken ashore next day and during interrogation, Friedrich Koch related what had happened inside the aircraft.

As a general rule, at this stage of the war, Luftwaffe aircrew shot down over or around Britain were fairly happy to be taken prisoner and often asked to be taken straight to a police officer or military personnel to whom they could formally surrender. A few spoke fluent English and quite a number of others had some grasp of the language, but most did not. The Intelligence view of this attitude was that the airmen were so convinced that a successful invasion was only a matter of days or weeks away, whereupon they would be released from captivity, that they were not too concerned about being taken prisoner and even welcomed a short rest from flying duties.

The Durham Light Infantry was an illustrious regiment by any standard and its history includes no fewer than eleven Victoria Cross awards, of which six came during the Great War, including that to Brigadier-General Roland Boys Bradford, who had risen to that position through the ranks from the very bottom. Born in the village of Witton Park, only a stone's throw from Cockfield, he was the youngest Brigadier-General in the British army and had achieved the rank through his outstanding ability and leadership. He was one of four brothers, all of whom were decorated during the Great War, but when his brother, Lieutenant-Commander George Bradford, RN, was awarded the Victoria Cross too, the family became unique in the conflict as the only one where brothers were awarded the ultimate decoration. Tragically, neither of them survived; nor did another brother, James Bradford, MC.

In July, as Churchill had predicted, the Battle of Britain began, and despite the great history and tradition in Durham for the DLI, it was to the RAF that I was inexorably drawn. It was the lasting memory from 1935 of that biplane along with the daily news broadcasts on the wireless about what was happening in the war and the descriptions of aerial battles in particular that became my greatest inspiration to join the RAF. After Dunkirk, it was mainly the RAF that repelled the Luftwaffe from our skies and then took the war to the enemy's homeland and, like so many young lads at the time, I identified with it all and wanted to be part of it; I wanted to do something for my country and I wanted to do it in the RAF.

Whilst 15th September would prove to be the turning point of the Battle of Britain in the south, the turning point for the north-east came a month earlier. At 12.47 on Thursday 15th August the air-raid sirens sounded around across much of the north-east, including Durham, Bishop Auckland and Cockfield. The whole area was under attack from a large Luftwaffe force which came across the North Sea in several waves of bombers, some of which were escorted by Me110 fighters. The attackers were met mainly by Hawker Hurricanes, those great workhorses of Fighter Command, together with some Spitfires.

The German intention was to saturate our defences over a vast area of the north-east, but Air-Vice Marshal Saul, DFC, Air Officer Commanding No.13 Group, was so successful in this, his first major battle of the war, that it also became his last, because the Luftwaffe never returned to the north-east in any great numbers again during daylight hours. From a force of 157 aircraft, the Luftwaffe lost sixteen bombers and seven Me110s whilst AVM Saul's defending squadrons ended the day more or less intact and without any fatalities amongst his pilots.

That is not to say that the attackers failed completely. The all-clear was sounded at 14.10. I was at work in Bishop Auckland and towards the end of the afternoon heard the news that Cockfield had been bombed. I was desperate to get home in case my family had been affected. I cycled the eight miles back to Cockfield as fast as I could, praying that no-one had been killed. When I arrived in the village it was immediately obvious that it had suffered from the raid but it could have been a great deal worse because twenty-eight high-explosive bombs and hundreds of incendiaries had been dropped. One HE had exploded in Front Street, excavating a crater across more than half the width of the great open space that lay between the houses on opposite sides of the road. Windows had been blown out, the medieval ceilings in some of the older houses had come down, and a byre with some outbuildings had been damaged. Most of the bombs, though, including the hundreds of 4lb incendiaries, had fallen on the open land of the Fell.

It was also fortunate for the village that many of them did not explode or ignite, possibly because they had been released too low to the ground and had landed on the soft coarse grass and heather of the moors. Over a hundred soldiers were sent to the area to search for and recover these unexploded bombs and incendiaries; but the locals got there first to bag a souvenir or two. Most families in the village had at least one. I managed to find two incendiaries which, completely oblivious to the danger, I stuffed into my saddlebags and proudly took to work the following day to show to my colleagues. At this stage of the war, these were highly prized trophies.

It later emerged that Göring had not sent this large bomber force all the way across the North Sea to attack the little village of Cockfield but instead it was making its way to the west coast, possibly as far south as Liverpool. Caught out by the strength of our defending fighter force, many of the Luftwaffe crews decided that discretion was the better part of valour, jettisoned their bomb loads and smartly turned east to escape. Unfortunately for Cockfield, as some of the crews were making this decision, the village lay beneath them. It was, though, an incredible stroke of very good fortune that no-one had been hurt and an immense relief for me that evening when all the family were once again safely at home and the house undamaged.

One of the Me110 fighters which had escorted the attacking bombers to Sunderland that day ran into the No.41 Squadron Spitfire of Eric Lock at 20,000 feet and became the young Pilot Officer's first victory. Three weeks later, on 3rd September, the squadron was posted to RAF Hornchurch in Essex where within a week he had added another eight victories, including three in one sortie. By the end of October he had twenty victories to his credit, been shot down three times, awarded the DFC and bar and had become Britain's highest scoring pilot of the Battle of Britain. He was a household name; someone whose deeds were celebrated and who truly could be described as a national hero, although he avoided the limelight as much as possible.

On 8th November, he was attacked by Me109s off Beachy Head and had to make a forced landing. Uninjured, he was soon back in the air. On the 17th his squadron attacked a force of seventy Me109s, overwhelmingly impossible odds, even for Spitfires. He secured two victories and then succumbed to those odds. Too badly injured to bail out, with wounds in both legs and his right arm, his aircraft damaged, he seemed finished. But his luck had not quite deserted him. One of the Messerschmitt cannon shells had damaged the throttle and it was stuck wide open, the lever having been blown off. In a matter of seconds, the Merlin engine accelerated the Spitfire out of the combat area at over 400mph.

For Eric, his problems were just beginning. Trapped in his fighter at 20,000 feet, hurtling through the sky at full speed, he could not hope to bail out or make a scheduled landing; a crash awaited him somewhere. Having descended to 2,000 feet and selected a field, he cut the engine and, only able to use one arm, brought his aircraft down in a successful wheels-up landing. Still unable to move, he lay bleeding in the cockpit for two hours in the cold November air until found by a couple of soldiers who made a makeshift stretcher of greatcoats and rifles and then carried him the two miles across ploughed and boggy fields for help. During this trek, the soldiers dropped Eric no fewer than three times but before his ordeal was over, he had passed out.

He was sent to Princess Mary Hospital at RAF Halton for surgery. He awoke to be told that he had been awarded the DSO to add to his DFCs. His further treatment over the next six months included skin grafts by Dr Archibald McIndoe at East Grinstead. He returned to flying in June 1941, joining No.611 Squadron as a Flight Lieutenant commanding B Flight, with which he quickly brought his victory tally to twenty-six confirmed, one shared, and seven probables. He was last seen attacking German ground troops on 3rd August 1941. Neither he nor his aircraft has ever been found. Despite his early death, he remains the eighth highest scoring British ace of the war.

Flt Lt Eric Stanley Lock, DSO, DFC*, Mentioned in Dispatches
[Crown public domain]

Flt Lt Eric Stanley Lock, DSO, DFC*, Mentioned in Dispatches, the Battle of Britain's most accomplished ace, is largely now forgotten by a public who are more familiar with those who survived. The young Shropshire hero is honoured on the Runnymede Memorial and is remembered in his home county, where a road near his family home is named after him, as is the members' restaurant bar of the Shropshire Aero Club at the former RAF Sleap. He is also remembered by the Battle of Britain Memorial Flight, whose Spitfire P7350 has carried the markings of his aircraft N3162 EB-G which he flew on 5th September 1940 when he downed two Heinkel 111s and an Me109 in the same sortie.

On that night, Thursday 5th September, whilst Eric Lock was celebrating at Hornchurch, I was proved wrong again; Hermann Göring must indeed have had Cockfield on his list of targets. Just before 23.00, I was on duty at the ARP station when the local air-raid sirens sounded. Before long we could clearly hear the approach of at least two bombers. By now, we were all used to the sound of aircraft engines and could tell the difference between ours and theirs; we knew that these were German.

The bombers must have been right overhead and not very high because the noise of the engines reverberated through the air. Then came the unmistakable soft wissssh sound of falling incendiaries as several sticks rained down upon the village just behind our HQ in the school. But Sir Robert de Cockfield was once again looking after his village that night because all the bombs fell onto the Lands Bank Allotments. The magnesium quickly started to glow, but with nothing much to catch light, the small fires that did flare up were soon extinguished. There was no damage to the village but most of the cabbages, onions and late runner beans were very definitely over-cooked. It was all another remarkably lucky escape for the village and the people living in Mount Pleasant and at the top end of Front Street in particular. These rows of houses form two sides of the allotments and could so easily have all been destroyed. Nevertheless, the loss of the allotment crops was a serious matter as these were important food supplies which had gone for that season; but it could all have been so much worse.

At home, when Mum heard the bombers, she had quickly got Grace out of bed and down the stairs. With no Anderson shelter, the two of them had taken cover under the dining table, leaving Dad to organise the three boys. It was all over in a few moments and the aeroplanes droned their way out to the east, the North Sea and home. The incendiaries were obviously left over from a raid either on one of the north-east towns or a target further to the west. After they had gone, the effort for us was to put out the fires that had started in the allotments.

Ten days earlier, in the darkness of the night sky on 24th/25th August, the pilot of a Heinkel 111, no longer sure where he was but reassured by his navigator that London lay far to the east, had opened the bomb-bay doors of his aircraft and released his load of high explosives. For the rest of their journey home, the unfortunate pilot and navigator were blissfully unaware that the explosions and fires that they had caused far below in the inky darkness of the blackout were in Fore Street, part of what is now the Barbican. Hitler had forbidden raids on London and next morning the crew's officers were summoned to Berlin.

Around such events does fate spin the wheel of history. Within twenty-four hours the RAF had bombed Berlin, and Göring was being called Meier, although not to his face. Hitler was incensed both that his capital city had been bombed and that his air force had allowed the RAF to reach it at all. He ordered Göring to switch targets from our airfields and defences to Britain's cities, especially London. The change in Luftwaffe strategy came just as Fighter Command was on the point of collapse from want of aerodromes and its pilots all but exhausted. In the bright sunlit sky on the morning of 7th September, the London Blitz began. The breathing space for Fighter Command enabled it to rebuild the aerodromes and ultimately win the battle.

The night of Thursday 14th November 1940 is one of that handful of immensely significant dates which resonate through British history. It is a date which is unforgettable to a certain generation of its people; it was the night that 449 Luftwaffe aircraft bombed Coventry in relentless waves for thirteen hours. The next morning, news of the almost total destruction of the ancient city centre, together with its magnificent fourteenth-century St. Michael's cathedral, shocked the nation. It was an unambiguous attack upon the civilian population, but far from being cowed, the raid hardened attitudes and strengthened the resolve of the nation to defeat such a foe. The official death toll was put around 554, although the exact figure has never been known because no-one really knew how many people were in Coventry that night. The King visited the city during the following Saturday and was visibly moved by what he witnessed. There is no doubt that what Churchill saw upon his own visit influenced him significantly and impacted heavily upon the developing plan for the strategic bombing of Germany.

Five days after the Coventry attack, in the Midlands town of West Bromwich, eleven-year-old Howard Parker went with his friend John Downing to John's home at 104 Oak Road. The house was also the local shop owned by John's parents, William and Eliza. The two boys were making model aeroplanes for a competition at school and having finished his own, Howard had gone to help John. After tea, he was about to return home before it got too late when at 6.53pm the town's air-raid sirens sounded their warning for the 185th time since war began.

Howard picked up his coat and headed for the door to go home but John's mother wouldn't let him go out into the streets with a raid about to start. She told the two boys to take John's six year-old sister Jean, with them and go and shelter in the cellar. A flight of stone steps led down into the cold, dusty storeroom beneath the shop. From the centre of the brick arched roof a single shadeless electric light bulb hung on its short plaited cable. Dust-coated cobwebs shimmered in the draught across the brick joints of the walls and ceiling. Various sized square tins and round drums for the shop jostled for space amongst the jumble of domestic paraphernalia stored on the stone floor. Along the back wall ran a brick barrel ledge about two feet high and two feet wide on which John's mother kept the vinegar drum and other bulk liquid containers ready for dispensing their contents into customers' own jugs and bottles. Not intended as an air raid shelter, the cellar lacked any form of comfort and so with nowhere else to sit, the children sat on the cold, hard, brick ledge.

The now familiar sound of enemy bombers with their unsynchronised engines vibrated overhead. In a repeat of Coventry, the first wave dropped thermite incendiaries designed to set the town on fire and act as a beacon for the following waves. Soon more bombers arrived releasing their high explosives, which added to the mayhem in the streets and the terror of the population.

There seemed little attempt to aim for industrial targets such as the railway sidings or the large gas holder at Swan Village; it was the town centre shops, houses and shelters that were hit. An early casualty was the District Hospital in Edward Street, where the medical officer, Dr William Walton, and the matron, Miss Evelyn Thomas, were blown off their feet as they stood talking. They would each later be awarded the George Medal for bravery whilst evacuating the hospital during the raid. Another loss was the Corporation gas showrooms in High Street, although for some this was a stroke of good fortune because along with the building, all the hire purchase records were destroyed including the details of who owed money to the Corporation.

In the Downing's cellar, the children listened with growing fear as the muffled crumps of exploding bombs became louder, and the booming thumps of anti-aircraft fire gathered intensity. Jean clung nervously to her big brother. They had not experienced a raid as heavy as this before. A series of louder explosions close by shook the cellar walls and the ground beneath their feet as the pressure in the room changed, sucking the air from their shelter and causing a vacuum in their ears. Now truly frightened, Jean began to sob. With shaking hands, John lifted her onto his lap. They didn't know it, but a few yards away 2a Richard Street South no longer existed and eight members of the Care family had been killed.

Then, an immense deafening blast above their heads shook the whole structure of the cellar. In that instant, everything changed. The light went out, plunging them into absolute darkness, and with the roar of an express train, the cellar door disintegrated as great lumps of brickwork, rubble, glass and plaster cascaded, bounced, and tumbled down the steps, blocking their only means of escape and covering them in a cloud of choking dust. From outside they could hear the crash of falling masonry and timbers as the structure of the Downing's home collapsed.

The Harrises' house next door but one had taken a direct hit, killing six of the family and demolishing houses on both sides. The moments of uneasy quiet that followed were broken by the intermittent thudding of collapsing masonry and the irregular ticking as fragile lime mortar fragments, spiders and cobwebs shaken out of the joints in the brick ceiling continued to drop onto the children's heads, the floor, and the tins; but it was the roof which had saved them from being crushed.

Terrified, Jean cried for her mother as John tried to comfort her. Howard groped his way in the pitch darkness to the cellar steps to see if they could get out, but it was hopeless. He couldn't find the steps at all, only the great pile of broken brickwork and smashed timbers where the steps should have been. The shop had been totally destroyed and John's parents, who had been locking up when the bomb exploded, lay dead amongst its ruins. The children were trapped and the only two people who knew they were in the cellar were now dead.

The sounds of ringing bells on fire engines and ambulances, the throbbing drone of the bombers, the booming of flak guns and the continued crump of explosions began to filter down through the jumbled ruins to the children beneath.

The bells became louder and then stopped. The children shouted and screamed but amongst all the chaotic noise outside their cries for help went unheeded. Deep in the cellar, their voices were too faint to be heard by the ARP wardens, firemen and police officers who were now risking their lives in the burning ruins of Richard Street South and Oak Road. Realising the hopelessness of their situation, there seemed little the children could do but to wait and hope that rescue would come. They had no means of tracking time other than by their own tiredness. Cold, frightened, hungry and thirsty, they huddled together for warmth and lay down on the stone floor, quietly crying until sleep overtook them.

Sometime later, Jean was awakened by the feeling of a warm liquid soaking through her thin dress. As she moved, she felt that the floor around her was wet. Unable to see anything, she woke John and Howard. During the raid, eleven water mains around West Bromwich had been fractured hampering the efforts of the local AFS, the Auxiliary Fire Service. However, the AFS team fighting the fires at Richard Street South and Oak Road had found an undamaged supply and during the night had poured thousands of gallons of water onto the burning ruins of the houses, including the terrace where the Downing's shop had once stood. It was that water, still busily being pumped, which had awoken Jean.

The boys soon realised that if they weren't rescued soon they could all drown. There was nothing good about their predicament but if there was, it was that the water was warm. Having been sprayed onto the burning buildings, it had become heated as it filtered through glowing brickwork, charred timbers and scorched earth to trickle down the cellar steps and walls. With no other choice, the three soaking wet children sat on the barrel ledge once more and hoped that the water would soon stop rising; but it was a forlorn hope and before too long they had to stand up.

The raid had continued for over nine hours and as the last of the bombers flew away to the east, they left behind more than two hundred people dead and a chaotic tangle of wrecked and burning buildings, collapsed services and exhausted Civil Defence teams frantically trying to locate people trapped in the ruins of the town. After the All Clear had sounded around 4.00am, Howard's mother Lily had waited for his return but when he hadn't come home by daylight she went to the Downing's shop where she knew he had gone after school. In Oak Road, she was met by an ARP warden who told her that she couldn't get to the shop, it had been completely destroyed and there were no survivors. He took the details from the distraught woman and later that day, Howard's name was added to the list of fatalities displayed at the Town Hall.

By mid-morning the fires were out and with everything dampened down, the AFS packed up and left, but with all that water in the ground, the level in the cellar continued to rise. Unbeknown to the children, the bodies of William and Eliza had been recovered and, certain that there were no survivors, rescue teams had been stood down before workmen with picks, shovels and wheelbarrows had started to clear the rubble and re-open Oak Road. It was with false belief that the children thought that rescue awaited them; no-one was coming for them.

Without even the faintest glimmer of light, the darkness of the cellar was absolute, bearing down upon the children. As the water slowly rose inside that black hole, fear gripped them. Why had none of their parents come to get them out? What had happened to them? Did Howard's mother know about the cellar? Had anything happened to her and his brother George?

The passage of time was now marked by the depth of water which had reached above Jean's chin. She was no longer able to save herself, and so John lifted her up into his arms. As he did so, Howard felt something solid bump against him; it was the family's wooden one inch diameter flagpole that was floating amongst the debris in the dusty scum and filthy water.

After hours beneath the ruins of the shop, with the brick ceiling only inches above their heads, it was the immense strength of character of these children which kept them from giving up. The flagpole gave them an idea, and with it renewed hope. Whilst taking turns to hold Jean, the boys used the floating flagpole like a battering ram to bang against the back wall in the hope that someone might hear the thudding, but outside, there was still too much activity and noise in the street for their efforts to be heard.

By around 3.30 in the afternoon, the water level in the cellar had risen to the boys' chins. They were exhausted from holding Jean who was slipping in and out of consciousness. They lacked sleep and food, and despite all that water, they were dehydrated. Although air had reached into the cellar, it had mixed with lethal coal gas from fractured pipes and become toxic. Time had almost run out for them.

Meanwhile, the workmen outside had finished for the day. They needed to get back to the depot before dark in case there was another raid. Loading their tools into a truck, they were about to go when one of them realised he had left his shovel among the ruins of the shop. Content to leave it until the next day, his friend persuaded him to retrieve it lest the foreman found out. He clambered over the pile of rubble that had been the Downing's home and bent down to pick up his shovel. As he did so, in the growing quiet of the gathering evening, he heard an unfamiliar sound. Listening hard, he thought he heard it again.

"Come on Alf, get a move on, were waiting."
"Shut up, I can hear something. I think there's someone under this lot."

The others jumped down from the truck and quickly joined Alf. They stood quietly, listening. Thud. "There it is again." Thud. It was the faint sound of the flagpole being bumped against the wall. In the now failing light, the team followed the sound towards where the back wall of the shop had once stood. The blast of the bomb had exposed the cellar wall below ground level and it was against this that Howard and John were still persevering with their battering ram. The men called out and with the last of their strength the boys shouted back. Quickly retrieving their tools from the truck, the men dug through the top course of exposed brickwork and opened a way into the cellar.

To their horror, water poured out and with it came the flagpole that had saved the day. Opening up a narrow hole and taking care not to collapse anything on the children, they looked inside. The water was almost over the mouths of the two boys who still held on to Jean, though she was now unconscious. Working rapidly, the escape hole was made big enough for John to pass the limp body of his sister to the waiting arms of a man with tears running down his cheeks. Then they helped John out, and finally Howard. In the meantime, one of the men had gone to the ARP Post to send a message for an ambulance. Twenty-one hours after their ordeal began, exhausted and suffering from gas poisoning, the children were taken to Hallam Hospital which was already filled beyond capacity. After the District Hospital had been bombed the night before, its patients had been evacuated to Hallam. Everywhere men, women and children lay stitched, plastered, bandaged, and splinted on beds, stretchers, and mattresses, in wards, in corridors and in the hallway while nurses and doctors tried to cope with the tide of human suffering that had come through the doors.

Because of the shortage of space, the boys were sent to different wards where they were treated for coal gas poisoning, pneumonia, shock, and dehydration. It was a fateful event that would separate the friends for the rest of their lives. Jean never regained consciousness and died a few hours later. John was deeply traumatised by the news that his parents had been killed and that despite his and Howard's desperate efforts, he had lost his little sister too. When he enquired about his friend, he was told that Howard was listed as dead. Believing that he alone had survived, he went to live with his elder sister in Birmingham, the only remaining member of his family. John later returned to West Bromwich for a few hours. The Duke of Kent visited the town and presented a number of awards to people arising from that terrible night, including a gold medal to John in recognition of his attempts to save his sister.

On his own discharge from hospital, Howard had the uncomfortable experience of reading his name on the fatality list, but since he is now almost ninety, he is sure that this was a mistake after all. It was many years though before he was free from the nightmares of those terrible hours. Howard's mother could hardly believe the message she received when told that her younger son was alive after all and in the Hallam Hospital. Nevertheless, she would never share any information about her family and so Howard's presence in the cellar was not disclosed to the local press, and thus his endurance and heroic efforts during that time have remained untold until now.

Half a mile away, another drama was unfolding and ARP dispatch rider Charity Anne Bick was about to become the youngest person ever to receive the George Medal. At the outbreak of war, fourteen-year-old Charity lied about her age, said she was sixteen and volunteered for the ARP as a dispatch rider, where she joined the team at the Brickworks office near her home in Maud Road. The men and women on the ground were not too fussy about checking ages; Charity was doing the same job that I and hundreds of other scouts were doing up and down the country so I can understand her enthusiasm and desire to be involved.

As the bombers approached West Bromwich on that Tuesday night, the air vibrated to the booming of the defending anti-aircraft guns while the searchlights weaved across the sky seeking the attackers. Within moments the first fires quickly sprang up from the hundreds of incendiaries that rained down upon the streets.

Charity and her ARP warden father rushed up to the roof of a shop which had been hit by an incendiary. Their stirrup pump failed, though and so, fully exposed to the falling bombs, Charity carefully splashed water from the pail onto the glowing magnesium core until it was extinguished and the building saved. But the old shop roof had been badly damaged and it collapsed, sending Charity and her father crashing to the floor below amongst the plaster and broken timbers. Suffering minor injuries, they returned to the ARP post. Just as they arrived, a massive explosion nearly blew them off their feet as three nearby houses were destroyed. All the other ARP wardens were on duty elsewhere so Charity borrowed a bicycle to take the vital message for help to the Civil Defence Control Centre.

The young dispatch rider made several attempts to get through to the Centre along dangerous streets and canal towpaths where bombs were falling, fires raged, buildings were collapsing in her path and shrapnel from exploding flak shells rained upon her. Several times she was blown off her bicycle by the blast from exploding bombs. At other times she jumped off to put out incendiaries by throwing them into the cut or elsewhere out of harm's way; bombs which at any moment could have burned her alive in seconds. Eventually, covered in mud and grime, she reached the Control Centre and delivered her message. Over the hours of the raid, Charity continued to dodge the bombs, fires and falling masonry as she cycled between the ARP post and the Centre to deliver her vital messages.

On 10th September 1941, Charity received her George Medal from the King for her outstanding courage and devotion to duty during that raid. The minimum age to receive the George Medal is sixteen but on that November night Charity was, in truth, barely turned fifteen. She is almost certain to remain the youngest ever recipient of the award.

Coventry and West Bromwich saw the start of the Luftwaffe's episodic blitzing of British cities. In addition to London, Southampton, Portsmouth, Hull, Bolton, Stockport and Manchester were amongst those that quickly followed.

I was determined that the war would not get in the way of my aim to be appointed King's Scout and worked at my various proficiency tests, which included making a detailed scale map of Cockfield, undertaking a solo three-day hike and camp, and then compiling a written hike and countryside report at the end. On another occasion, to prove my axe-man skills and abilities, I met Lord Barnard in one of the tree plantations on his estate where his forester had marked three trees for us to fell. After felling the first one by way of demonstration, the Commissioner handed me the axe and watched me drop the remaining two.

Not long afterwards, as another part of the badge I was working towards, I had to swim the length of one of the Park's lakes under his supervision. Even though we were all used to the cold in the north-east, I still remember how chilled the water seemed as I waded in at the start of the swim. Then, as the pool deepened, it became bitterly cold and my muscles began to cramp. It was only by gradually increasing the speed of my stroke that I was able to keep my circulation going and the blood surging through the straining muscles.

I had by now achieved nine proficiency badges. In 1936 I had received my Tenderfoot and Second Class attainment standards; in 1938, Cyclist and Gardener; in 1939, Ambulance, and by this time in 1940, Civil Defence, Engineer, Farmer, and Pathfinder.

Almost every night when not involved in scouting, and sometimes afterwards too, I had my Civil Defence duties. In addition, I was working Monday to Saturday lunchtime at Wilson's and was at night school studying for my drawing office examinations one evening each week. Later, when the threat of invasion had passed and I was stood down from some of my Civil Defence work, I was able to spend more time at scouts and also started to learn more about the RAF.

The autumn of 1940 brought dark days for Britain. After the fall of France, we stood alone. Victory in the Battle of Britain had thrown us a lifeline, earned us a breathing space, but the Luftwaffe, much less the Third Reich, was far from defeated. The menace of the U-boat wolf packs in the Atlantic was taking a growing toll of devastation upon our shipping that plied the trade routes from the Americas and, once round the Cape of Good

Hope, those from the Far East. We were no longer able to use the Suez Canal as the Mediterranean was too dangerous for convoys which would have all fallen prey to U-boats and dive bombers. Whatever we did not produce, grow or mine from our own land had to be imported and our two navies were fighting both the enemy and the sea to bring in every last commodity that we needed to survive. Like Bomber Command's campaign, the Battle of the Atlantic would become a continuous struggle throughout the war in Europe, lasting from the first to the final day.

All our cities were bombed. Some, such as Hull, Clydebank, Plymouth, Manchester, Liverpool, Portsmouth, Glasgow, Southampton, as well as the more widely reported targets of London and Birmingham, were bombed so severely that whole areas were razed. Hull was so badly bombed that the government became sufficiently concerned about public morale that its name was censored out of the news and simply referred to as a city in the north of England.

Some of my scouting badges and photographs

Chapter Five

" The Rising Sun of Imperial Japan,
Long ago eclipsed,
Honoured man's inhumanity to man,
But Kohima's, immortal words still say,
'For your tomorrow we gave our today'."
Of War – Kenneth Ballantyne [1998]

January 1941 heralded three events of great significance to me. The first was my sixteenth birthday on the 8th, and then on the 20th the government's new fire-watching regulations came into effect. All men and women aged between sixteen and sixty had to register for forty-eight hours per month part-time Civil Defence work, which for most people mainly meant fire-watching duty. I quickly registered and added fire-watching duties to my busy rota, although my other Civil Defence work meant that I was already doing much more than the required basic hours. The third event was that in the middle of all this the Air Training Corps [ATC] was launched for boys between sixteen and eighteen. In the first six months, over 200,000 cadets were recruited, including me. I had filled my time to overflowing with things to do.

It was whilst attending my evening classes that I heard the Air Training Corps was to form a new squadron based at Bishop Auckland Grammar School, and so, together with two other scouts from a different troop, I joined No.1407 Squadron. The ATC was very new. The government had come to realise the value of the very popular Air Defence Cadet Corps, formed three years earlier and had agreed to take it over. The ATC came into being on 5th February. Like most teenagers, we didn't think about the appalling risks associated with aircrew in wartime; it all seemed very exciting, which is probably why so many young lads volunteered. Here was a chance to fly when flying itself was still a new and novel activity, and one which most people had never experienced. Before the war, only a relatively few people could drive a motor car; even fewer had ever flown, but the ATC was going to help us to join that club. There was also the issue of patriotism. It was a huge motivator for me and for millions of others during the war. We were desperate to get involved, to do whatever we could to help beat this enemy who threatened our very way of life and everything that we held dear. It wasn't just the rich who loved this country; as a generation we were brought up to be patriotic. Not everyone shares that same general feeling of patriotism today, which is a serious problem for Britain. If people have no pride, no belief in their country, they are lost as a nation.

Me as an ATC cadet with No.1407 Squadron – February 1941

At 750 feet above sea level and only about fifteen miles from the coast Cockfield had afforded me a good view of the aerial daytime combats of 1940, which had increasingly ventured inland and at times had given me a grandstand seat to what was happening. Later, high above the coastal plain, fire watching in the village gave us all a balcony perspective of the night-time bombing of the county's east-coast towns and cities. We could hear the air-raid sirens of Middlesbrough, Stockton-on-Tees, Darlington and Durham very clearly, as well as Bishop Auckland's. The sky became laced with the complex pattern of weaving searchlight beams probing the darkness, seeking out the bombers that flew across the area, some destined for the west coast, others turning to go further north. Soon our guns would start and I could hear their dull thud and see the flashes against the blackness of the land. I never really knew whether the gunners were firing in hope or at a visible target. I remember thinking, why can't they just shoot it down; they must be able to see it with the searchlights. Before I was very much older, I learned that it was not, thankfully, that easy, especially without the help of radar-controlled predictive flak.

Over the next two years I watched these scenes unfold with a growing desire to revisit this treatment upon our enemies as they continued to devastate homes and lives in the county I loved. However, because I was in a reserved occupation I knew that I was unlikely to get the opportunity to fulfil this wish. Nevertheless, I had long ago made up my mind that I would volunteer for the RAF if the chance presented itself and so it was with RAF service in mind that I had joined the ATC; it was the first step along the way and would give me a taste of what it was like.

The RAF was very particular about its recruits; wanting to fly and volunteering for aircrew was not enough. Aircrew training was rigorous, demanding, specific and tailored to each position in the aircraft, and the lives of an operational crew depended on many things, including the character of the individuals in that crew. Whilst volunteers coming from the ranks of the ATC were not treated any differently, they were looked upon favourably in the recruitment process. I trained with the ATC each week learning the basics, including how to salute, the ranks and insignia of the Service, the RAF structure, and aircraft identification. Scouts had taught me to march but now I learned to do it to RAF commands.

The Royal Air Force came into being on 1ˢᵗ April 1918, the amalgamation of the Royal Flying Corps and the Royal Naval Air Service, creating the world's first, largest and most powerful independent air force, with over 20,000 aircraft and 300,000 personnel. In the intervening years since then, it had experienced mixed fortunes. At the end of the Great War, the Army and the Admiralty wanted to take back control of their aircraft and lobbied for the RAF to be disbanded. The Prime Minister of the day, David Lloyd George, gave the Air to Winston Churchill as part of the War Ministry. Churchill was air-minded having learned to fly in November 1913 and one of his first appointments was to bring Hugh Trenchard back as Chief of the Air Staff. Together they saved the RAF at a time when the government continued to make stringent cuts to manpower throughout the service, closed aerodromes and scrapped aircraft. By March 1920, only 3,280 officers and 25,000 other ranks remained from the original 300,000. The Women's RAF had been disbanded altogether.

Ironically, it was trouble in the Empire, Somaliland and Iraq in particular, which became pivotal in securing the future of the RAF. Had it not been so, we would not have had a unified air force capable of defeating the Luftwaffe in the summer of 1940. In the early years following the Great War, the Service had not only proved that it was invaluable for Empire policing duties but had demonstrated that it could be much more effective than ground troops and at a fraction of the cost, which greatly pleased the Treasury if not the army. Out in Iraq at this time, there were four young RAF officers who had outstanding careers ahead of them and upon whom we would rely heavily during the war; they were Squadron Leaders Roderic Hill and Arthur Harris, together with Harris's two flight commanders, Flight Lieutenants Robert Saunby and Ralph Cochrane.

The swingeing cuts imposed by the government were not constrained to the RAF but applied to all the services pursuant to what was then known as the 'Ten Year Rule'. This guideline, surprisingly proposed by Winston Churchill as Secretary of State for War and Air and first adopted in August 1919, estimated the scale of our armed forces based upon the assumption that Britain and the Empire would not fight another major war for at least the next ten years. In 1929, the rule rolled over and was not abandoned until 23rd March 1932. Its renewal very nearly cost us the war before it had even begun.

The Royal Navy in particular had felt the true implications of the policy, to the point where in April 1931, the First Sea Lord, Admiral of the Fleet Sir Frederick Field told the Committee of Imperial Defence that the Navy had been cut beyond the point where it could protect Britain's trade and sea communications in the event of a war. He reminded the Committee that new warships could not be designed and built and their crews trained at a few months' notice. The Air Ministry similarly lacked animation. It was not until 1934 that the House of Commons passed an expansion programme for the RAF which, over the following three years, led to thousands of young men joining up. For many it was an escape from unemployment, for others it was the fulfilment of a dream. Whatever the reasons, these were the men who the RAF took to war in 1939.

Between February and May 1941, Göring's bombing strategy turned to our dockyards, ports and naval bases along the south-west and west coasts; Plymouth, Cardiff, Swansea, Merseyside and Clydeside were systematically attacked as part of the attempt to starve us into submission by severing the convoy lifeline across the Atlantic.

As spring turned to early summer that year, the momentum of the war still remained firmly with the Nazis. The 9th May though brought the sweet smile of fate upon the beleaguered British, even if only a handful of people were allowed to know it at the time. The day was also one of reckoning for Fritz-Julius Lemp, the man who had infamously sunk the passenger liner *Athenia* on the first afternoon of the war.

At around midday, convoy OB318 and its escort group, which included the corvette HMS *Aubretia* and the destroyers HMS *Bulldog* and HMS *Broadway* led by Commander Joe Baker-Cresswell in *Bulldog*, was off Greenland's Cape Farewell when it was attacked by two U-boats, *U-110* commanded by Kapitänleutnant Lemp and *U-201* commanded by the more senior Korvettenkapitän Adalbert Schnee. Lemp moved in and torpedoed two merchantmen in quick succession. Whether

89

because he was tired or had become a little complacent, he made two fatal errors when he failed to notice the proximity of HMS *Aubretia* and, anxious to confirm his hit, he left the *U-110*'s periscope up too long. *Aubretia*'s lookouts saw the telltale streak in the water and even before Lemp's second volley of torpedoes had struck, the corvette attacked with depth charges.

U-110 weathered the attack, but after *Bulldog* and *Broadway* joined in, the onslaught was so great that Lemp was forced to surface, whereupon the U-boat's gun crew started firing at the British ships. *Bulldog* prepared to ram and, believing his craft to be imminently doomed, Lemp shouted, "Last stop, everybody out". His crew needed no second telling and promptly dived into the sea. At which point, Baker-Cresswell quickly appreciated the potential to capture the U-boat and veered away at the last moment. As he swam towards the now waiting *Bulldog*, Lemp too saw that his boat along with all her secret equipment and code books was about to fall into British hands. He began to swim back to his vessel but was lost to the sea before reaching it.

While the surviving submariners were pulled from the water onto his ship and quickly moved below, Baker-Cresswell ordered Sub-Lieutenant David Balme to lead a boarding party onto the floundering submarine. Having crossed the choppy water in *Bulldog*'s whaler, Balme, with pistol in hand, scrambled onto the U-boat's deck. Needing to use both hands to climb and then descend the conning tower's wet ladders, he holstered his revolver, very conscious that he now presented himself as a sitting duck to any enemy sailor who had remained on board.

It was a very different world that greeted David Balme inside the U-boat. Standing in the control room, the uneasy quiet of the abandoned vessel accentuated all the little noises which he would otherwise not have noticed. The steel plates creaked as the boat gently rolled with the swell of the sea and he could hear the muffled slosh of water in the bilges. From somewhere near the stern came a rather alarming soft hissing sound. The control centre was lit by an eerie blue glow which cast a dim light across the unfamiliar dials, levers and gauges. Somewhere, something was ticking.

Inside his chest, the young sub-lieutenant could hear his heart pounding, his whole body tense and strained. Was anyone left on board, had scuttling charges been set, was lethal chlorine leaking from the batteries, was the craft already slowly sinking with him inside it? With his revolver drawn again, he slowly and cautiously made his way through the separate compartments of the U-boat. The food of an unfinished meal lay abandoned on the table, personal possessions were scattered on bunks, Lemp's cap remained perched where he had left it on the back of the small captain's table. Balme was reminded of the *Mary Celeste*.

By now he had been joined by the rest of the party and they set about stripping the U-boat of its secrets; its codes, ciphers, equipment, books, logs, charts, records, orders, documents, wireless sets, anything that looked as if it might be important. The officer organised a human chain up through the conning tower to load as much as possible into the whaler.

Cyril Lee, a stoker in the party, examined the engines of *U-110* but decided it was too dangerous to try to start them. Meanwhile, telegraphist Alan Long had found a strange-looking typewriter in the wireless room and showed it to Balme. "This is a funny sort of machine, Sir. It looks like a typewriter but when you press the keys something else comes up on it." The officer recognised it as some sort of coding equipment and ordered it to be unscrewed and taken to the whaler along with all the books and documents they could find to go with it.

What the two men had found was an undamaged, operational Enigma machine. They also recovered the daily settings until the end of June and the Kurzsignale book, the special shorthand codes used by the U-boat service to minimise the length of transmissions and therefore reduce the chance of detection at sea. It was everything and more that the code breakers at Bletchley Park had dared to dream of. The boarding party of Balme, Long, Lee, Sidney Pearce, Cyril Dolley, Richard Roe, Claude Wileman, Arnold Hargreaves and John Trotter spent six hours on *U-110* stripping it of everything and anything that looked as if it just might be worthwhile. During this time, Baker-Cresswell sent across some sandwiches for them and whilst eating his at Lemp's table, David Balme secured the U-boat commander's cap as a trophy and also a pair of very fine binoculars for his own use. By now, fears for their safety had grown and the party was ordered back to *Bulldog* at around 18.30.

U-110 was taken under tow to Scapa Flow but sank before arriving there. It is likely that, when the Admiralty realised what had been recovered, the U-boat was allowed to quietly sink to preserve the illusion that the Enigma machine and its secrets had also gone to the bottom of the Atlantic. Sub-Lt Balme's party and everyone involved in the incident were sworn to utmost secrecy. Dönitz's Kriegsmarine remained convinced that the *U-110* had been sunk in the action and never knew that Bletchley Park was now able to decipher all U-boat messages. The ability to do so, though, had to be tempered with caution so as not to alert the enemy to the security breach. It was a gift which would necessitate the Admiralty and the War Cabinet making some uncomfortable decisions in order to preserve the secret.

David Balme was awarded the Distinguished Service Cross and Allen Long the Distinguished Service Medal, whilst Cdr Joe Baker-Cresswell and *Aubretia*'s captain, Lt.Cdr Vivian Funge Smith were each awarded the Distinguished Service Order. Later, when David Balme was promoted to Lieutenant-Commander, he was the youngest officer in the Fleet to hold that rank. As for HMS *Bulldog*, at the end of the war in Europe, she sailed to Guernsey and hosted the formal surrender of the occupying German troops in the Channel Islands.

The importance and significance of Bletchley Park to the British war effort was unknown to most people and indeed unimaginable to many. The men and women who worked there in the utmost secrecy, even from each other, piece by piece stitched together the cloth of Intelligence fabric on which the war was being fought. Another vital part in the code-breaking picture came to light by pure chance and a seemingly innocuous act by an unknown German private in the Wehrmacht. At the end of August a Lorenz cipher operator sent a 4,000-character coded message from Athens to Vienna. The message was not properly received in Vienna and the operator there compounded the coming mistake of his colleague when he asked in plain language for it to be repeated. The Lorenz operator re-sent the message but, critically, did not bother to change the key settings on his machine before doing so as his orders required. Thus Bletchley Park's interceptors not only heard the same message twice, but, crucially, knew that it was the same message.

Five months later, the outstanding mathematician Bill Tutte and his team had, by a process of reverse engineering, discovered the complete logical structure of the Lorenz machine. It was an accomplishment which was later described as one of the greatest intellectual feats of World War Two. We now had the ability to decipher all the messages of the German army as well as its navy.

Bombing operations to Germany were not yet the efficiently planned and coordinated massed raids that they would become the following year. In 1941, operational crews took off for night raids more or less whenever they wanted to with navigational aids that comprised mainly a sextant, a pair of compasses, a map, and a watch. Consequently, despite the commitment and optimism of crews, the actual accurate target-hit success rate was about five percent.

Whilst the Merchant and Royal navies were fighting a very personal war to keep the supply lines open, the army's two main areas of engagement were the Far East and Mediterranean theatres. Across North Africa, General Erwin Rommel's Afrika Korps pushed hard from the west against the British 8th Army in repeated attempts to capture the Suez Canal and the oil fields of Persia and Iraq that lay beyond. Over the next twelve months, the Pathé Newsreels at cinemas reported that the Germans had captured Tobruk, then that the 8th had retaken it, then lost it, and then recovered it; backwards and forwards the port went between the two sides until finally settling into British hands.

For the families on the Home Front, there was no relief. Shortages became the normal state of affairs; rationing tightened and even onions became so scarce that there were none to go with the tripe. At 8.15 each morning, after my father and I had gone to work and the others had gone to school, my mother would listen to the *Kitchen Front*, a daily programme on the Home Service which broadcast fuel and food-saving tips and recipes for housewives.

In April 1940, Lord Woolton, who as Frederick Marquis had been a social worker and then managing director of Lewis's, had been appointed as the wartime Minister of Food; the man responsible for overseeing rationing. A year later, *The Times* of 26th April published the recipe for Woolton Pie, the creation of Francis Ladry, the chef at the Savoy. The ingredients were 1lb each of diced carrots, potatoes, cauliflower and turnips [swedes], three spring onions, vegetable extract, chopped parsley and one teaspoonful of oatmeal. The crust was wholemeal flour or mashed potatoes. There was no meat since it was heavily rationed and this made a tasty alternative. During the war, many recipes were vegetarian out of necessity.

Frederick James Marquis, 1st Earl of Woolton
[photograph: Dutch National Archives, The Hague, Fotocollectie
Algemeen Nederlands Persbureau (ANEFO), 1945-1989]

Although the pie wasn't particularly popular, Lord Woolton was, and despite the hardships that rationing brought, his personal charm wooed the public even when he was extolling the virtues of meatless rissoles, sugarless cakes, and tea without tealeaves. He brought his business skills to the job and only rationed those items of which he had enough to go round, even in small quantities. His motto could well have been 'it's a small thing that won't divide'. This policy engendered a sense of fairness and trust amongst those who were struggling to survive the hardships of war.

He also believed in dietary education and introduced Dr Carrot and Potato Pete along with the *Kitchen Front* on the wireless and Food Flashes, short films in the cinema. Rationing, which continued until 1954, meant that we ate less fat, sugar and meat, but many more vegetables and, because we walked or cycled most of the time, we took more exercise. Because of the wartime shortages rather than in spite of them, we became a fitter and healthier generation than any before or since and Lord Woolton can take a fair amount of the credit for that achievement.

June brought the most startling and exciting news that we had read for a very long time when the newspapers were full of Hitler's decision to turn on his erstwhile ally, Stalin; on 23rd, the Germans invaded Russia. As it had been for Napoleon 130 years earlier, turning east would prove to be Hitler's undoing.

On the other side of the Atlantic, though not as isolated as many Americans thought it was or wished it to be, the United States had nevertheless made its position clear at the outset of the war: it was not going to be drawn into another pan-European conflict between the old enemies and declared its unequivocal neutrality. It was content to trade with all the belligerents whilst remaining at arm's length from the fighting, even when American citizens were caught up in it and killed. 1940 was election year and President Roosevelt sought a third consecutive term in the White House on a platform of American neutrality.

In late May, Roosevelt was so sure that Britain could not resist the Nazis and that Churchill would surrender that he had a secret meeting with the Prime Minister of Canada, McKenzie King. Roosevelt sought to urge McKenzie King to abandon Britain, ensure the transfer of the Royal Navy to Canadian ports before a

British surrender, thereby denying the ships to the Germans, and thus secure the North American continent. The Canadian leader was horrified at the suggestion and, after informing Churchill of Roosevelt's assessment of British chances and of his plan, wrote in his diary, "*It seemed to me that the United States was seeking to save itself at the expense of Britain, that it was an appeal to the selfishness of the Dominions at the expense of the British Isles.*"

Prevailing American attitudes were made clear when its ship, the SS *Robin Moor* was sunk by *U-69* on 21st May 1941. Republican Senator Gerald Nye blamed Britain for the sinking, Democrat John McCormack asserted, "*It was very unfortunate but there is no reason now to get unnecessarily excited over this incident*", and fellow Democrat Senator Pat McCarran agreed. Then, in a reference to the earlier sinking by Japanese warplanes of the USS *Panay* on the Yangtze River near Nanking on 12th December 1937 whilst she was evacuating American personnel, Republican Melvin J Maas remarked, "*Japan…not only failed to rescue survivors but machine-gunned them afterward, and we didn't go to war.*" So determined was Congress to keep America out of the conflict that even the torpedoing of the destroyer USS *Reuben James* by *U-552* on Halloween 1941 with the loss of a hundred US sailors failed to ignite Capitol Hill, although it took the precaution of suppressing the news of the sinking from the public. It wasn't that Britain was without friends in America; there were many who wanted to join Britain's struggle against the tyranny and domination of the Nazis, but as minorities so often do, the isolationists shouted the loudest and Congress sat on its hands.

Joseph Grew, the United States Ambassador to Japan, was a career diplomat and seasoned officer in his country's Foreign Service. He had been the Ambassador there since 1932 and had seen the rise of Japanese militarism. An ally of Britain and America in the Great War, Japan now looked to dominate the Pacific region and all that lay in it. On Monday 27th January 1941, Grew secretly reported to Washington that he had learned from the Peruvian Minister to Japan, Ricardo Screiber, of a plan by the Japanese to attack the American fleet at Pearl Harbor. The possibility was discounted by Admiral Stark, Chief of Naval Operations at the base and the officer responsible for providing intelligence to the C-in-C of the Pacific Fleet, Admiral Kimmel.

With the passing months, Grew became increasingly worried about Japanese military plans, and on 17th November again urgently warned Washington, this time that an attack might come suddenly and unexpectedly. The battleships of the Pacific Fleet remained at anchor and Congress remained in denial. Sunday 7th December changed all that. The following day Congress voted to declare war on Japan. The first woman to be elected to Congress, pacifist Jeanette Rankin, voted against the declaration just as she had done in 1917. However, whereas in 1917 she had had some support, this time she was a lone voice. Even staunch isolationists such as Joseph Kennedy, father of the future president, were silenced by the ruthlessness of the attack at Pearl Harbor and the subterfuge which had preceded it.

In Britain, the news of the attack was greeted with joy and excitement, albeit tempered by sorrow for those who had been its victims. The expectation that America would now enter the war, with its seemingly limitless resources of men, women, materials and equipment, was eagerly anticipated. The year that had started so bleakly and had been so difficult to live through might yet end more hopefully. But it was a short-lived hope.

I joined my family around the table for tea after I had arrived home from Wilson's on Thursday evening. As usual, Dad had the Mullard switched on ready for the BBC news, but when it came we were stunned; the Japanese had sunk the battleship HMS *Prince of Wales* and the battlecruiser HMS *Repulse* in the South China Sea north of Singapore. It was the first time that capital ships had been sunk by air power alone and signalled the end of such ships in the future. Our Far East Fleet was rendered ineffectual, the Americans were preoccupied and struggling with the aftermath of Pearl Harbor; the Japanese, who were already making their way down the length of the Malayan peninsula towards Singapore, had almost total control of South-East Asia.

The first American troops arrived in Northern Ireland at the end of January, and then on 15th February, Singapore fell. Known as the 'Gibraltar of the East', Singapore was the major British military base in South-East Asia and the centrepiece of strategic planning for the area. But culturally, it was so much more than that. Singapore was a British institution; it was the embodiment of the

British Empire, it represented everything that was great about Britain. It was the Raffles Hotel, the comfortable, elegant and sophisticated living that was the colonial lifestyle, but with it had come a certain complacency and arrogance amongst the military. The defence planning had not properly anticipated a land attack through the jungles of Malaya. One consequence of this was that when the great 15-inch naval guns were turned to fire inland, it was with mainly armour-piercing shells which had little impact on infantry. Had they been supplied with high-explosive shells, Japanese casualties would have been much greater, and although the guns would probably not have been decisive, the invaders would have had to fight much harder for their victory.

Perhaps the greatest Japanese atrocity in the battle for the colony was the massacre at Alexandra Barracks Hospital when all the patients, doctors and nursing staff were brutally bayoneted or shot. When Lieutenant-General Arthur Percival surrendered to Lieutenant-General Tomoyuki Yamashita on 15th February, it was to hand over some 130,000 British, Empire and Commonwealth troops to his enemy, all of whom would be kept in appalling conditions and brutally treated. Most would be used as slave labour on various building projects, including the infamous Siam to Burma Railway, or locked away in Changi POW camp. Churchill described the fall of Singapore as 'the worst disaster in British military history'. Only the loss of Gibraltar itself could have had greater impact.

When the likely success of the Japanese attack became apparent to the owner of Raffles Hotel, MS Arathoon, he resolved that they would not have the family silver. Whilst Japanese troops crossed the Straits of Johor in collapsible boats, trusted Raffles staff buried the entire collection of precious hotel silver, including the famous solid silver beef trolley, beneath the floor of the Palm Court. The invaders never found it even though they frequented the hotel throughout their occupation. The silver stayed under the Palm Court until the Japanese finally left the hotel on 4th September 1945, whereupon Arathoon instructed its recovery.

HMS *Repulse [photograph in public domain - US Navy]*

HMS *Prince of Wales [photograph in public domain - US Navy]*

From time to time in life a passage of literature, a poem, a song or a piece of music all have the ability to be instantly recognisable and universally associated with an event or a time in history. In 1915, Hans Leip, a young school teacher who had been conscripted into the Imperial German Army wrote a poem about a nurse he knew. The poem remained the private sentimental jottings of a homesick soldier until 1937, when it was published with the title, 'Das Lied eines jungen Soldaten auf der Wacht' [The Song of a Young Soldier on Watch]. It was given its evocative tune by Norbert Schultze, and in 1939 German chanson singer Lale Andersen recorded '*Lili Marleen*'. Hardly a hit, the song sold around 700 copies and faded into obscurity.

After the Nazi occupation of Yugoslavia in 1941, the Germans used the powerful transmitter of Radio Belgrade to broadcast propaganda and programmes to their troops across Europe, the Mediterranean and North Africa. Whilst going on leave to Vienna, a lieutenant at the station was asked to bring back some more records from the Reich radio station in the city. There weren't many but he collected what he could find, including, hidden underneath a pile of old papers and record covers at the bottom of a cupboard, a copy of '*Lili Marleen*'.

Back in Belgrade, the song was played and the homesick soldiers of the Wehrmacht and the Afrika Korps adored it and adopted it. However, the sentimental ballad was so far removed from the rousing Teutonic music of the Nazis that the propaganda minister, Joseph Goebbels, forbade further plays, fearing it reminded the troops too much of home and their missed loved ones. In response, German soldiers and airmen everywhere wrote in their thousands asking for it to be played again and even General Erwin Rommel urged Goebbels to change his mind because of the morale value the song provided to his troops. Reluctantly, Goebbels relented and the song became the signature tune of Radio Belgrade's Soldatensender programme, *Messages from Home* being played every night as the last song at 21.55 before signing off.

However, the soldiers of the British 8th Army and 6th Armoured Division which faced the Afrika Korps across the desert sands also listened to the Soldatensender programme and eagerly awaited Lale Andersen's honeyed voice each night. It wasn't long before they too adopted the song and an English translation was provided. The song, which won Lale Andersen a gold disc for a million sales after the war, was subsequently recorded by many artists, including Vera Lynn and Marlene Dietrich, who it was that changed the spelling to *Lili Marlene*. It was a song and tune which became instantly recognisable and associated with the Second World War by both sides, transformed from obscurity to immortality by the hand of fate and the tenacity of a German lieutenant.

One of the great joys about true stories is that they are so often stranger and more astounding than fiction. In truth can be discovered the immense resourcefulness of the human spirit and in particular the will to survive. Throughout most of the war the threat to shipping and their crews from U-boats extended far and wide. Kapitänleutnant Carl Emmermann was the first commander of *U-172* and in the autumn and early winter of 1942 took his vessel on its third patrol. They had left their base at Lorient on 19th August to prowl the waters of the South Atlantic, and by 23rd November were on the equator around 750 miles east of the Amazon estuary. Standing in the conning tower early that morning scanning the far horizon through his binoculars, Emmermann picked up the faint telltale wisp of smoke from a ship's funnel.

The British ship SS *Ben Lomond*, which the year before had been part of convoy OB318 and the *U-110* Enigma machine incident, was steaming slowly and alone en route from Cape Town to Paramaribo, capital city of Suriname, with a cargo of ballast, when Emmermann saw her smoke. In the still, calm, blue water of the southern Atlantic *Ben Lomond* was struck by two torpedoes at 14.10 and sank inside two minutes. Of the fifty-four men on board, only six managed to escape. *U-172* surfaced and Emmermann questioned the survivors in the water. Then, having satisfied himself that neither the Master, John Maul, nor the Chief Engineer, Clement Craig, were amongst them, left them to their fate. This seemingly callous act was in strict accordance with his orders from Großadmiral Karl Dönitz contained in the infamous Laconia Order which followed the torpedoing of the liner RMS *Laconia* by *U-156* near Ascension Island two months earlier. After the sinking of the *Laconia*, three German U-boats, *U-156, U-506* and

U-507, surfaced and whilst some of the crews machine-gunned the circling sharks, others pulled men, women and children from the water, took the life boats in tow and gave food and hot drinks to the hundreds of survivors in their charge. All went well until an American Liberator arrived on the scene and indiscriminately bombed everybody, even though *U-156* commander Kapitänleutnant Werner Hartenstein had sent an uncoded message to the British in Freetown explaining what he was doing.

Among the six men who had escaped from the *Ben Lomond* was the Second Mess Steward, Poon Lim. Unable to swim very well, the Chinese-born steward had managed to pick up a life jacket and jump into the sea. In the commotion of the rapid sinking, Poon Lim became separated from the other seamen and slowly drifted away, supported by his life jacket. After about two hours, he caught sight of a life raft nearby and struggled over to it. Whilst the raft was his saviour, it also presented him with some difficulty. It was about eight feet square and made from six empty oil drums with wooden boards forming a platform which was some three feet out of the water. It was with no little effort that Poon Lim climbed onto the raft, but as he sat on the platform recovering from his exertion, he felt the great relief at being out of the reach of the marauding sharks that cruised these waters. He gazed out across the glassy surface of the ocean in every direction but could see only pieces of the flotsam and jetsam that had escaped from the *Ben Lomond*. There was no sign of the other survivors or any other vestige of human life; he was entirely alone.

The raft contained a reasonable survival kit including forty litres of water in a jug, several tins of biscuits, some chocolate, a bag of sugar lumps, some flares, two smoke pots, a torch and some rope. It had no means of propulsion and so Lim could only drift on the wind and currents in the hope that he would be picked up before too long. He carefully rationed his consumption of the food and water supplies, but as the days slipped by without rescue, this resourceful man from Hainan Island set about preparing for a longer stay. He collected rainwater in a canvas life jacket cover, made a small fish hook from the torch wire and a larger one from a nail out of the raft. He caught fish as often as possible and cut them up with a knife he made from one of the biscuit tins. The cut fish he hung up on the rope to dry, there to be eaten in leaner times ahead.

At first he counted the days by tying a knot in a piece of the rope, but after a while he gave up and counted full moons instead. Then a huge storm blew up from the south-east. Frightened that he would be swept off his sanctuary, he tied the rope around his wrist and secured the other end to the raft. Lim survived the storm but it ruined his dried fish and contaminated his fresh water. Days later, and almost at the end of his endurance, he caught a seagull and drank its blood to survive. Strengthened, he was able to fish again, including catching a shark, the fins of which he dried as a delicacy! Nearly twelve weeks had gone by when at last he saw a freighter approaching, but despite his signals, it carried on by even though he knew the crew had seen him.

Not many days later, a flight of American Navy aeroplanes passed overhead. One of the pilots saw him, circled round, and dropped a marker buoy nearby. Lim must have wondered if he was ever destined to be rescued because within the hour another powerful storm hit him and washed away the buoy. As the storm subsided and the sea settled, a U-boat surfaced not half a mile away and began gunnery drills, shooting at seagulls. Once more, he was ignored by the crew. Then one afternoon, after more than four months drifting alone across the South Atlantic on his raft, he noticed that the water had changed colour and was no longer the deep blue of the ocean. What he was seeing was the silt sediment being washed out to sea from the Tocantins River, part of the great Amazon basin; he was nearing land.

On 5th April 1943, after 133 days on his raft, he was picked up by three Brazilian fishermen and taken in to Belém. He spent four weeks in hospital and then Poon Lim returned to Britain where he was awarded the British Empire Medal by King George VI in recognition of his unparalleled achievement. The Royal Navy too had much to learn from this humble second steward and incorporated his experiences and skills into its survival at sea manual. Poon's was a battle not only with the elements and physical survival, but also an emotional and psychological one to overcome the fear, desolation and loneliness he had experienced during those months adrift. In the end, it was his strength of character, his skills, his wits, and his determination to survive which had brought him through.

Poon Lim had survived on a life raft longer than anyone else had ever done. When this was pointed out to him, he replied, "I hope no-one will ever have to break that record." So far he has had his wish.

Poon Lim on his raft [photograph in public domain – US Navy]

Chapter Six

"And Crispin Crispian shall ne'er go by,
From this day to the ending of the world,
But we in it shall be remembered-
We few, we happy few, we band of brothers."
Henry V, Act IV – William Shakespeare

On Saturday 2nd January 1943, six days before my eighteenth birthday, I went to the RAF recruiting office in Durham with my friend Joe Teasdale. I had found a way out of my reserved occupation status at just the right time. Desperate for operational aircrew, the government had relaxed the rules. If I volunteered for aircrew duties, I could join the RAF and then, if I overcame all the hurdles along the way, I would be able to go to war in an aeroplane. If I stumbled at any point, I would be straight back to Wilson's. On that cold January day, Joe and I offered our services to King and country. The first hurdle was a very quick medical hardly worthy of being called 'an examination'. We were informed that we were classified A1 fit, which we already knew, and told to go home and wait for the RAF to contact us.

The next scout meeting was the monthly Commissioners' gathering and, as usual, Lord Barnard's chauffeur glided the Rolls Royce to a silent halt with the back door directly level with where I was standing at the bottom of Esperley Lane. As we drove to Cockfield, the Commissioner, knowing of my desire to join the RAF, asked me how I had got on in Durham. I told him that I had formally volunteered and been provisionally accepted. He was very pleased and advised me to keep a diary and take a camera with me throughout my service, as many people did even though both were strictly against the rules.

There had been a few changes at scouts since the start of the war, perhaps most notably we had lost our scout master, Leslie Young, who had been replaced by Mr Clinton. Les Young's peacetime trade was a joiner/cabinet maker for Lord Barnard. His home was thirty miles away, but in the 1930s, very few people outside the south-east of England were able to commute that distance each day and so Les had been given the use of three rooms in Raby

Castle. In the early years of the war, together with some of the other older scouts, I would go to Les's rooms where we would make home implements and decorate items which were sold in the village to raise much-needed funds for the scouts. Then, around 1941, Les got married and moved out of the castle and into an estate cottage. He may have been a reservist because not long after this he was either called up or volunteered for the army and became a sergeant in the Royal Artillery, where he served as the commanding NCO of a Martello tower in the sea approaches to London.

These round towers were built across the British Empire during the 19[th]century, mainly as coastal forts. They were constructed with very thick walls and a flat roof, on which was mounted a gun emplacement. By the latter part of the century, the towers had become obsolescent, but because of their sturdy construction most had survived, and indeed many still do. That solid construction with a 360° field of observation and their self-contained design made them once more defensively important structures. Equipped with anti-aircraft guns, some were brought back into use, and it was from one of these forts in the Thames estuary that our scout master conducted his war.

Others left the troop too; I would simply be another in a line of departures. Sid Best joined the Royal Marines and served on a small ship that brought back the wounded Canadians after the abortive attack on Dieppe. After that he was posted to Iceland to support the protection force there, whose job was to prevent a German invasion of this most strategically placed island. I met up with him on one of his home-leave visits during which he told me that anyone posted to Iceland had to take a canvas coffin with them as part of their kit because of the paucity of trees on the island!

Two other scouts joined the army whilst Joe Teasdale and I followed Jack Rand into the RAF as aircrew. Jack, who had been Troop Leader, served with Coastal Command flying Sunderlands, and after the European war ended was posted to SEAC, the South East Asia Command. On one occasion he was detailed to land his Sunderland on an extremely small lake in the Burmese jungle, there to pick up several captured high-ranking Japanese army officers, each of whom was bound hand and foot to prevent their suicide, and bring them back for interrogation. It was a particularly difficult mission to fulfil but Jack managed to safely deliver his important prisoners, an accomplishment which earned him the DFC.

Meanwhile, Joe spent the war as an air gunner with Bomber Command, during which time he was awarded the DFM for shooting down a night fighter. There was a keen interest in the RAF amongst the apprentices at work and in addition to me, Wilson's lost another three to the Service, one of whom served in the Far East flying in Beaufighters, but sadly he did not survive and was lost on operations over Burma. Another local lad who was lost over the jungles of Burma was Simon, the eldest son of the Secretary of State for War, Anthony Eden. A navigator with No.62 Squadron, twenty-year-old Pilot Officer Simon Eden lies in the very beautiful Taukkyan War Cemetery.

During the Great War, his father had served on the Western Front with the King's Royal Rifle Corps, which was initially recruited from the agricultural labourers of County Durham, and with whom he fought at the Somme. During that battle he was awarded the Military Cross for saving the life of his sergeant, a decoration he rarely mentioned even when describing the incident that led to it. In 1916, at the age of nineteen, he became the youngest adjutant on the Front, and two years later when appointed brigade-major of the 198th Infantry Brigade, was the youngest officer in the British army to hold that rank.

The other person who was very pleased to know of my impending entry into the RAF was my Uncle Alf Beadle, one of my mother's two brothers who had gone through the Great War. It wasn't so much the advice that he gave me that I valued but a possession that I carried with me on every operational mission, his Great War Service pistol. The Webley Mark VI was a .455 calibre weapon, and once I became operational, I was able to draw the ammunition for it from the station armoury. I carried it down my flying boot along with my sheath knife and it became a sort of lucky charm for me. It was also a great comfort to know that should I have to parachute into enemy territory and things not look too good, then at least I would have the chance to take some of them with me.

This might sound a little melodramatic but we already knew that some crews who had been shot down, especially over or near the target they had just bombed, were subjected to mob rule and hanged from lampposts, sometimes with their own scarves. Others were murdered by the SS or the Geheime Staatspolizei, the universally feared and despised Gestapo.

Having been accepted for aircrew in principle, some weeks later I received a letter and travel warrant instructing me to attend the RAF Recruitment Centre in Doncaster for the Aviation Candidates' Selection Board assessment. Joe and another ATC friend from the nearby village of Copley were also called that day.

The assessment was carried out over three days, which meant that we had two nights to stay at the Centre, but because several of us there were ATC and used to being away from home from time to time, we got up to all sorts of antics, probably enjoying ourselves more than recruits were supposed to. On one of the nights we had a huge pillow fight during which someone's pillow landed on my face. I threw the pillow back over the beds but unfortunately it hit the light in the centre of the room. The lamp swung wildly on the end of its plaited cable, crashed into the ceiling and smashed the Bakelite shade, the shattered pieces of which showered down in all directions. That put an end to that game. A little while later, I received a bill from the RAF for a replacement shade.

The interview process was divided into four parts. The first was a medical examination, which, although a little more detailed than the Durham one, was still fairly superficial, essentially being designed to ensure that each recruit had four limbs, could walk, talk, see and hear, and did not suffer from any obvious disease or impairment. A much more thorough examination would come later down the line. Next was a series of written tests, including general knowledge and intelligence. The intelligence test was very simple to start with but gradually became more difficult as the paper progressed. There was also an elementary mathematics paper. Then we had a series of basic aptitude tests designed to determine which particular job in the aircraft each one of us would be most suited to. Lastly, we were interviewed individually by the serving RAF officers of the Selection Board.

I had applied to be a pilot but the Board informed me that whilst I was considered suitable for pilot training, the PNB [pilot, navigator, bomb aimer] scheme was over-subscribed and that what were needed more urgently than pilots were flight engineers and air gunners. Consequently, with the level of my apprenticeship examination attainment, I was recommended for FE training. I was very happy with this; it was aircrew and I was going to be able to fly. At one period during the recruitment drive, this selection scheme was so short of air gunners that, as an incentive, those volunteers who passed the training were promised an immediate commission.

Before I left, the officer made it very clear to me what the risks faced by aircrew were. With such low chances of survival, he asked me to confirm that I still wanted to move on to the next stage of consideration. I desperately wanted to fly and, like most people, I took the view that it would always happen to the other chap. I confirmed my resolve to him. After that came my attestation. I signed Form 2168, my Notice Paper containing the conditions upon which I was to be employed by the RAF as a volunteer for the duration, swore my Oath of Allegiance to the King, and received my service number, 1591101.

I was told to go home and await my call-up papers, which would include instructions about where I was to go next. Whilst I was waiting, I received a letter of welcome to the RAF from Archibald Sinclair, the Secretary of State for Air. I also continued my apprenticeship at Wilson's but now with a new purpose.

Easter 1943 was very late, with Good Friday falling on the 23rd April. The month was generally quite warm, but on 7th, devastating gales swept Britain only to return for the bank holiday weekend and make a misery of people's brief respite from work. Everything certainly didn't shut down for a bank holiday as in peacetime, but whilst production continued as usual, additional time off was given. For those working on the factory floor, especially munitions workers, these breaks were an important opportunity to get some fresh air and sunshine. It was a rare opportunity to perhaps have the chance to spend time with a husband or wife, girl or boyfriend.

The weekend also celebrated an important psychological point on the Home Front. The government used the significance of Easter in our Christian country to lift the ban on the ringing of church bells on the Sunday as thanksgiving for deliverance from the threat of invasion. It was the first time since June 1940 that the bells had rung out across the land from steeples and towers great and small. The relaxation was for Easter only and the congregations which filled the churches made the most of it. We really had seen off the threat of invasion; the spectre of Nazi jackboots marching up Whitehall and through our villages no longer haunted us.

Mid May brought news of what would become the RAF's most famous bombing raid of the war; the outstanding attack on the Ruhr dams by No.617 Squadron. The Möhne, the Eder, and the Sorpe dams held back the waters of three immense reservoirs which fed the factories of the industrial Ruhr valley. The first two structures were breached, but the human cost was very high. Eight aircraft were lost, along with fifty-three airmen, and another three were taken prisoner. On the receiving end, something in excess of 1,650 people died, almost all from the flood waters that were released.

The raid would prove to be a huge propaganda coup but also a great missed opportunity as Bomber Command failed to follow up the attack with conventional high-level raids to prevent the rapid rebuilding of the two dams and the resumption of the hydro-electric power they produced.

By now, I had passed all the tests for another three badges; Missioner and Blacksmith in 1941 and Handyman earlier this year. Only the Camper badge stood between me and Scout First Class. I desperately hoped that I would be able to achieve this before my call-up came. At the end of June, Lord Barnard hosted another of the many scouting weekends at Raby Park, only this time it was the highly competitive scouting and camping event which was attended by six local troops. After Jack Rand left to join the RAF in 1941, I was appointed Troop Leader and thus it was for me to lead the 1st Cockfield to victory and the coveted competition trophy.

The entire weekend was one long competition. Everything we did, from the way the tents were put up to the food we prepared, from the conduct of the troop to the specific challenges, were all observed and marked by the monitors. Finally, at the end of the weekend, the results were collated, the scores added up and the 1st, 2nd and 3rd places awarded. The winners were the 1st Cockfield Troop. I was immensely proud of all the scouts in the troop who had worked so hard to win this trophy against some very tough opposition. Scouting was the most popular activity for both boys and girls from all walks of life and those involved in it devoted much of their leisure time to learning the skills that were taught. The weekend was a double personal triumph for me. I had led the troop to victory and had also successfully completed my Camper badge, which brought with it the Scout First Class badge.

My call-up papers came on 12th July 1943, within a fortnight after the scouting competition, and so the presentation celebrations were put off for the time being. Enclosed with my orders and travel warrant to London was a notice which stated: "*You will be taken on strength from the date you report for duty and will also be issued with uniforms etc as soon as possible thereafter. You should therefore bring with you the minimum of personal requirements.*" I was to report to No.1 Aircrew Reception/Receiving Centre, at RAF Regent's Park, although upon arrival, the actual assembly point was Lord's Cricket Ground, the home of English cricket and the MCC, which was being used as the Induction Centre for RAF aircrew for the duration.

Despite wartime rationing and shortages, we had pride in our appearance in 1943, and without exception, every one of the thousand or more recruits was dressed smartly in a suit, blazer and flannels or sports jacket and trousers. We each carried a little brown suitcase containing the bare necessities and stood waiting for our names to be called out by the sergeant conducting the roll-call. Had I been wiser, had I known then what I know now, I might have taken a few moments to look around at the fresh, freckled faces of the young men who stood there, fain to fight, and ponder upon how many would still be alive when peace returned; the answer was fewer than half.

As the roll-call progressed, we were divided up into 'flights' of sixty men, each one given an identification letter to go with the intake number. I was part of No.5/107/A Flight. Each Flight had an NCO in command. His first order to us was to put down our cases and stand to attention. A neat row of brown cases appeared on the grass next to their owners and we stood to attention. Then came the order 'at ease'. It was immediately apparent who had been in the ATC, the police cadets, Boys' Brigade or some other disciplined organisation. Some of those who had not had no idea what to do but quickly copied the rest. Our corporal introduced himself and told us a few of the basic rules governing our stay at RAF Regent's Park, which, stripped of all waffle, boiled down to the fact that we were not free to go into London whenever we wanted and would do as we were told.

After that we were called to attention and marched off to have our kit issued. A variety of local business premises had been requisitioned and were utilised by the RAF for kitting out each intake of recruits. As well as the extensive grounds of Regent's Park, some of the requisitioned buildings were also used for fitness training and overflow eating places. We were issued with our uniforms and other kit, everything from tunic to gas mask, steel helmet to housewife. Included in the kit was a white cap insert which we wore to denote that we were aircrew under training. At this stage, our uniforms were Service Dress or 'Best Blues'; we would be issued with battledress when we got to our ITW, Initial Training Wing. For now, this was all that we needed. All the items were set out on the Scale of Issue, including any variation from that printed on the form.

With my kitbag loaded and slung over one shoulder and that last vestige of civilian life, my little brown suitcase, in the other hand, I joined the squad to be marched to our billets, which were in various blocks of flats scattered around St John's Wood; for A Flight, St James Close, Prince Albert Road, became home. Our training as airmen had begun. In the four weeks that each intake spent at RAF Regent's Park, the emphasis was heavily upon making a start at getting the raw recruits fit, used to wearing the uniform, accustomed to military discipline and responding to orders without question.

The RAF had the use of the whole of the Park, including the Neo-Georgian Winfield House, built in 1936 by the American heiress Barbara Hutton on the site of the earlier house which had been destroyed by fire that year. The house, which is now the residence of the US Ambassador, had been requisitioned for the war, and in 1943, some very fortunate Balloon Squadron airmen and WAAFs were billeted in it together with various other equally fortunate RAF units.

In 1829, the owner of the original house, Francis Seymour-Conway, 3rd Marquess of Hertford, bought the very distinctive clock from the tower of St. Dunstan-in-the-West just before the church was demolished. Founded at the end of the 10th century, St. Dunstan-in-the-West was one of the very oldest churches in London, along with St. Martin-in-the-Fields and the RAF church, St. Clement Danes, and may have been founded by St. Dunstan himself in his final year as Archbishop of Canterbury. The 3rd Marquess had hung the clock on the front wall of his house which thereafter quickly became known locally as St. Dunstan's. At the time of the First World War the house was in the hands of the American financier Otto Kahn, who lent it to a new charity which had been founded to look after blinded service men and women. The charity took its title from the house and that is how St. Dunstan's got its name.

In our block of flats, four were allocated to a bedroom, which just about gave us room to swing the proverbial cat around. The beds, which will be very familiar to a certain generation, were iron framed with a wire mesh on which we laid the thin mattress 'biscuits'. By now it was afternoon and none of us had eaten since breakfast. We changed into our uniforms, packed our civvies away in our suitcases, tied them with string, wrote our home addresses on the label supplied and left them downstairs to be collected. The RAF took them to one of the mainline stations from where they were sent on. It would be some years before those clothes were needed again. We were now marched over to the London Zoo main building in the Park for a mug of tea and a 'wad'. It was here in the visitors' restaurant that we took all our meals, and no doubt some wag suggested the zoo was an apposite venue for the assembled company!

113

Afterwards, we were ordered to collect a towel and wait outside. A few minutes later, our corporal marched us to the nearest swimming pool and told to us to strip off, even though we had no costumes to put on; what a sight that was! We then lined up about ten at a time, jumped into the pool and swam as many lengths as we could. I was an accomplished swimmer, so it was enjoyable for me, but it was a struggle for some and a terrifying experience for those who couldn't swim at all. But that was the object of the exercise; the RAF needed its aircrew to be able to swim in case of a ditching and this was the surest way of finding out those who could and those who couldn't.

Back in our billet, we set about making up our beds, complete with hospital corners, and marking every piece of clothing and equipment with our own service numbers. The mattress biscuits and blankets were already in the room, stacked on each bed by the previous occupant. There were no sheets or pillow cases; they were not provided to recruits at ACRC! Next we tried to understand the Air Diagrams on Form 1385 which showed how our kit should be laid out for daily bed inspections and weekly kit inspections. The daily bed inspection required the bed to be stripped, the bedding folded and wrapped in a blanket folded long ways so that the folded bedding inside could be seen, looking a little like a sandwich, and stacked on the mattress biscuits along with certain other items of kit. This is sometimes referred to as a 'boxed bed', although strictly speaking, a boxed bed has the folded bedding hidden by a second blanket folded around the bundle at 90 degrees to the first, thus creating a true box. The weekly kit inspection was everything on the bed in the designated order as shown in the diagram.

The next day, each Flight was taken in turn to the RAF barber, whether anyone needed a haircut or not. It is, or was, a sort of military tradition that the first act was to give each recruit a short-back-and-sides, even though most of us had one anyway because only women, girls and a few bohemian artists grew their hair long and wore ponytails. Then we were inoculated against diphtheria, typhoid and smallpox, a wonderful cocktail of drugs. A few had bad reactions and needed to be admitted to the sick quarters, which had hospital status.

The inoculations were followed by a very detailed medical examination, with the emphasis being upon the examination, which stripped away all dignity and left nothing to the imagination. It also included an X-ray for tuberculosis and anyone found to be suffering from TB was immediately confined to sick quarters. At the end of the process, the doctor had to be satisfied that each recruit was FFI [free from infection], or able to be treated in the sick quarters until FFI or, worst of all, was unfit for aircrew duties. If his finding was the latter, the recruit's services were dispensed with. Whether the RAF had some other use for him would depend upon the doctor's particular findings and conclusions; if there was a doubt, the recruit was rejected.

To add the final touch of excitement to the day's delightful activities, each airman had to visit the RAF dentist. Any tooth which gave the slightest hint of concern was filled, without the benefit of either a gum-numbing injection or a high-speed drill. If filling was not an option, the tooth or teeth, as the case might be, was removed. Finally, we were each issued with our Identity Card, Airman's Service Book, which the airman always carried except on operations, and Pay Book, which was retained by the RAF. In addition, our two identity discs were issued, but for the time being they were kept with the airman's Pay Book until we started flying. I was paid 3s/6d a day, which included 6d per day war pay, and I received it, less any deductions, in cash fortnightly at the pay parade.

After four weeks of marching, swimming, drills, kit inspections, fatigues, aptitude tests and lectures on the administration and organisation of the RAF, King's Regulations, RAF law, signals, mathematics, and the use of weapons, we had come to the end of our time at Regent's Park. All in all, I had enjoyed my time there. Much of what we did was simply an extension of the training that I had been receiving in the ATC, and many of the skills I had learned in the scouts stood me in good stead throughout my RAF years. The postings to the various Initial Training Wing stations for the successful recruits came through and I was sent to the specialist centre for flight engineers, No.21 ITW Torquay, re-designated No.3 from September.

Straight after an early breakfast on Wednesday 11th August, I joined my kitbag and some other fledgling flight engineers in the back of a 3-tonner for the short ride to Paddington station, where we caught the train to the West Country. Reading, Newbury, Westbury, Taunton, Exeter, the Great Western 'Castle'-class engine raced along the familiar route, smoke streaming from its stack whilst its miscellany of passengers chatted, dozed, read, completed crosswords, or simply watched the English countryside pass by. With Exeter behind us, the most delightful but potentially most dangerous part of this whole journey was about to begin. The line took us down to the estuary of the River Exe, then alongside the shore, across the headland of Dawlish Warren and once more within feet of the English Channel, through Dawlish and on to Teignmouth. Trains on this section of track were vulnerable to Luftwaffe fighter bomber attacks, mainly by Ju88s, but we were lucky and passed through unhindered to Torquay, where we arrived late in the day.

Our billets were in the Devonshire, Dorchester, Park Hall, and Regina Hotels, which had been requisitioned for use by the RAF. Once again, the dormitory was made up of the maximum number of beds that could be squeezed into a room. There were four in my room at the Dorchester. However, the great luxury that we now enjoyed was sheets and pillow cases, which were issued to us more or less as soon as we got there; the mattresses, though, were still the ubiquitous biscuits.

The next day, I received my battledress issue, training syllabus, aircrew lecture notes and a pamphlet entitled, 'YOU are going to be a FLIGHT ENGINEER'. I wasn't sure whether this was an order, a challenge or an attempt at humour, but since training personnel have no sense of humour, I quickly discounted that option. The pamphlet briefly set out the six-week training regime during which we would be taught the basic principles of the subjects that we would study in much greater detail when we moved on to the next stage, which would also have a more practical aspect to it.

At Torquay we completed our instruction of RAF law, administration, organisation and discipline, and gas attack procedures. Drill and physical exercise were part of every day's

116

timetable except Sundays. Today, when every house is built with an inside bathroom and a shower and when there is a multi-billion-pound industry in men's cosmetics and toiletries, it might seem strange that personal hygiene and sanitation were also taught. It was, though, indicative of the housing conditions of many pre-war families that this most basic facet of service life was included in the curriculum. Pride in one's appearance and hygiene standards fed into the overall culture of personal and collective discipline.

The Dorchester Hotel, Torquay

Reveille was 06.30 each morning followed by breakfast half an hour later. The day was filled with a combination of classroom lectures, practical demonstrations, drill, and fitness sessions until 18.00. Sundays started at 07.00 and were free of formal training exercises. There was compulsory church parade each Sunday morning, a tradition which reflected the importance of religion in both the services and society more generally, especially in a time of war. Lights out was 22.30 whatever the day.

Whilst the evenings were technically our own, there was little time to relax as there was kit to be cleaned, boots to be bulled, guard duties, inspections and fatigues to be done, and exams to be revised for. We were examined at the end of each week and at the end of the course. To pass was mandatory for progression. Anyone who had just failed by a whisker was given extra training; substantial failure resulted in the airman being removed from the course and transferred to General Duties Section.

Swimming was strongly encouraged, as was dinghy drill. The likelihood of a returning aircraft having to ditch in the sea was fairly high. Flak, fighter damage or a lack of fuel were the most common causes. Consequently, it was in each airman's own best interests to be able to swim and to have practised dinghy drill. Later on, when we were on our squadrons, dinghy drill became an important part of our continued training and practice on those days that we were not on operations. Nevertheless, squadron commanders expected crews to have more than an elementary understanding of the procedures before they got to their stations.

Since Torquay was on the coast, we were able to replicate reasonably realistic sea-ditching conditions in which to practise dinghy drill by dropping off the quayside into the water whilst wearing full flying kit. This I usually enjoyed, but on one occasion I felt a little unwell and therefore decided to avoid the session. Unfortunately, a fair number of the other cadets chose to do the same thing, though in their case it was simply to avoid getting cold and wet. As if scripted, that was the day that the instructor decided to check to see how many of us had our swimming costumes; it was not many, which cost us seven nights' jankers, cleaning and dubbining football boots.

We were issued with some of our flying kit for use in this dinghy training as well as for some of the other exercises relating to aircraft during the second half of the course. This kit included flying boots, a Mae West life jacket, emergency whistle, parachute harness, warm socks, three pairs of gloves [silk, wool and chamois], leather gauntlets, flying helmet complete with oxygen and communication mask, goggles and an all-in-one flying suit together with a second kitbag to put it all in. In true military custom, everything was recorded on a form, in this case Form 667B. Battle damage excluded, the RAF never lost any kit, only airmen lost kit, and if they did, sooner or later it had to be paid for, as wireless operator Arthur Atkinson discovered to his cost.

In April 1944, No.61 Squadron ended a detachment to Coningsby and returned to its base at RAF Skellingthorpe. The Squadron's bulk equipment was transported by road but lighter items were loaded into their Lancasters. After landing at the base, the aircraft were parked at dispersal and left while the crews located their billets. This done, they returned to the aircraft to collect their own equipment. Much to Arthur's dismay, when he climbed back into T for Tommy he realised that his flying boots, which he had left in the rear of the aircraft, were nowhere to be found.

He was detailed for operations that night and so hastened to the station stores in the hope of borrowing a pair of boots, at least for the night. His plea was met with a flat refusal by the storekeeper, whose explanation was as logical as it was callous, "That's all very well, but what if you fail to return; I will be short of a pair of boots. You can buy a replacement pair." Flying boots were expensive, which is why someone had helped themselves, and it would have cost Arthur more than a week's pay to replace them. Left with no other choice, he flew that night in his uniform shoes.

The wireless operator in a Lancaster not only occupied the warmest seat in the aircraft but also controlled the heating system, and so instead of purchasing replacement boots, he flew that operation and the rest of his RAF service wearing shoes. He was eventually demobbed in 1946, but when he came to hand in his flying kit, he was still short of his flying boots. Despite having risked his life on more than thirty missions over occupied Europe on behalf of his country, his efforts were not considered to be worth a pair of boots and he had to pay up. The RAF always gets its kit one way or another.

A few years ago, Arthur read the book *Keeping Watch* written by former WAAF, Pip Beck, who described her experiences in the flying control tower at various Bomber Command stations, including Skellingthorpe. She told the story of how her feet were always cold until some kind airman gave her a pair of flying boots which he had obtained from an unknown source! It seemed that here was the answer to Arthur's mystery and he didn't begrudge her warm feet in her time of need. Out of interest, Arthur looked up the dates of Pip's time at Skellingthorpe against his own but their service hadn't overlapped and so they couldn't have been his boots after all. He does, though, like to think that the recipient of his 'donation' was a WAAF as pretty as Pip Beck rather than some sweaty airman.

It was inevitable that my intake would include a number of other scouts from across the country and we got together on a regular basis throughout our training. As we passed through our training, two of these lads became particular friends, Tom Marton from Oxford and Jack Mately from Leeds. Happily, they both survived, although towards the end of the war Tom's service concluded in a way I could never have guessed.

At the end of the six weeks' course, I passed all the examinations and moved on to the next stage of my training at St. Athan. However, before travelling to South Wales I had two weeks' home leave. The County Commissioner had asked me to telephone his secretary whenever I was home on leave and to make arrangements to visit him at Raby Castle and let him know how I was getting along in the RAF. I used one of the two new telephone boxes in the village to ring the castle and made the arrangements to visit the following day. Lord Barnard greeted me warmly and we went through to one of the many rooms, where his wife brought us tea. No longer was I the 'boy' scout but a young man training for war, reflected in the manner of my reception.

He had kept in touch with my parents and so knew that I would be home at the end of the month. To coincide with my leave, a scout 'camp fire' had been arranged for Friday evening in St. Mary's Church Hall at which I would be presented with the winners' trophy from the June camping competition together with my Scout First Class badge. When Friday came we had such an enjoyable evening that for a few hours the clock was turned back to the 1930s and the more innocent time of those pre-war days. The local newspaper even sent along a reporter to cover the story. The Cockfield Scout and Guide bands provided the music and other local Brownie and Wolf Cub packs helped with the entertainment. Lord Barnard, in his role as County Commissioner and on this occasion accompanied by his wife, Lady Sylvia, congratulated the troop and presented me with the South-West Durham Competition Trophy and then my Scout First Class achievement badge for which I had worked so hard over many years.

Then he sprang his surprise upon me; I had also been appointed King's Scout. It was not an automatic appointment upon making Scout First Class but was dependent upon the County Commissioner's personal recommendation to King George VI; it was a rare achievement. I have always tended towards self-deprecation, but in that moment I felt an immense pride within myself, not just for the achievement but for my many years of tenacity. With war raging, my Civil Defence duties, my apprenticeship work, and night school to attend, it would have been very easy to let the scouting slip. It was a hard enough goal to reach in peacetime; in wartime it had been twice as difficult, but I had never lost my enthusiasm, interest or enjoyment, and now I had joined a very small and exclusive band of scouts at the pinnacle of the movement.

Lord Barnard had deliberately not said anything to me on Tuesday but had kept the award back as a surprise. I was overjoyed as he handed me the King's Scout badge and the coveted red and white all round shoulder cords. The Commissioner was very generous with his congratulations but I knew that in addition to my own efforts, my achievement had much to do with the considerable encouragement which both he and Leslie Young had given to me and indeed to all our scouts over the years. This was the fulfilment of the ambition which had dominated, guided and motivated my childhood and teenage years, and was an immense privilege. Along with countryside pursuits, scouting had been my greatest love when I was growing up, and the following week, whilst still on leave, I went into Durham to have my photograph taken in full King's Scout uniform.

All too soon, my leave was over and it was time to return to the RAF. I caught the bus to Durham station and then the train to Paddington, where I changed for Cardiff. From the Welsh capital it was a local train to the newly upgraded halt at St. Athan. Since I was now lugging two kitbags around with me between postings, I was very pleased to see an RAF bus waiting there to take the newly arrived cadets to the base.

Torquay trainee flight engineers - I am 6th from left in the 3rd row back

The Vickers Wellington – the mainstay of Bomber Command during the early years of the war

Chapter Seven

"Any landing you walk away from was a good one"
RAF axiom

Planned in 1936, RAF St. Athan was opened on 1st September 1938 as No.4 School of Technical Training and included a substantial maintenance unit facility. In June 1942, it started to train flight engineers as the heavy four-engine bombers, the Stirling, Halifax, Lancaster and American Liberator, joined the war. The introduction of these large aircraft, like the invaluable Sunderland flying boat, demanded a highly trained flight engineer to be responsible for and manage their multiple engines and complex fuel, oil, electric, pneumatic and hydraulic systems. The FE was responsible for *"the technical maintenance of his aircraft, on the ground or in flight. Before flight, testing the serviceability of the engines, instruments and ancillary equipment; the calculation of fuel requirement relative to the bomb loading and to ensure the safe return of the aircraft and crew safely to base. In flight, ensure economical use of fuel, periodically record all instrument readings, operate emergency systems if required, carry out emergency repairs; act as Second Pilot or Air Gunner when required."*

This is what I had now come to St. Athan to learn. The training was superb, well organised with the best of equipment and instructors, covering a vast and varied number of topics, including techniques and disciplines. It was here that we built upon the basic knowledge that we had acquired at ITW in the theory and principles of flight, navigation, meteorology, airframes, Merlin engines, carburettors and magnetos, electrics and instrumentation, pneumatics, hydraulics, oil, air flow, fuel systems and logs, vacuum, cooling, oxygen and heating systems, armaments, aerodrome procedures, and much more. Interspersed with all the learning, a fairly rigorous fitness régime was maintained.

Christmas 1943 came and went. Although the day was free from any lectures and we were treated to a pretty good Christmas dinner, there was no home leave. The next day, it was business as usual. It wasn't until the end of the tenth week of the course that we were given seven days' leave. I was glad to get home again and have a break from all the intensive learning, even though I was certainly enjoying what I was doing. When we returned to St. Athan, we were given the option of which four-engine type of aircraft we preferred to fly. The reason for the choice, which was given only to flight engineers, was simply that the engines and their relationship to the aircraft as a whole were different in each of these aircraft types. From that point on, each recruit concentrated upon that type for the rest of his training; I chose the Lancaster with its Merlin engines.

The intermediate stage of the course lasted for seven weeks, at the end of which we enjoyed another seven days' leave. This time, when I returned, it was not to St. Athan that I went but to the Avro factory at Woodford in Cheshire, now part of Greater Manchester. In 1924, Alliott Verdon-Roe moved his aeroplane factory to Woodford from Alexandra Park Aerodrome in south Manchester. By 1943, it was the main Lancaster bomber construction, assembly and test factory, and I would spend two weeks there on the 'Manufacturer's Course' gaining a greater understanding of how this famous Rolls Royce engine was put together, its component parts and its idiosyncrasies.

Together with another St. Athan trainee, I was given digs at a house in Wilmslow. As part of the very tight security surrounding the bomber production, we were told to report to the local police station when we arrived. Having done so, we had our identities thoroughly checked. Once satisfied that we were who we were supposed to be, a Police Constable escorted us to our digs and told us which bus to catch in the morning for the factory. Our landlady was a cheery soul and looked after the two of us very well. Her husband and son were both away on active service and having trainees under her roof perhaps helped to ease the worry she must have carried.

We were not troubled by the Luftwaffe whilst I was there. Manchester had suffered its worst bombing at Christmas 1940, raids which over two nights had radically changed the built environment of the city. However, although the bombing had largely stopped by 1943, on Christmas Eve the following year, forty-five V1s were launched at Manchester from Heinkel aircraft over the North Sea. Of these, fourteen fell into the sea, but the remaining thirty-one made landfall as far apart as Newport in Shropshire and Spennymoor, close to my home in County Durham. My fortnight at Woodford was really interesting but it rushed by all too quickly, and back at St. Athan the intensive training programme picked up where it had left off.

We were, though, not isolated from the world and each day we read the newspapers, which religiously printed the censor-approved details of the war. The fall of Singapore was the last substantial failure in the war for the British. It was followed later that year by the success of the 8th Army in North Africa, and although there were to be many months of bombing yet to endure together with failed operations along the way, the mood was increasingly one of optimism that we would eventually win. We also knew that the war could not be won without an invasion of occupied Europe, but we had no idea when it would come.

Whilst I had been at Regent's Park, the first invasion of Italy had taken place on 3rd September, followed by the Italian surrender five days later. Then, just as I started at St. Athan, came the news that Italy had changed sides and declared war on Germany. This was very bad news for Hitler, not because the Italians were a particularly strong ally, but because of Italy's geographical location. By changing allegiances, the Italians had offered up what Churchill called 'the soft underbelly of Europe'; an easier way into Germany. That was not how it turned out, though, for all those involved in the Italian campaign, for in addition to fighting the enemy, they also had to contend with the most destructive of nature's forces when Vesuvius erupted in March 1944. By then, our troops had become bogged down in Italy. The Germans, commanded by Generalfeldmarschall Albert Kesselring, had replaced Italian troops and sought to defend Italy in a series of 'lines' across the country, resulting in bitter and costly fighting for both sides.

RAF Bomber Command still remained the only force able to attack Germany, and because the British public wanted to know more than anything how the war in Europe was progressing, that is, what damage we were inflicting upon Germany, the newspapers continued to report the activities of the Command, its successes and our aircraft losses, or at least those approved by the censor. Since we were busily training to become aircrew mostly destined to join Bomber Command, these losses were of immense and intense interest to us. In February and March, towards the end of the Battle of Berlin, the Command suffered its greatest numerical losses of the war in three raids which came in quick succession.

Leipzig, Berlin, and Nuremberg cost us 245 aircraft lost, together with those that crashed on return to Britain; seven, and sometimes eight, young men in each aeroplane. Throughout our time at St. Athan, we had tried to make light of the almost daily tally of losses by drawing humorous cartoons and annotated sketches of possible scenarios in our text books, usually involving the fate of our instructors; but losses on this scale could not be laughed off. In a rare display of compassion, the RAF actually discharged one of the cadets on my course. Briggs had an elder brother who was posted MBK, Missing Believed Killed, on operations. There were only the two of them in the family.

Earlier in the war, the RAF was not so sensitive to such matters, but perhaps the unbearable, though certainly not unique, tragedy of the four Garland brothers, all of whom served in the RAF, weighed heavily upon its conscience. Following the death of Flying Officer Donald Garland VC at Maastricht, by 1943 two of his three elder brothers had also died; their remaining brother would be killed in Holland before the war ended. Thus for Briggs, it may have been that even as early as the beginning of 1944, the RAF neither wanted nor needed to risk inflicting such pain on yet another family.

As we progressed through our training, we became more confident in our abilities, more comfortable as cadets; we enjoyed more freedom and the fun that it brought. During training, we were billeted in the station barracks, which were actually hundreds of single-storey wooden huts in rows of twelve. Each hut accommodated sixteen cadets and had a small room at one end for the NCO. After the fortnightly pay parade, many lads celebrated with a few beers in one of the local pubs before wandering back to barracks in time for Lights Out. What goes in usually needs to come out, and during the night the need arose. This was winter time in west Wales and so rather than go outside in the wind and rain to the lavatory block, the deed would often be done in a fellow airman's boots, which were usually neatly placed at the foot of the sleeping innocent's bed. Next morning there was always trouble, swearing, accusations and much amusement by all but the unfortunate victim.

Sometimes at the weekend we would have a night out in Cardiff, after which we would catch the local train back to St. Athan. The carriages on these trains almost always had compartments with a corridor, and so to help our meagre pay go a little further, we used a trick or two to avoid everyone in the group buying a ticket. Because of the blackout, there was no lighting on the trains for fear of attracting the attention of a passing Luftwaffe intruder aircraft. Having pooled our money to buy the correct number of tickets less two, we would find an empty compartment and then the two lads without tickets would climb up into the two luggage racks and lie down in them. Once the journey started, the ticket collector would come along in the normal way, but because of the blackout, he only had a small pencil torch and so stood in the corridor to check the tickets as we handed them to him through the compartment door. Should he try to look into the darkness of the compartment, the correct number of bodies would be seated, but the two lying in the luggage racks had a free ride.

Another favourite ruse involved a little creativity, and cadets whose homes were too far away to visit by rail on a twenty-four-hour pass became very adept at forging travel warrants. This is how it worked. Upon returning from a legitimate weekend away, a cadet would ask a friend to meet his train at the station when it got in, together with an extra platform ticket, or else to pass one through the railings to him at a pre-arranged point. The returning cadet would then hand the valid platform ticket to the collector at the gate as he left the station whilst retaining the legitimate railway warrant, which he could then alter with a new date for future use.

To give us both the training and the feel of being in an actual aircraft, salvaged cockpits were used. This allowed us to simulate and practise pre-flight checks, take-off procedures, 'flying for economy' and landing procedures. There was also a tethered airframe on which we practised running up the engines to full throttle. However, the constant noise associated with this became a problem and St. Athan became a pioneer of flight simulators.

In January 1944, after successfully passing the first part of the course at St. Athan, I was reclassified as AC2 (Grade B). Whilst this didn't amount to a promotion in the usual sense, it did signify an important stage in my training. It also meant a pay rise of two shillings a day, which was not to be scoffed at and enabled me to send some money home for my parents to help them out.

We came to the end of the syllabus in midMarch, were given some revision time and then into our examinations, which were a mixture of written and oral tests. They were very detailed and intense, but at the end of it I had passed with an above-average mark. I now received my flight engineer brevet and a real promotion to the rank of sergeant, which was the minimum rank for aircrew. I also had a doubling of my wages to ten shillings and sixpence a day. During the evening of Thursday 30th March 1944 I proudly sewed my sergeant's chevron stripes onto my best blue and battledress tunics, and removed the white cadet flash from my cap in readiness for our passing-out parade the following day.

As I did so, little did I or anyone else know that within a few hours, Bomber Command would be suffering the most disastrous raid in its illustrious history: Nuremberg. On Friday morning, it was a very sombre organisation that evaluated the night's fiasco and, as the scale of the losses filtered through to all levels of the Command, at St. Athan, like elsewhere, we could hardly believe what had happened. Although the training regime never missed a beat, the raid inevitably had the effect of concentrating our minds upon what we had signed up to do.

The raid had gone ahead even though a reconnaissance aircraft had reported clear skies all the way to the target, with 10/10 cloud over the city. The moon that night was also particularly bright and shone for the whole outward leg of the mission. The defending fighter pilots didn't have to guess the target; they could see the bomber stream as clearly as if it was daylight. Ninety-five aircraft failed to return from Nuremberg and a further fourteen crashed whilst trying to land back in England. The raid was a complete disaster of the highest order. It had achieved nothing and cost the lives of 535 airmen, with another 180 captured as prisoners of war or lying wounded in Britain. It brought an end to the Battle of Berlin.

The night did, though, produce a Victoria Cross, awarded to twenty-two-year-old Pilot Officer Cyril J Barton of 578 Squadron from RAF Burn, the captain of Halifax LK 797. Still some seventy miles from Nuremberg, his aircraft was attacked by night fighters, which resulted in the loss of the intercom system, the machine guns, and one engine. Although his aircraft was now defenceless, Barton pressed on to the target, coming under further fighter attacks on the way.

Then, in a communication mix-up, his navigator, wireless operator and bomb aimer bailed out. Against all odds, they reached Nuremberg, where P/O Barton released the Halifax's bombs. At this point the propeller blades of the damaged engine broke up and flew off. Flying on three, the pilot turned his battered aircraft for home. It wasn't long before his flight engineer realised that precious petrol was seeping away from damaged fuel tanks. With the strengthening headwind it would be touch and go. Using his experience, Cyril Barton managed to avoid the heavily defended areas and, despite the worsening condition of the weather and his aircraft, crossed the enemy coast and headed towards Yorkshire. However, without his navigator, he was unaware that the wind had pushed him out over the North Sea, and by the time that he sighted the coast near Sunderland, he was ninety miles north of his base and almost out of fuel.

In quick succession, two of the three remaining engines spluttered to a stop, their fuel spent. Barely able to remain airborne on the last engine, the Halifax shook violently as it approached stalling speed. Moments later it crashed in the railway cutting at Ryhope Colliery. The two gunners and flight engineer scrambled from the twisted wreckage with only minor injuries, but in a cruel twist of fate, their brave young captain was not to join them. The posthumous Victoria Cross awarded to Pilot Officer Cyril Joe Barton was both the sole VC of the Battle of Berlin and also the only one to a Halifax aircrew member during the entire war.

With the end of my course came a week's leave, which gave me the chance to go home and relax whilst I tried not to dwell upon the terrible losses of aircrew at Nuremberg. Again I went to the scout meeting and helped out. I also had news of my ATC friend from Copley village who had joined up with Joe and me at the beginning of 1943. He had been accepted for pilot training and sent out to Canada but had unfortunately failed to reach the required standard. After his return to Britain he was eventually seconded as a Bevin Boy and sent down the mines. Largely forgotten about until very recently, around ten per cent of all conscripts became Bevin Boys and there is no doubt that for some at least, fighting the claustrophobia of that work each day took a huge amount of courage.

My next posting was to RAF Scampton in Lincolnshire and the Aircrew Commando Training School there. Originally known as Brattleby, the aerodrome was first opened in 1916 with temporary wooden huts, six hangars and no recognisable runway. With the end of the Great War, the aerodrome was closed and by 1920 everything had been removed and the land returned to farming once more. Closed but not forgotten, the aerodrome was re-opened as part of the air force expansion programme of the 1930s in response to Germany's rearming. Now called RAF Scampton, it came into being on 27th August 1936.

In addition to Guy Gibson for his part in the Dambusters' raid and his leadership over a sustained period, the station was home to two other outstanding Victoria Cross recipients. Flight Lieutenant, later Wing Commander, Roderick 'Babe' Learoyd of No.49 Squadron was honoured for his courage and determination in pressing home the attack on the Dortmund-Ems Canal in the face of intense and overwhelming defensive flak on 12th August 1940.

The following month, Sergeant, later Flight Sergeant, John Hannah from Paisley by Glasgow, was the wireless operator in a Hampden of No.83 Squadron flown by P/O Connor when it was hit by flak and machine-gun fire over Antwerp on 15th September 1940. The ensuing blaze was so intense that it forced the navigator and air gunner to bail out. Hannah, though, stayed behind and, while the aircraft's own ammunition exploded around him, he fought the fire even when it melted the floor beneath his feet. First he used the aircraft's extinguisher, then his parachute, and finally his bare hands to quell the flames, and in so doing saved the life of his pilot, who was able to bring the battered and burned aeroplane back to Scampton. Connor was awarded the DFC and John Hannah, the Victoria Cross. Sgt Hannah was only eighteen years of age at the time of his action and is not only the youngest ever RAF recipient of the Victoria Cross but was also destined to be the youngest recipient of the award from any of the services during World War Two.

By the time I arrived at Scampton for the Commando course in early April 1944, the aerodrome was closed to flying while the old grass runways, which were no longer suitable for the increased bomb load capabilities of our heavy four-engine aircraft, were upgraded to concrete ones. No.617 had moved to Coningsby before going on to Woodhall Spa, whilst in August 1943 No.57 Squadron, which had provided three crews for the Dams' raid, had gone to the newly constructed airfield at East Kirby. Then, on 15th November, B Flight was moved a quarter of a mile across East Kirkby aerodrome to form No.630 Squadron.

The Commando course was designed to teach aircrew how to use the various little pieces of equipment that were included in our escape kit in order to evade capture, along with survival and unarmed combat methods should we be shot down over enemy territory. The old 57/617 Squadron crew rooms became our lecture hall, and in one of them the models of the three Ruhr dams, which had been used by Gibson's men as part of their training, were still on display and made fascinating viewing. After this course, I was posted to No.1660 Heavy Conversion Unit at RAF Swinderby where, because of a shortage of Lancasters, we flew the Short Brothers Stirling for our heavy bomber training. These Stirlings had been withdrawn from operations as increasing numbers of Halifaxes and Lancasters became available to squadrons. However, the idiosyncratic characteristics of this particular type led to some interesting and dangerous experiences for us.

The course at Swinderby was a double one lasting for three months; the first part was the Heavy Conversion element, which trained us to fly the large four-engine aircraft. The second was the Operational Training element, where we formed ourselves into the final combination of individuals who would make up each crew.

131

My first course was with an all-Canadian crew who had most probably done all their basic training in Canada before being transported to Britain for the final stages of training. All flight engineers were trained in Britain prior to being crewed up and I flew as 2nd engineer with this crew.

The Stirling was designed to fly with two pilots, hence the need for two FEs. For take-off and landing, the 1st engineer sat in the co-pilot's seat. After take-off, he would go back to his proper seat behind the cockpit and I would sit in the co-pilot's seat. The purpose of this first course was to give us practical flying experience as flight engineers before we teamed up with a permanent crew.

With the constant demand upon aircraft to be available for use, it was inevitable that maintenance suffered. Accidents and incidents were a common occurrence but we just got used to them, although the fewer you experienced, the better it was for everybody. The little ones, we all learned from. The major ones, the serious injuries, the fatalities, we tried to put to the back of our minds; it did not do any good to dwell upon these things, it got in the way of concentration and learning; the training programme had to carry on, come what may.

Several times during the three months that I was flying from Swinderby, I experienced one of the common problems in heavy bombers, that of tyres bursting on take-off or landing. Familiarity with this event bred neither contempt nor complacency; it was a most unnerving experience and not one to be recommended. The Stirling's original wingspan design had been reduced down to 99′ overall so that it would fit into the standard T3 hangars. Because of this, the tyres were manufactured to 6′ diameter, the effect of which was to increase the angle of attack of the wings to the air for take-off. The trouble was that any twisting of the tyres by a bit of line-up adjustment during take-off or landing, especially with a crosswind, caused the steel-wire moulding inside the tyre to fracture, breaking the walls and piercing the inner tube, causing the tyre to burst under the pressure.

Another particular problem with the Stirling was the propensity for its engines to catch fire, a very unhealthy habit when airborne and one that I experienced on HCU with the Canadians. One night, we had been in the air for about an hour and were at about 17,000 feet when the starboard outer engine suddenly started to trail flames, which were getting larger by the second. The 1st engineer operated the fire extinguisher, cut the engine and feathered the propellers. The pilot began to gradually lose height. I could feel my heart pounding inside my chest as I watched expectantly to see if the flames would subside or whether I was going to have to bail out, which is something that we had not had, and were not going to have, any training for.

For some reassurance, I checked that my parachute was to hand. After about five minutes, the combination of the extinguisher and the warmer air at the lower height seemed to work and the flames flickered and gradually died away. Our navigator set a course for Swinderby and we headed for home with as much haste as the remaining three engines would allow.

The Short Brothers Stirling – the first of Bomber Command's four-engine 'heavies'

Not only had we been at risk of the fire spreading to the rest of the wing and bringing the aircraft out of the sky, but we were also in danger of being seen by any prowling Luftwaffe intruder which could have finished us off very easily. Stirlings were particularly prone to engine fires, often caused by problems with the cooling system. The large circular engine oil cooling radiator slung below each radial engine would start to freeze at altitude from the bottom upwards, causing the engine to overheat and catch fire, as had happened to us.

On another occasion when we had been on a bombing exercise, one of the practice bombs hung up in the aircraft bomb bay, but then after we landed back at Swinderby, it dropped out onto the hardstanding and exploded. It wasn't a huge explosion as it was only a practice bomb, but it was enough of one to cause some damage to the aircraft and would have seriously injured or killed anyone standing close to it.

Most crews experienced quite a few problems during flying training and there were many accidents during the programme. Casualties in training accounted for fifteen percent of all Bomber Command losses during the war. The aircraft were old, worn out, poorly maintained and over-flown in order to meet the endless demands to supply crews to operational squadrons. There were several fatal crashes even during the period I was at Swinderby.

At odd times we did manage to have a night off in Newark or else we cycled down to a dance at Morton Hall, which was No.5 Group's HQ and quite close by. Walking back from there on my own one night, I came across a hedgehog in the road and it gave me an idea. I gently gathered up the little creature in my forage cap and carried it back to camp, where I quietly slipped it, including all its many fleas, into the bed of a sleeping airman and then waited! It's a good job he didn't know it was me.

One evening, when night flying was cancelled early, I borrowed a bicycle from another airman and together with three other lads, cycled into Newark. After an enjoyable time there, we set off back to camp, but as bad luck would have it, we were stopped on the way by the police and I was reported for riding my bike without lights and was subsequently fined five shillings by Lincoln Magistrates, even though I had pleaded the blackout in mitigation. I know that I had broken the law and the police were doing their job, but I did feel a little aggrieved that the magistrates did not have a better understanding that in a few weeks' time I would be flying over Germany risking my life by taking the war to the enemy. I was tempted to point out to the bench the irony that on such occasions I would be riding my whopping great Lancaster bomber which would also have no lights on it! Ah well, *c'est la guerre, c'est la vie*; at least I can laugh about it now.

Improvements and advances in aeronautical technology and procedures have made flying today a relatively safe form of transport and leisure pastime. Putting aside the deliberate destruction of an aircraft in flight by terrorists or by some other act of sabotage, crashes are now very rare occurrences. It was not always so. In the early days of aviation, most pilots learned by trial and error, usually their own, although the smarter ones also took heed of others' mistakes. The Great War brought technical advances to these rudimentary machines and to our understanding of the natural forces which played upon their fragile frames.

The war in which I had elected to fight as aircrew had brought larger, faster and more efficient aircraft, but the dangers associated with flying them had also increased. Everything happened much faster, there was more to go wrong, the pressures of training meant that maintenance was often skimped or skipped altogether, the aircraft were packed with a deadly cocktail of highly explosive bombs, ammunition, petrol and electrical equipment, there were many more aircraft crammed into the skies, be they over Britain or over occupied Europe, and collisions were many and often, and the enemy had developed more efficient and sophisticated methods to bring us down; flying had become a very dangerous occupation.

From the moment he stepped into the aircraft for his first training flight, the average life expectancy of an RAF airman became progressively shorter. By the time he became operational, it was as little as seven missions. Consequently, serious relationships with women were not recommended. Whilst I was at Swinderby, I knew one very pretty WAAF who had lost three successive boyfriends in flying accidents at the station and inevitably became known as a 'chop girl'.

Chop girls very quickly acquired a reputation that they were best avoided. I'm sure that most, like the one I knew, were perfectly nice girls; it wasn't that sort of reputation that they had. In wartime, it was the much worse reputation of being unlucky. In a highly male-dominated service, all girls were in great demand, and the prettier they were, the more attention they attracted. But bad luck just seemed to accompany some of the prettiest. In RAF slang, anyone who was killed was referred to as having 'gone for a Burton', after the beer advertisement at the time, or alternatively as having 'got the chop'. Thus, if the boys that a girl stepped out with then got killed, she would be known as a chop girl and suitors very quickly dried up.

It was during the second part of the course at Swinderby that I teamed up with the rest of my crew. They were: Flight Sergeant Jerry Monk [pilot], Flying Officer Len Knowles [Bomb Aimer], Sergeants Jim Kenealy [Rear Gunner], Jock Gillespie [Mid-Upper Gunner], Joe Baldwin [Wireless Operator] and Bill Whenray [Navigator]; it was with these six men that I would go to war as their Flight Engineer.

One day in early June there was a complete shut-down at Swinderby and the skies around us were eerily quiet. There was no flying, no leave, nothing outside the confines of the base. We carried on with our ground training wondering what it was all about. The next morning, Tuesday 6th June 1944, we understood: D-Day had begun and the Second Front had opened. Everyone, including the Germans, had known that it was coming and that it would be soon, but we hadn't known exactly when or where. Now, everyone knew it was Normandy. That day was also our first OTU flight as a full crew and, although we were not involved in the Normandy landings, it would not be long before we were, bombing the Wehrmacht and the Waffen SS positions to break their defences and help open the way for our ground troops to move up into France and on towards the Rhine and Germany.

We were accompanied on our first three flights by one of the instructors, P/O Olsen, whilst we practised circuits and landings time and again, and then three-engine flying. After that he let us go solo on circuits and landings. The next exercise was fighter affiliation and corkscrews, for which P/O Olsen joined us again.

The flying training now seemed very thorough and hectic; it was also relentless. We trained constantly for six and a half days every week, all hours, day and night. We were put into aircraft and practised take-off, cross-country navigation, bombing, fighter affiliation and corkscrews, aiming-point photography and landings, time and time again. With each take-off, the law of averages increased the hazards and the chances of an accident.

Mitigating that average was our mounting expertise, ability and fusion into a crew working together as a team; it was a race against the odds, as it would continue to be when we became operational. As well as acquiring the necessary skills, we would have to have the essential element of luck, and enough of it to see us through; only time would tell.

One June day, we took off to practise high-level bombing, but after we had been in the air for about half an hour, the starboard outer engine spluttered, coughed and cut out. It didn't matter what I did, it would not re-start. There was nothing for it now but to turn back to base, glad that we had practised flying on three earlier that week. It was an uncomfortable flight back to Swinderby as we were all very conscious that should we lose another engine, we and the aircraft would be tested to the limits to get back at all. We radioed the Watch Tower to explain our predicament and were cleared to land. This was now the most vulnerable part of the whole trip; to lose the starboard inner now would spell complete disaster. The only saving grace was the daylight; it was midafternoon. Jerry brought the Stirling down first time and a combined audible sigh of relief swept through my headphones as we safely sped down the runway before turning onto the peri-track and heading for our dispersal.

Later that night, three other crews were not so lucky and a wireless operator, a bomb aimer, three flight engineers, and a pilot were all killed. Amongst the three Stirlings lost was one which exploded. There were rumours afterwards that this had happened because one or two of the crew had been smoking during the flight, which was strictly against the rules. The problem here was that the fuel-priming systems for each of the four engines were located inside the fuselage, causing a constant smell of petrol and accompanying fumes. Shorts had manufactured the Stirling on very similar lines to their highly successful Sunderland flying boat where they had had to install the system inside the aircraft, and so they simply incorporated the same design on the Stirling, a feature which sometimes brought such disastrous results. Lancasters and Halifaxes had their fuel-priming systems located outside the fuselage, in the undercarriage wheel arches, and so this type of internal explosion couldn't occur.

We were lucky in our hut to each have a single bed because in 1944 the station was severely overcrowded, with some 3,000 aircrew at any one time all going through training on conversion and OTU courses in addition to the permanent flying and ground crew staff on the base. To overcome the shortage of accommodation, many of the huts had been fitted with bunk beds. This overcrowding also led to many accidents and crashes both on the ground and in the air, but such was the pressure on the throughput of aircrew that the situation was not resolved until the end of the European war.

Amongst those thousands of men I managed to meet up with Ashley Wilson, who came from Cockfield and lived at the newsagents in Front Street, opposite St. Mary's Church. Ashley was a few years older than me and was married, but I had known him at home in much the same way that I knew everyone in the village. He was an AC1 ground staff at Swinderby and as I got to know him better, we became pals. The fact that I was a sergeant and outranked him was completely irrelevant; we were simply friends from the same village. Since Ashley was married, he only went to the occasional dance, but for the single men on the station, each and every one of these occasions was an important opportunity to unwind and forget the hard training we were going through. Ashley was only too pleased to help me out and so when there was a dance in the airmen's mess he would lend me his tunic to wear. Sergeants were not normally permitted into the airmen's mess except on duty or for an open-invitation occasion, so I would not have been allowed in to their regular dances wearing my own tunic. But thanks to Ashley, I was able to lindy hop, big apple, quickstep and waltz my way through many more happy evenings.

The training was hard and relentless at Swinderby but I enjoyed myself and made good friends. One particular friend was Vin Taylor, who I flew as 2nd engineer with and who would be posted to East Kirkby. Another was Bill Burr, who seemed so much older than the rest of us though he was only twenty-seven! Bill, who had been a pharmacist before joining the RAF, used to look out for me and was very kind, but because of his good nature, I couldn't resist playing all sorts of pranks on him. Inevitably, the day came when he had the opportunity to reverse the tables. Late one morning, I was in bed fast asleep after having been night flying. Bill and some of the other students carefully carried my bed outside and across to the other side of the road with me still in it, sleeping like an innocent.

Relocating me in broad daylight was bad enough but their true intentions were arrantly mischievous as they continued to carry me a little further, then oh so very gently, lowered my bed to the ground – directly outside the main entrance to the Waafery. It wasn't long before female voices, fresh air and the heat of the sunshine on my face broke through my sleep. As I began to sit up, I quickly realised that this time it was me who was the victim of the joke and that my predicament was the source of much amusement to all the WAAFs who walked past my bed as well as to my so-called friends. With few alternatives, I took the most pragmatic option; I lay back down, pulled the blankets over my head and stayed there until Bill and the others carried me back to the billet, accompanied by plenty more laughter and giggles from the Waafery.

When returning from a night out in Newark, some of our students managed to 'acquire' a side of bacon from a loaded railway meat wagon due for transportation. Before leaving the station, they hid the bacon inside the greatcoat belonging to one of the group, and with it slung over his shoulder, brazenly handed in their tickets to the collector at the exit. Back at the camp, the bacon was hidden inside an air-raid shelter ready to be cut up later and then cooked in the billet. Bacon, like almost everything else, was still strictly rationed and as young men we always seemed to be hungry, so in addition to a very welcome change from wartime RAF food, the bacon would be quite a treat.

A side of bacon was both valuable and traceable. Someone had noticed that the meat wagon had been tampered with, remembered that RAF lads had been in the station at the time and put two and two together; the local police became involved and the game was up. The bacon was retrieved from the air-raid shelter and the students were put on a charge. They were very lucky that the CO at the time, who I think was Air Commodore John Whitworth, DSO, DFC*, managed to keep the offence on the base to be dealt with by the RAF and the students didn't end up in front of the magistrates charged with a number of felonies.

By the 14th July I was finished at Swinderby, and the next day, together with my crew, I moved to No.5 LFS, the Lancaster Finishing School at RAF Syerston on the other side of Newark; I had reached the very top of my training programme. The next two weeks would be spent familiarising ourselves with the Lancaster, and then we would be posted to an operational squadron; for us it was to be No.630 Squadron at East Kirkby.

Our Stirling stands in the background after we had completed another training flight. I am 3rd from right

Chapter Eight

*"In Bomber Command we had to lay on, and more often than not,
carry through, at least one and occasionally more than one major battle
every twenty-four hours. That was a situation which no naval or
military command had ever had to compete with. Navies fight two or
three major battles per war. Armies, maybe a dozen. We had to lay
on, during my three and a half years, well over a thousand."*

**Air Chief Marshal Sir Arthur Travers Harris,
C-in-C, RAF Bomber Command, 1942-1945**

The dull-blue RAF 3-tonner rattled along the road whilst we
jogged, swayed and bounced about in the back swearing
oaths of doom upon the head of our erratic driver, who,
isolated in the front cab, remained oblivious to our plight. Finally
he swung the vehicle through the main entrance to Royal Air
Force Station East Kirby. With a squeal of brakes, he brought the
truck to such an abrupt and vicious halt outside the guardhouse
that we were all thrown into a heap at the front. With grateful
thanks that our journey was at last over, we, the seven young men
of Jerry Monk's crew, clambered out of the back, retrieved our
kitbags, and as each one passed the cab, left the young AC2 behind
the wheel in no doubt about what we thought of his driving. We
trooped into the guardhouse where Len Knowles, the officer in the
crew, reported our arrival to the duty corporal. We were the latest
sprog crew to arrive for an operational tour of duty with No.630
Squadron. It was Sunday 30th July 1944.

RAF East Kirkby, now the Lincolnshire Aviation Heritage
Museum and home to one of only three mobile Lancasters in the
world, was a new No.5 Group Bomber Command station. Work
had started on the aerodrome in 1942 and it had opened on 20th
August the following year. The Lancasters of No.57 Squadron
had arrived nine days later. Then, on 15th November under Wing
Commander M Crocker, DFC, 'B' Flight moved across the airfield
to form No.630 Squadron equipped with Mk111 Lancasters and
given the code letters LE. Its motto was *Nocturna Mors*, Death by
Night. Shortly afterwards, East Kirkby, whose codename was
Silksheen, became No.55 Base, No.5 Group, responsible for the

administration and aircraft maintenance of the satellite stations at RAF Spilsby and RAF Strubby. The Greenwich meridian dividing east from west passes right through the centre of the aerodrome.

December had brought a change of commanding officer when Wing Commander John Dudley Rollinson, DFC, assumed command of the squadron. On the night of 28th January 1944, in the depths of the Battle of Berlin, Bomber Command sent 677 aircraft to the big city. No.630 Squadron put up eleven of its Lancasters for the raid; two of them failed to return home that night, including Rollinson's. The loss of the CO brought another change and the very popular twenty-nine-year-old South African Wing Commander William Inglis Deas, DSO, DFC*, arrived to take over.

Shortly after our own arrival on the squadron, we were interviewed by the latest CO, Wing Commander LM Blome-Jones, DFC. He left us in no doubt that spirits were far from high as both squadrons at East Kirkby had suffered heavy losses on operations over the last two months, including recently that of W/C Deas in the raid on the flying bomb store at St-Leu-D'Esserent on the night of 7th/8th July. Deas had been on his 69th mission and had been a huge loss to the squadron. No.630 had lost thirty-eight crews in the last seven months, including two consecutive COs, and morale was very low; it affected everybody, as we were about to find out.

We were part of A Flight, but when we first arrived at the station there was no available aircrew accommodation for us and so for the first month we shared the living accommodation with some of the ground crew NCOs, apart from Len, who was in the officers' mess. The billet was sited out in the farmland which surrounded the base, alongside a wood and quite a distance from the sergeants' mess. The station buildings were well dispersed around the aerodrome as a defence against enemy attacks, which we did experience on a couple of occasions whilst I was there. We also had a flying bomb attack. We were the only aircrew sharing with ground staff but they were a good bunch and made us welcome. One of them had a copy of Richard Tauber's recording of 'My Heart and I', and a favourite game and likeable nuisance was to keep playing it over and over again on the wind-up gramophone.

By the end of the week we had had a few days to settle in and Friday 4th August brought our first flight in an operational squadron aircraft. Around 14.00 hours we went over to dispersals to carry out an air test on a repaired Lancaster, ME739 LE-F. We were accompanied by Flight Lieutenant Walters, the squadron test pilot, who was there to see how well we performed and whether after all our training we really were ready for operations.

The first thing that I noticed about the aircraft was the better quality and higher standard of everything around me. I had been used to the tired, unreliable, clapped-out workhorses of Training Command, whereas this newly repaired Lancaster was a lovely aircraft to be in. At 14.30, Jerry eased LE-F from the dispersal and, full of confidence, we began our flight test. Whilst Jerry flew the aircraft, my job was to record the handling and readings throughout the test and then write up the report. After we had completed the air test, Flt Lt Walters began to put us through our paces and asked that the two gunners should report a simulated fighter attack. As each gunner reported an attacking enemy fighter, Jerry would put the Lancaster through a corkscrew evasion manoeuvre, that is to dive, turn, climb, turn, dive, turn, climb and so on. When viewed as a diagram, the manoeuvre resembles a corkscrew, hence its name, and it is the most stressful flying procedure of all on both the bomber and the crew, especially those without seat harnesses, who tend to be thrown about inside. It is also guaranteed to induce airsickness in all but the strongest of stomachs.

At the end of this little exercise, we felt that we had performed quite well, the squadron test pilot did not share our confidence. He told us in no uncertain terms that if that was the best we could do as a crew, we had no hope of ever surviving a full tour. In fact, we would be lucky to survive anything and would be sitting ducks to the experienced German night-fighter pilots waiting for us. He said that we should not worry about the wings coming off in our corkscrews because the way we were flying, someone would very soon shoot them off for us, and he added that if we wanted to return from our first mission we had better pull our fingers out and get ourselves combat ready in the few days we had left to do it. It was a very sobering moment for us and we were all pretty shaken by his comments.

With that, Walters took the controls and showed us how the corkscrew should be done. It was an incredible experience and a remarkable demonstration of fine airmanship. The end result was that it gave us all quite a shock as we realised just how bad we really were, especially as we had thought that we were fairly good and ready for ops. Consequently, Flt Lt Walters' report comments about Jerry's flying abilities were not good. I felt sorry for Jerry because during our training up to this point, no flying instructor had said anything like Walters' remarks to us or given us any cause for concern. When we talked about it later, we decided that because of the age and doubtful serviceability of the aeroplanes that we trained on, the instructors were reluctant to put too much pressure on their airframes and that as long as students demonstrated the rudimentary skill of the manoeuvre, they were passed.

After nearly an hour, we landed and the Flight Lieutenant left us to it. At 15.50, we were back in the air; we now knew that we had some serious practice and work to do if we were to have any hope of survival.

The next evening, I was in our billet writing a letter home to my parents when two junior officers came into the room. The pilot introduced himself as Flying Officer Fenning and he was accompanied by his navigator. Fenning told me that they were on the Battle Order for a daylight raid the following morning and, to my surprise, added that it had been decided I was to fly with them on the raid as a temporary replacement for their own flight engineer, who was sick. I left my letter, collected my battledress tunic and forage cap and went with them across to the picket hut to book an early-morning call for me.

I didn't sleep very well that night; a mixture of excitement, apprehension, the dawning realisation of the dangers that awaited me, and an overwhelming desire to perform well for this battle-hardened crew disturbed my usually comfortable sleep. It seemed that I was to start my war with a crew I had never met before and it was very important to me and for the reputation of my regular crew that I did not let them down, especially after our less than auspicious performance the day before.

Early next morning, I walked the half-mile across the airfield to the mess for the customary pre-op meal of bacon and two eggs and to meet the rest of Fenning's crew. After breakfast, it was a one-and-a-half-mile walk through East Kirkby village, past the Red Lion, the only pub, and along a strictly unauthorised short cut through a private orchard, to the crew rooms. I would make this walk with my own crew many times at all hours of the day and night over the next eight months. The apple trees were laden with fruit which slowly ripened as the autumn progressed and, tempting though it may have been, we never stole any of them. We did, however, buy many pounds of them from the owners, which was far more worthwhile because it ensured our regular supply of fresh fruit during a time when such items were strictly rationed.

At the crew rooms, we were thoroughly briefed about the raid, especially by the Intelligence Officer, whose information was particularly detailed. The target was to be the V1 flying bomb sites just north of Paris at Bois de Cassan on the banks of the Seine. Then, we each collected our escape kit, coffee, chocolate, orange juice and other rations, got into our flying kit and finally, and most importantly, collected a parachute. The chatter that had accompanied breakfast had gradually dwindled away. Now everyone was occupied by their own thoughts about the mission ahead. Would our fighter cover turn up? What would the flak be like? Would there be as many enemy fighters as expected? Would we get back? They were amongst the questions I would ask myself every time.

Fully kitted and carrying my parachute, rations and small case of forms and paperwork, I went outside to the waiting crew bus and clambered in with an ungainly effort. At dispersals around the peri-track, the bus disgorged its young men seven at a time. Finally, it was our turn. There in the bright light of the Lincolnshire countryside on that Sunday morning stood PD253 LE-D for Dog, fuelled, bombed-up, ready. Now we were at the aircraft I could focus on my job and the butterflies which had flitted and fluttered inside me since the night before disappeared. All my attention was on the aeroplane and the part I had to play in helping to complete our mission successfully.

After carrying out our individual checks, both outside and inside, F/O Fenning and I started the engines, ran them up, throttled them back again and then eased the Lancaster out to join the queue of aircraft slowly making their way round the peri-track.

When we reached the head of the runway, Fenning applied the brakes and I went through the thirteen-point pre-flight check with him. With OK for take-off, at 09.34 he released the brakes and we started to roll down the concrete strip. At last I was going to war; this is what I had trained so hard for during the last twelve months. Fenning's right hand was on the two forward throttle levers and my left hand was on the two rear ones as together we eased them forward, building up the speed of the heavily laden aircraft. When the tail came up, he put both hands onto the control column so that he could, together with the rudder pedals, hold the Lancaster straight. I now had full control of the four throttle levers and gently pushed them forward, opening up the engines to full power, then 'through the gate'. By pushing the throttles through the gate, I had squeezed the very last ounces of power from the four Merlin engines; there was nothing in reserve if she didn't lift off.

I looked out of the cockpit at the runway rushing away beneath our wheels. The roar of the engines at full throttle was deafening, exhaust flames were licking back over the engine housings and wings, the thin black line of the boundary hedge at the far end of the runway began to take shape, but the Lancaster stayed steadfastly earthbound. Quickly I scanned the cockpit instruments then glanced to my right to check engine oil pressures, temperatures, coolant, fuel pumps. They all looked fine. I looked forward again and could see all the features in the hedge with alarming clarity. I suddenly realised that we were not going to make it. God! My war was going to end before it had begun, here at East Kirkby in a massive explosion on the airfield boundary.

Then to my horror, on the other side of the hedge and directly in line with us I saw a group of children who had stopped on their way to church to watch us take off and were now excitedly waving to us. Our own deaths were going to be tragic enough, but we were going to wipe out these young lives too. Time seemed to stand still amongst the agony of these thoughts; then the bouncing stopped, the runway dropped away and a moment later the

146

boundary hedge zipped by beneath us in a blur, our wheels clearing it easily.

The feeling of relief was followed by one of great delight as I looked back and saw the children laughing, still frantically waving, straining against our backwash, revelling in the thrill of being right underneath us as we took off just feet above their heads. After we had returned from this mission, I was told that the Fenning crew were well on their way to completing their tour and that the pilot had deliberately kept the Lancaster down until the last moment to give the children the excitement they were waiting for. It wasn't the first time he or other pilots had done this. I just wish I had known that as we were hurtling down the runway towards them.

The undercarriage came up and locked in with a comforting clunk as we continued to climb away from the airfield and head towards the V1 site upon which we intended to deposit 13,658lb of high explosives. Clear, accurate marking and bombing was top priority on such a target. The usual procedure in these cases was for a photo reconnaissance aircraft, usually a Mosquito or a Spitfire, to over-fly the target and check the weather conditions and visibility. If considered to be unsuitable, the mission would be called off to prevent French civilian casualties. We were part of the first wave of the attack and were to be accompanied by a fighter escort which was to join us at the French coast. Before then, the bomber stream formed up and flew south to Beachy Head. We had not trained for formation flying as had the Americans and so it would not be true to say that we flew in formation, more a sort of general gaggle heading in the same direction. From Beachy Head we flew across the Channel to Dieppe where we were to meet up with our fighter cover.

As we neared the French coast, we expectantly watched for our fighter escort to appear. Presently we crossed the coastline where, far below like spilt ice-cream, the waves were bursting upon the rocky headlands each side of the heavily defended Dieppe harbour. Ahead, the clouds were building and darkening; the weather was deteriorating towards Paris. Like everyone in that band of aircraft, I scanned the sky for the comforting sign of friendly fighters. Mosquitoes, Spitfires, Mustangs, Thunderbolts, we didn't care what they were just as long as they turned up to protect us from the waiting Me109s and Fw190s. Moments later, it was not our fighters that filled my vision but my first encounter with enemy flak; innocent-looking dark puffs of perfidious smoke in the sky ahead, and then it was all around us, each one designed to bring an aircraft down, like a pheasant shot by a 12-bore. The shrapnel rattled against the sides of the Lancaster and I felt the aircraft buck and lurch with the closeness of some of the explosions.

Above us, there appeared a solitary Lockheed P-38 Lightning. We pressed on, though now searching the sky for enemy fighters with a greater urgency. As a force, we were not trained or equipped for daylight raids without proper fighter cover, and once the enemy radar operators confirmed that we were on our own, Hell would be unleashed upon us. As we approached Paris, the clouds rolled in and bubbled above us in banks of boiling grey. Over on our starboard side I could see the Eiffel Tower standing tall and clear above the streets and buildings of the French capital. Our target lay a little further ahead to the north-east but now those thickening clouds gave us some protection against fighters coming down from above.

The pathfinders had marked the target well with green Target Indicators on the aiming point, but the bombing became scattered as some of the Master Bomber's instructions were misunderstood and many aircraft held onto their load for fear of hitting French civilians. I stood up and folded my seat back against the fuselage side so that if we were hit, it would not get in the way of the cockpit area crew getting to the forward escape hatch. The two gunners would leave by the rear access door. The bomb aimer was in the nose lying on his 'couch' overlooking the sights. We started our run-in and I was more vigilant than ever for fighters as there was very little flak over the target, a sure sign that they were about.

Then I saw the first Me109 coming in fast on our starboard bow, middle to low down and about 200 yards away. In that position it wasn't readily visible to our mid-upper gunner. The Lancaster ahead of us was flying straight and level, already releasing its bombs as the fighter closed on it. I could see the little flashes from the 109's wing cannons as the pilot attacked the cockpit and nose area of the bomber.

I grabbed Fenning's right arm and shouted, "Fighter, fighter, 109 coming in starboard bow, attacking Lanc ahead, cockpit area."

Our front turret, which was normally operated by the bomb aimer, was now unmanned. I realised that the fighter was going to peel around and attack another aircraft, probably us. I turned to Fenning at my left shoulder and asked if I should go down and man the turret. Very quickly he shook his head.
"No, you stay there. If he attacks us, be ready to pull me out of my seat and take over if I'm wounded."

Sure enough, the fighter did come round again, but we were passing over the target at around 180mph and by then we had moved on through the sky. Flying in an opposing arc, when the 109 came in again it brought him behind us and lined up on the following aircraft in the stream. We dropped our bombs on the target, held steady for the aiming-point photograph and then turned for home. Although untroubled by fighters, the return flight was particularly rough as the weather steadily worsened, tossing the Lancaster around like a leaf on the breeze. I had never suffered from air sickness, even when Flt Lt Walters had shown us how to corkscrew properly, but the two cans of fresh orange juice that I had drunk on this trip sat heavily in my stomach and almost proved to be my undoing.

After five hours' flying, we entered Silksheen's circuit at 3,000 feet, gradually dropping down in 500 feet steps as each aircraft below us landed safely until finally it was our turn. Fenning's luck had held and had put him in the right place to miss both attacks by the Me109. That was just how it was; survival or disaster hung upon a gossamer thread of chance. You could help your luck by being well trained and as good a crew as possible, but in the end you needed luck to survive. Three Lancasters were lost on this raid, one of them a No.630 crew whose luck had run out. Whether they were one of the aircraft attacked by the 109, I don't know, but we subsequently found out that all the crew survived the crash and became prisoners of war.

After we landed, we also found out what had happened to our fighters. That Sunday morning, the PR flight picked up the deteriorating weather conditions over France and advised that the mission be scrubbed. It was, and the fighters were stood down, although I don't know how the Lightning ended up with us. Perhaps its pilot, like the first wave of the bomber stream, did not receive the message to abort and so had pressed on with us to bomb the V1 site.

When the debrief was over and I had had another plate of bacon and eggs, I returned to my billet, suddenly very tired. But there was to be no rest straightaway as my crew were there, impatient to hear what the raid had been like; did we hit the target, what about the flak and the fighters? I kept my answers as matter of fact as I could and glossed over the attacks and how close we had come to being shot down. It would not have served any useful purpose; they were going to find out for themselves very soon and Jerry had his 'dickie' trip to come first, when he would fly as second pilot with another crew on an operation. During the raid, so much was happening and so quickly that I didn't have time to think about the fighter attack, but afterwards, that night, the scene replayed over and over in my mind. It was something that I would learn to control, at least whilst I was on ops.

At 00.40 next morning, I was once more airborne for a thirty-minute night flying test with the Fenning crew, after which I went to bed and gladly slept solidly. I was now officially operational and after breakfast checked the Battle Order in the mess for that night, more to start the habit than expecting to find anything. But there it was in plain black type: Sgt E Watson FE to fly with F/O Fenning. My insides lurched. Well, I suppose it showed that Fenning must have been happy with my performance, so that at least was some consolation. During the morning, we went out to our aircraft at its dispersal to visually check it over, having already done the NFT.

We were to be part of a large and mixed force of 1,019 aircraft that were to attack various targets in the Normandy battle area. There were several aiming points for the raid and with a bomb load that night of 13,737lb, ours was Sequesville la Campagne, a German troop strong point in front of the Allied force. On the way back, our aircraft developed a problem with its pneumatic system and we diverted to RAF Gaydon in Warwickshire, an OTU station which had a runway long enough to land a Lancaster on. We returned to base the following day flying through a heavy storm on the way. Shortly after we landed I was met by our navigator, Bill Whenray, who told me the news that Jerry had been promoted to Flying Officer. We were all very pleased for him although sorry to see him leave the billet and move to officers' accommodation.

Each of the different trades in the aircraft tended to get to know one another as we mixed at the specialised briefings, talked to each other about technical details, and so on. I had briefly got to know a sergeant flight engineer named White from another crew and the Bois de Cassan raid was his first mission. He was a decent sort of chap and I was sorry to learn that it was his aircraft that had failed to return.

Back with my own crew, on Wednesday night we took off at one minute past midnight for a 'Bulls-eye' training session. Flying at 20,000 feet, we practised escaping from a searchlight cone. The enemy's searchlights were grouped around a single radar-controlled central light which was slightly blue. Once this picked up an aircraft, the other lights in the group would be brought onto the target aircraft to form a cone from which escape was very difficult. The flak batteries, usually 88mm and 105mm, would then concentrate on that aircraft to shoot it down. When it came, it would be a terrifying experience.

On Friday, Jerry went on his dickie trip. The force attacked the U-boat pens at Bordeaux and La Pallice, dropping 2,000lb armour-piercing bombs bang on the target. All the crews returned safely. However, a few weeks later, when the pens were captured and inspected by the Allies, it transpired that despite the very accurate bombing, the roofs had not been penetrated, which is a testimony to the strength of the structures and the engineering skills of the Germans.

On Saturday night it was Jock, our mid-upper's, turn to go on a raid. Gradually we were collectively gaining a little operational experience. Then on Sunday, we were on the Battle Order as a full crew for the raid that day; it was to be our first mission together as the complete crew we had formed at Swinderby. Having given the engines of our aircraft a full run-up, we waited for the briefing. However, when it came, it was a stand-down for all crews, which gave us the night off. Instead of flying, I went to the camp cinema to see *The Life and Death of Colonel Blimp*. Released the year before, it was a complex but highly enjoyable story which spanned the time from the Boer War through the Great War and into the present conflict. Scots actress Deborah Kerr played three different women in her roles opposite Roger Livesey. Filmed in full Technicolor, it was magnificent.

My crew: Front row L-R – Ted Watson, Jim Kenealy [Rear Gunner]
Jerry Monk [Pilot] Bill Whenray [Navigator]
Back row L-R – Len Knowles [Bomb Aimer] Jock Gillespie [Mid -
Upper Gunner] Joe Baldwin [Wireless Operator]

Monday morning, and we were on the Battle Order again. It was to be another daylight raid where the target was Quesnay Wood, again in the Normandy area. We were given a bomb load of 13,649lb of explosives; since this was our maiden mission, there was no overload.

We flew to the west of Reading and then over the New Forest, crossing the coast at Lymington, clipping the Isle of Wight at the Needles, and then across the English Channel. Here we were treated to a bird's-eye view of all the frenetic activity that was going on beneath us in the aftermath of D-Day. Royal Navy ships and merchant convoys were moving through the Channel, heavily laden supply vessels and naval escorts were crossing to Normandy, the Mulberry Harbours were a hive of activity of men and vehicles scurrying about with directed purpose like so many ants. On the invasion beaches, wreckage of landing craft, tanks and more vehicles lay scattered along the sandy shores. Then as we crossed the coast and flew inland, the immense damage to the coastal towns came clearly into focus.

Quesnay Woods lay near the high ground that rose above the main road from Caen to Falaise. Flying towards the target it was easy to see the activity of our own forces and evidence of the desperate fighting that was going on upon the ground in the battle for Caen. The town was of vital strategic importance to both sides. Once it fell, the Allies would pour out of Normandy into France, and the road to Paris and thence to Germany would lie open; thus the enemy defended relentlessly. Military Intelligence believed that the wooded areas of Quesnay concealed large columns of Tiger tanks, along with associated troops and armour.

As soon as the first bombs started to fall on the wood, the 12th SS troops in there knew that they were the target and had to get out or be annihilated. From my seat high above the scene, I could see the tiny figures of infantry streaming out of the trees in all directions, trying to escape the perdition that we had unleashed. But there was worse to come. As the men, tanks and armour were caught in the open ground, Typhoons, Spitfires and P-51 Mustangs swept down upon them with 60lb rocket-projected warheads. Even the mighty Tiger tank was no match for the speed and destructive power of these fearsome fighter aircraft. There was little chance of escape and survivors must have been few.

But this was 1944, and although there were occasions when highly trained specialist crews carried out pinpoint accurate attacks on targets, we did not have the technology to slot a bomb into a letterbox. Consequently, despite the best efforts of Bomber

Command crews to hit only the aiming point, bombing accuracy often became scattered, suffered creep-back or was influenced by other factors such as cloud, communication mix-ups or enemy fighter attacks. There were seven different targets associated with this raid, and at one of them, Canadian and Polish ground forces were mistakenly bombed when they used the same-coloured flares as the Master Bomber was using to mark the targets. In a completely unrelated incident, the Canadian artillery was machine-gunned the following day by RAF Spitfires and USAAF Mustangs.

The next day, Tuesday 15th August, was the start of the invasion of southern France and the Allied breakout from Normandy was under way. For Bomber Command, our targets this day were nine Luftwaffe night-fighter airfields in Holland and Belgium in readiness for a renewed bombing offensive against German cities. The daylight raid involved 1,004 Lancasters, Halifaxes, Mosquitoes and a Lightning. For our crew in ND412 LE-H, the target was the Deelen field, one of the main airfields and control centres for the Nachtjager squadrons, the enemy night-fighter force. This would be a Paramatta raid, which was the Command code for visual bombing of the target in clear weather.

As the attacking bombers closed upon the airfield, the defenders put up such an intense flak barrage I was sure that sooner or later we would all be hit. Looking out of the cockpit windows, the sky seemed full of those dark, treacherous puffs of smoke; soon our aircraft reeked of cordite as shrapnel rattled and bounced against the Perspex. Then there was a huge explosion just ahead of us and LE-H rocked and bucked as the heavy concentration of fire found its mark and the aircraft in front took a direct hit in the bomb bay. The Lancaster just blew up in a massive fireball and disintegrated before our eyes. An engine, with the propellers still turning, somersaulted above our heads whilst part of the wing sliced away through the air. Thousands of pieces of aeroplane, large and small, fell away to the earth, some trailing flames as they went. On the ground, little fires showed up where the burning pieces landed, while in the air, a pall of drifting smoke was all there was to show of that proud machine and the seven young men it had contained a few moments earlier.

I had never seen anything like it, nor could I have imagined the horror of what I had just witnessed; it stunned both Jerry and me. Moments later, though, we too were on our bombing run and had a job to do, but it took an immense effort of concentration to focus upon it and not the vision of that explosion. Later we learned that this aeroplane had come from our satellite airfield at Spilsby and had been piloted by Flt Lt Geert AC Overgaauw from Amsterdam. None of us dwelt upon it then, though it would be a long time before the images finally faded from my consciousness: but even after all these years, just occasionally, it still haunts a dream.

The single P-38 Lightning that had accompanied us on this raid had taken off from nearby Coningsby, flown by Wing Commander Guy Gibson as a mission observer.

Operations were relentless as the Allies sought to drive the enemy out of occupied Europe, and Wednesday evening saw us preparing for a night-time raid. This time the target was the port of Stettin in eastern Germany, now Szczecin in Poland, on the Baltic coast. We knew early in the day that whatever the target was, it would be a long flight there and back because the aircraft was being given plenty of fuel and a lighter bomb load of 8,021lb to compensate for the extra weight of petrol.

We took off at 21.05 and headed out low over the North Sea. The route took us past the Friesian archipelago, where we woke up its string of flak ships. We made landfall just north of Cuxhaven where the force started to gain height and divided, some going on to attack Kiel while the major part headed east. From here to Stettin we ran the gauntlet of fire as we passed through successive flak and fighter belts. I looked down to see strings of white balls slowly climbing towards us, growing bigger, closing faster, then zipping past at an alarming rate. Going off into oblivion. The quantity of anti-aircraft fire that the defenders put up was frightening, and at times I couldn't see a way through it. We flew to the north of Hamburg and Lübeck, each time coming under an intense barrage of flak. The sky seemed full of searing flashes of brilliant orange shell bursts followed by mucky black smoke. These bursts momentarily illuminated nearby aircraft and lit our cockpit in a seemingly constant staccato of flashes.

Nearing Rostock, the bomber stream turned south-east, hopefully tempting the German controllers into thinking that Berlin was the target, since Mosquitoes had already been in and attacked it, and sending their fighters there. For a little while the flak was left behind but the fear and threat of those fighters remained ever constant. After another turn to the east, we reached the target, only to find that it too was very heavily defended. Our aiming point was the dock area above which the searchlights wove a labyrinthine snare of illumination whilst the 88mm ack-ack guns sent up a lethal barrage of explosive.

Above the port, a box barrage of exploding shells came so close that it almost brought disaster to us as the Lancaster bucked and lurched, stuttered and shuddered. We could not have been prepared for the intense ferocity of this onslaught. Fear gripped my stomach as I realised that death could come at any moment. Jerry struggled to hold her steady on our bombing run, but we put our load right onto the aiming point. With the photograph captured, more in urgency than relief, we turned north on the first leg home. Glad to be away, I tried not to think about what dangers the darkness held as we headed towards the Baltic coast.

Although there had been no moon, we had been flying beneath the brilliance of the starlit heavens since we had left Stettin. Lurking unseen below, a fighter pilot could pick us out as we passed across the face of those perfidious pinpoints of light, but now, thankfully, the clouds were beginning to build up and obscure our betrayers. The course home took us down the Baltic, sweeping wide of the flak ships and shore batteries, then over the northern tip of Denmark and out across the North Sea. When Bill Whenray our navigator announced that the coast of Denmark had slipped away beneath us and we were heading out over the featureless blank expanse of the sea, I allowed myself to believe that we were almost safe.

Startled, I ducked involuntarily as suddenly out of that black void two rockets trailing fiery tails flashed across our path a few feet in front, followed by the fighter passing over our cockpit. Jock Gillespie, the mid-upper, got off a few rounds, but the German was gone. We had no real defence against rockets and I thought that we were about to meet our end in a watery grave of the North

Sea. There was only one chance of surviving another attack. I pushed the throttle levers through the gate to give us full speed while Jerry banked the aircraft towards the nearest clouds. The first billows of dark mist had no sooner washed over the cockpit when Jim Kenealy in the rear turret reported another two rockets passing underneath us. But these were well wide of the mark and must have been fired more in hope than expectation of success; we had been saved by the cloud cover which had come not a moment too soon. I didn't see the fighter that attacked us but it would most probably have been a Focke-Wulf FW190A fitted with rocket tubes.

More than seventy years later, I can still vividly recall the whole mission as one of utter terror. I was only nineteen; neither life nor training had prepared any of us for the fear we experienced that night and would do again on raids to come. We appeared to roll from one flak and fighter belt to the next, with the darkness making it all seem so much worse. Although it gave us cover, it also hid our attackers. It felt as though we had been under almost constant fire all the way there and all the way back. I also clearly remember my feelings as we approached East Kirkby aerodrome at about 05.15 in the darkness of the early morning after nearly eight and a half hours flying. We were all just desperate to get down.

We came down the stack, entered the funnels, applied full flap, and closed the throttles as the wheels touched down at the start of the runway. An immense feeling of relief washed over me as we gradually slowed then turned onto the peri-track. It was as if a huge weight that had been pressing down upon me had been lifted. I thanked God that the raid was all over, but at the same time the stark realisation dawned upon me that we would probably not survive this lot. If all or most of our other raids were like this one, I didn't see how we possibly could. It was a very common reaction and emotion by operational aircrew, especially after a particularly perilous mission.

The perceived wisdom was that once you had survived five operations, you were beginning to get the hang of it and gaining valuable experience. That was not how we saw things. It had been a terrifying night. Any novelty of being operational, any naivety at being involved in the bombing campaign which might have existed in my mind before this night was brutally swept aside at Stettin. There were no illusions about the great dangers which faced bomber crews on each mission, nor that I would probably die very soon. I suddenly felt much older than my years.

Whilst flying, especially on operations, we all depended on each other. We truly were a band of brothers, for the survival of each one of us depended upon everyone playing their part. We didn't talk about the fear we felt; we didn't need to. We were all frightened every time we flew out on a mission because we knew that death awaited the unwary and the unlucky. We had volunteered for this job and it had to be done, but Stettin changed me, and there was worse to come.

Bombing up with a 4,000lb 'cookie'

I got up around midday only to find that we were detailed for another raid that night. However, it was later scrubbed, much to our relief, and I caught up on some much-needed rest.

Friday brought us another operation to another target, this time a daylight raid on the flying bomb sight depot at Lisle Adam, north of Paris. We took off at 12.10 in ME845 LE-Q with a bomb load of 13,700lb. Two of the 158 Lancasters that took part in the raid were lost. One of them was shot down on the return leg. The aircraft was flying ahead of us when it was hit and I became transfixed on the events that followed. As the Lancaster started its final downward journey, I watched for the crew to emerge. First one then a second dropped from the forward escape hatch, their parachutes blossoming a few moments later. Despite the engine fire and the inevitable end, the aircraft remained steady in its descent. Then two more crew fluttered from the rear door, the gunners. Finally, a fifth body dropped from the forward hatch and the five parachutes floated away behind us like dandelion seeds on the wind.

The Lancaster, now close to crashing, still maintained its steady angled plane towards final destruction. All this time it was being followed down by a Mosquito whose pilot relayed a running commentary confirming that five of the crew had bailed out safely. It seemed likely that the pilot and probably the flight engineer had sacrificed themselves by staying at the controls and had ridden their aircraft all the way down to give the rest of the crew as much chance as possible to get out safely. Then the Lancaster hit the ground, bounced, hit it again and slewed around in great shower of sparks, earth, dust and vegetation. The whole scene had by now slipped away behind us and it was lost from my view, but the Mosquito pilot continued his commentary. He could see figures that he thought were French farmers running towards the wreckage and that they were helping the remaining crew to get out before the fire spread.

There is a temptation to believe that in the past, the weather was always seasonally compliant, but it was not always or even often so. During the next week we were detailed for four further raids, Königsberg twice, Brest and an unknown target, but they were all scrubbed because of bad weather. It was an opportunity for other things. I had a session in the Link Trainer, an oral examination by the Engineering Leader, attended an engineering lecture by the same officer and spent some time in the Intelligence section and library, which was open most of the day to aircrews. Here one had access to unbelievable Intelligence information about our targets and the progress of the war. I also paid my first visit to the town of Boston, where I went to the pictures.

Relaxing on a cookie!

Getting close to one of my engines
Note the scorch marks from the exhaust

Chapter Nine

Adolf Hitler Strasse in Darmstadt was the target for 25th August. The town, which we were told was a rail communication link and home to a large chemical works experimenting with bacteriological warfare and gas production, had not previously been attacked by Bomber Command. The raid was a failure. The Master Bomber had to return early and his two deputies were shot down. The low-level Mosquito crew could not locate the target, the marker flares were dropped too far west, and the bombing was scattered.

The following night it was the port of Königsberg in eastern Prussia, now Kaliningrad, which is administered by the Russians although never formally given to them after the war. It was not how I would have wished to spend a Saturday night and was also at the very extreme of our range; any crew suffering even slight fuel loss in a fighter attack or engine inefficiency would not get home. Take-off for us was 20.00 on a mission which would last 11 hours 15 minutes. To compensate for every last drop of fuel we carried, the bomb load was only 8,000lb.

The port had been the capital of East Prussia but was now the main base for the regular German army, the Wehrmacht. By 1944 it was only 70 miles from their Russian Front. Routed over Sweden, it was to be a round trip of 1,900 miles. It was Bomber Command's first attack on the city, and with no overload tanks, careful engine handling and flying at a lower altitude than normal was very important. During the afternoon, all crews went out to their aircraft, ran up the engines, checked all the equipment, then taxied and parked them in line at the head of the runway ready for take-off. Engines were shut down and then the fuel tanks were topped up again to the very brim, squeezing in every last drop of petrol. This was a very unusual procedure, and although at this stage we didn't know where the target was, we knew that it was going to be an extremely long trip and that getting back would be touch and go on the fuel alone, never mind enemy action.

After the evening briefing, meal and kitting up, it was out to the waiting aircraft, start up engines in succession from the lead and straight into an immediate take-off, after which we would fly at low altitude and at the most economic engine revs. As part of our bomb load, we carried a new flame-throwing incendiary which was designed to create extra-large fires amongst the wooden buildings in the streets of the port. The Germans were caught completely off guard that night and only four Lancasters were lost.

The most memorable part of the trip was when we flew over the brilliantly lit Swedish city of Malmö. After having lived through five years of the blackout, when going anywhere after dark was so difficult, it was such a joy to behold. Not too far below, the lights in the houses and streets twinkled and glowed in the darkness like so many inviting beacons of hope. But Sweden was a neutral country and here we were violating its air space, consequently it had to retaliate with flak and night fighters.

However, the Swedes had no desire to see Hitler win the war and this was a game that they were very good at playing. The searchlights were pointed vertically into the sky and did not weave; the flak was deliberately aimed to miss our aircraft and their ancient bi-plane night fighters flew around us with their navigation lights on. We were ordered not to fire upon any of their fighters unless we were attacked, which of course we weren't. At 07.15 on Sunday morning, almost out of fuel and desperately tired but safe, we were diverted to Longtown, just outside Carlisle.

There was no church parade for us that morning; instead we blissfully slept in our temporary accommodation before flying back to base in the afternoon. We more or less followed the line of Hadrian's Wall across to Newcastle and then down the coast before banking in to East Kirkby. On Monday we had to take a kite to Bottesford HCU and bring another one back. This time, though, I made the return trip in the rear turret. It was a strange sensation; I saw nothing coming and everything going.

The Battle Order beckoned us again on Tuesday night and once more it was to be Königsberg. It seemed that the PR pictures taken after Saturday's raid did not show sufficient damage to the dock area and commanders wanted another effort. The route remained the same, over neutral Sweden. The pre-take-off procedure with the fuel was repeated and we were airborne at 20.15, this time with a bomb load of 8,232lb.

In the gathering darkness, the bomber stream of 189 Lancasters headed out across the North Sea. Over the northern tip of Denmark, the German flak batteries put up a barrage which was soon left behind. Long before we reached its shores, I could see the waiting lights of Sweden shimmering like the allure of a siren's call. They had lost none of their appeal. The trip was going well and we continued to hope that we would catch the enemy off guard again by coming back so soon after the last raid. Above the Swedish mountains we turned to the Baltic and Königsberg. Ahead, I saw smudges of cloud beginning to drift across the stars, thickening as we neared the port. Then thin wisps washed over us, a ghostly shawl which stretched out and silently enveloped our aeroplane.

Suddenly, two streams of tracer zipped past the cockpit. In the rear turret, Jim fired a short burst in reply before we disappeared into the cloud, hidden from our attacker's view. The Ju88 had crept underneath us and fired the deadly upward-pointing twin-cannon *Schrage Musik*. Our luck had held and we had been saved in the nick of time by the clouds. We had lost him but had increased speed and so arrived at the target ahead of schedule.

The Master Bomber that night was Wing Commander J Woodroffe, probably No.5 Group's most experienced. What had earlier saved us now brought trouble because the target was totally obscured by low cloud and Woodroffe would not commence the attack. For twenty minutes the Lancaster crews awaited his orders, patiently circling Königsberg, while, with mounting tension, we endured the heavy flak and scoured the sky for fighters. To port, the hesitant glow from a burning aircraft pierced the dark as the flames grew, only to be quickly followed by another. Then, two aircraft collided. There was a blinding flash with orange flames dropping from the sky before a massive explosion ripped the two aeroplanes apart, sending burning wreckage in all directions. Down through the clouds the pyre tumbled, leaving only a fading glow to mark its passage until it too was gone and the darkness returned. Still we waited. Salty sweat leaked around my goggles and stung my eyes. A rivulet of cold liquid trickled down my back. My heart raced. It was that intense fear again.

The terror had not yet ended and another huge yellow flash lit up dozens of other aircraft, some uncomfortably close to us. The blast turned to a firework cascade of a thousand pieces of aircraft that tumbled earthwards, leaving behind an eerie green, blue, red and orange figure hanging in the air like a scarecrow. We had been told to mark down the exact location of each of these explosions because they were special scarecrow shells which the Germans had developed to resemble an aircraft explosion and designed to frighten us. Well, they worked, but it wasn't a special shell at all. After the war we found out that what we had witnessed was indeed an aircraft exploding from a direct hit in its bomb bay.

With each passing minute our nerves were stretched ever tauter. Then at last, Woodroffe found a break in the cloud and ordered the crews to begin the attack on their allotted aiming point. Thank God for that. Round we came to ours, opened the bomb-bay doors and, with no little relief, dropped our explosives and incendiaries on the target. With the sudden loss of weight, the Lancaster too gave a sigh of relief and rose up in sky as if to say that she had had enough and was ready for home. Normally, I would open up the engines after bombing and get us home as quickly as possible, but we didn't have the luxury of enough fuel to do that; it would need to be a steady trip back or we might well not make it.

Hardly had we left the target area when we were again attacked by another Ju88. Our gunners returned his fire as we corkscrewed, twisted and turned and finally sought the sanctuary of the clouds, hoping that we had convinced him we were not an easy target. But he was experienced and anticipated where we would be likely to emerge from the clouds; when we did, he was waiting for us. As he attacked again we corkscrewed into the next bank of cloud, but we knew he was still out there. By now we were somewhere out over the Baltic and greatly concerned at his persistence. Eventually, though, we did lose him in the heavy cloud cover, but we were now off course.

Our navigator Bill resumed our course for the return route home, and then Jerry and I saw heavy flashes in the clouds ahead of us. We knew that there was a severe electrical storm over a large area but these flashes were immense and we concluded that they must be gun fire. The only gun fire of that magnitude in this area would have to be over the target. Convinced that we had become disorientated during the encounters with the second Ju88 and that we were now heading back to Königsberg, Jerry turned the Lancaster through 180 degrees, away from the gun fire. Jerry and Len both had repeaters of the master gyro-compass which, now he had turned the aircraft around, were showing that far from flying away from Königsberg, we were heading straight back to it. That night we were in PD253 again. Before take-off, the ground crew had warned us that another aircrew had experienced electrical problems with the DR [distant reading] compass causing desynchronisation in this aircraft.

With this warning in mind, as a precaution, Jerry sent Joe Baldwin, our wireless operator, to check the reading on the master compass unit which was located close to the rear door. While the aeroplane bumped and jigged through the clouds, Joe precariously picked his way past the Elsan and between all the various bits and pieces of equipment that we carried inside the fuselage, some of which were now scattered across the floor, until he got to the master compass. When he returned to the cockpit Joe had good news and bad news. The good news was that the gyro-compass was working perfectly well after all; the bad news was that we now really were heading back towards Königsberg and into the path of other returning aircraft.

In double quick time, Jerry banked the Lancaster hard round again through another 180 degrees, but now we were even less sure of our position. At this range we were well outside the reception reach of our Gee radar navigation aid and so were going to have to rely on old-fashioned dead reckoning and compass readings. There is an old adage in the RAF that aircrew are never lost but are sometimes temporarily unsure of their exact location. Well, that was us and so we decided that the best start was to lose height and head out across the Baltic towards friendly Swedish airspace. Desperately watching out for enemy fighters, we invested some of our scarce fuel and flew as fast as we could across the Baltic's black and menacingly icy waters, hoping that it would not be too long before we saw land and could get a definite fix.

Presently, we saw the warm, welcoming lights that shone through the windows of the houses in a Swedish fishing village which we hoped was near Karlskrona. With the approach of land, we gained more height, turned west and followed the coast until we were able to pinpoint our exact position. However, by now I was seriously concerned about our fuel. We had taken off with almost nothing in reserve and our various changes of direction, extra flying time over the target and increased speed over the sea had more than used what little we did have. I told the skipper that I had serious doubts whether we could get back to England if we followed the projected route given to us at the briefing.

Jerry consulted Bill and Len over our options. We were faced with a stark choice. We could take a shorter, more direct route back which would use less fuel and ensure we had enough to get home, but we would be on our own, or we could throttle back even further and follow the planned route, hope to be amongst other returning aircraft and trust our luck that the fuel would hold out. I felt it probably wouldn't, so we would have to ditch in the North Sea with all its attendant risks, including never being found.

The shorter route was equally unattractive as it involved flying over enemy territory. We would have to fly very low to avoid being picked up on German radar and would be an easy kill for any fighter that found us. We had not been trained for this sort of low-level night flying and it was a highly dangerous strategy but a necessary one if we were to have any chance of getting home. Jerry told Joe and the two gunners the situation, and as a crew we opted for the shorter, albeit more perilous route.

Had our path simply been across the sea, it would have been relatively straightforward, but of course such things never are. From where we were off the Swedish coast, we would fly across southern Sweden, passing just south of Malmö, before slipping across Denmark's many islands, flirt with northern Germany and out into the North Sea well south of the Seaplane base on Sylt. Bill had planned the route to be as direct as possible, over the least amount of land and to keep us well away from the heavily fortified

Frisian Islands with their string of flak ships. If we had to ditch there was still little chance that we would be rescued. We had become the architects of our own destiny, whatever it be.

Bill and Len spread out all the topographical maps on Bill's curtained-off navigator's table to identify the areas of high ground, power lines, and tall buildings such as church spires along our route. All went well until we were near Malmö, when the Swedish batteries mistook us for a lone Luftwaffe aircraft and tried to shoot us down. Not returning fire, we raced on, glad to reach the Baltic again where Jerry brought the Lancaster down as low as he dared. We were so low that I could easily make out the rolling waves and the tumbling white horses on their crests. At that height, our greatest danger was flying into a ship.

Ten minutes later, the scattered islands off the Danish east coast were zipping beneath us. Then ahead I could see the phosphorous sparkling in the waves breaking along the shore of Klinholm Havn. Jerry gently pulled up the nose of the Lancaster and she roared across the ground at barely 200 feet while Bill checked our landfall point and read off the contour heights. If there were any flak batteries here, they were either asleep or unable to believe their eyes. Len had left Bill with the maps and had come back to the front turret to help Jerry and me search for fighters, electricity pylons, rising ground and other fatal obstacles.

On we flew, alone, vulnerable, audacious, daring to hope. Islands, inlets and shorelines flashed beneath us as we thundered on at 200 miles per hour, the Merlin engines throbbing their powerful rhythm. My eyes began to hurt from the strain of staring into the dark, and I admired the air gunners who did this hour after hour on every mission. Another fifteen minutes passed and the land began to flatten, a coastline came up and we were over the waters of the Femer Bælt. Then we were south of Denmark, flying over northern Germany. Lakes, fields and woods rolled away beneath us in our relentless urgency. At this height, the darkness held on and covered us in our hour of need as we impertinently intruded upon the enemy's slumber. It would have been naive of us to think that our dash for home had gone unnoticed; our progress and course were being plotted and telephoned ahead.

167

Daylight was not far away and if we were not close to England when it came we would be dead in the water, literally. The first faint fingers of grey light began to steal upon the unsuspecting darkness away to the east. Ahead, rolling mounds of sand dunes were rushing to greet us, and beyond them lay the open expanse of the North Sea; the last lap; almost there. Suddenly, out of the murk there below us was row upon row of wooden huts, their doors open, shafts of weak light spilling out onto the sandy ground betraying glimpses of the scurrying figures beneath; soldiers up and about going to their ablutions or breakfast. We had over-flown a military camp and their gunners were waiting for us. Bright balls of 17mm incendiary light flak zipped up and straddled our aircraft, threatening to end our little game. A punctured fuel tank now would be a disaster.

Instinctively, I pushed the throttle levers forward to give us full power, Len in the front turret and Jim in the rear opened up with all six .303 guns strafing the flak batteries, and Jerry dropped the Lancaster's nose, dived down over the dunes and out to sea, almost skimming the wave tops. I calculated that we had just about conserved enough fuel to keep the power on for twenty minutes or so to let us put some distance between ourselves and the enemy coast, just in case the camp had scrambled the Luftwaffe.

There was 400 miles of sea in front of us before we reached the Lincolnshire coast, and although Sylt was forty miles to the north, we could yet be caught if we hung about. The clouds which had twice saved us this night began to lighten and could help us no more. The Merlins continued to push us along at full speed, barely a hundred feet above the wave crests, until after twenty minutes with no sign of pursuing fighters, I eased the throttles back and heard the engines respond to my nurturing.

Anxiously, I watched the fuel gauges, the temperatures, the revolutions, the oil pressures. Everything needed to work efficiently if we were to get back to England. We were too low to bail out and still too far away to be rescued. It took two long hours to cross the North Sea but eventually, there, waiting for us in the morning light, was England. We were going to make it, and after 10 hours and 50 minutes of flying, we touched down safely at

07.05, back at East Kirkby once more. With the relief came the exhaustion. We could hardly believe that we had been successful, pulled it off and escaped unscathed, but despite that exhaustion, it felt so good.

The ground crew welcomed us back and thanked us for returning their aircraft to them more or less in one piece. The squadron aeroplanes actually belonged to the ground crews; they were their responsibility, as aircrew we simply borrowed them for each mission. With that wonderful flair for administration upon which the British Empire had been built, before each mission, the captain of the crew had to sign to take over the aircraft from the ground crew. On our return and before leaving the dispersal area, Jerry would ensure that the NCO in charge of our ground crew signed for the Lancaster's safe return.

We gathered up all our kit, papers, charts, parachutes and Thermos flasks, and climbed into the waiting truck, which took us to the operational debrief. As always, the room was smoky, noisy and brightly lit by the almost shadeless light bulbs that hung on long cords from the ceiling. With a pleasant smile, a young WAAF welcomed me back and handed me a steaming mug of hot tea and another one in which was my tot of navy rum. Most lads had their rum in the tea, but I always preferred to drink mine separately.

Our escape across the Danish peninsula had brought us home twenty-five minutes sooner than we were expected, but for now the Intelligence Officer was more concerned to know about the target, the weather, the flak, the fighters, the searchlights and a dozen or more other details of interest to him.

After an egg-and-bacon breakfast, I snatched a few hours' sleep. When I awoke, it was not to go on leave as I had planned but to the news that it had been postponed for five days, which was a big disappointment. The squadron was short of crews and the demands that were being made upon it meant our leave was put on hold. We were edging towards being considered as an experienced crew and as such were needed on the station. Hard on the heels of our leave postponement, Jerry and I were told to report to the CO, Wing Commander Blome-Jones. The following morning we explained what had happened over Königsberg, the reasons for not following the planned route home, and our early arrival. He understood the predicament we had found ourselves in, accepted the decisions we had made, and was satisfied that we had not unnecessarily endangered the safety of our aircraft. Nevertheless, we had been lucky, as fifteen aircraft had failed to return from the mission.

Königsberg brought our missions for August to an end. The weather had been lovely for most of the month. Apart from a few thunderstorms and some early-morning mists, the sun had shone most days. A crew was tour expired and left the squadron so we moved from our ground crew billet across to the aircrew site. Over the next few months we would experience one of the hardest aspects of being on an operational base, crews who failed to return. When the debriefs were over, when no more aircraft were limping home, when the arrival time for a crew remained blank on the plotting board, we knew they were not coming back. Beds that were neat and un-slept in, the photograph of a pretty girl that gazed silently back from a locker top, chairs that remained empty at breakfast, the remembered image of a face, was all that was left. We moved on.

Whilst the members of each individual crew knew one another very well, we all knew everybody to some extent but, more importantly, we all shared the immense risks and that made us one. There were about 150 aircrew on the squadron at any time and you eventually got to know them all by sight if not by name. When we lost someone, the custom was to drink to them the next night in the mess, hope that they had become a prisoner of war rather than perished, and then put them to the back of your mind. Most people knew someone who had been killed or was missing from this or some other squadron or amongst the many civilians who were lost in air raids, but it wasn't only life that had to go on but ops too; that is why we were there.

The belongings of airmen who failed to return were very quickly removed from the billets by the Committee of Adjustments. Letters, photographs, personal papers and other possessions were returned to the family with a letter from the CO. A bicycle or car would be auctioned amongst fellow aircrew members if the family did not want it returned to them. I bought a bicycle that way and it served me very well until it was auctioned again when I left the Squadron. A small car could be bought for as little as £5 and the new owner would eventually receive the petrol coupons.

Each separate trade had its own small room at the crews' rooms site. It was in these rooms that we met during the day when not on any specific training. We received our daily ration of olive oil capsules in between discussions, demonstrations, and instructions about relevant developments or new techniques led by a section leader, usually someone on his second tour. These crowded little rooms were so much a part of our time on the squadron because, in addition to the instructional sessions, it was here that we relaxed, chatted and, as the autumn and winter months beckoned, enjoyed just sitting around the warmth from the stove. One day, however, some prankster acquired a piece of wood, put a nail through the end and hooked a Very cartridge onto it. He then climbed up onto the roof of the FEs' room and lowered the cartridge down the chimney into the stove. The cartridge exploded, the stove jumped about 6″ off the floor and, thinking we had been bombed, we shot out of the door to be greeted with cheers by the waiting crowd.

For crews at East Kirkby and the surrounding stations, the most popular off-duty venue was the Gliderdrome, a dance hall in Boston. Many lads met up with local girls there and relationships developed and blossomed, but inevitably there were occasions when someone had to carry the message that a boyfriend had failed to return from ops the night before and would not be coming again. I had been going there for a few months when a flight engineer from another squadron told me that he had recently married a WAAF, the ceremony having been carried out by the Squadron Chaplain, and that he had spent his wedding night, not with his bride, but with his crew on an operation over Germany! The Gliderdrome still thrives today. The original was destroyed by fire in May 1959, but it was rebuilt and opened again on 27th January 1960. The music has changed and the young men and women are no longer in uniform, but plenty of them still work in the factories and the fields.

I awoke to hear the rain driving against the windows of the billet and the wind rattling the roof. It was Sunday 3rd September 1944, the 13th after Trinity and the 5th anniversary of the start of this war. The Command's targets that afternoon were six Luftwaffe aerodromes in Holland with an attacking force of 675 bombers. For us it was Deelen once again, where the enemy had some sixty aircraft lined up ready to fly back to Germany to defend the Fatherland against the approaching Allied forces. We flew into better conditions and bombed from clear skies. A little over three hours later, all the squadron's aircraft were back at East Kirkby after a highly successful mission.

The next day, at last, we received our leave passes and left the camp at around 13.00 in yet more driving rain and gale-force winds. I travelled to Lincoln with Bill and Jock before going on to Darlington, and reached home later that evening. It was so good to taste my mother's cooking again. I filled the next week with the unadulterated pleasure of doing all the things I would have done had there been no war, and even the unseasonable inclemency of the weather did not dampen my spirits. I cycled around the Cockfield lanes; I met up with my friends Terry Holmes, Percy, Curley, Eric and Freddie. We went to the pictures and to dances in Copley, Cockfield and Bishop Auckland. We sold tickets around the villages for the Cockfield Sports Day, which was held each year on the Recreation Ground on the second Saturday in September. We went to Enid Anderson's party the day after and had a marvellous time there. I went to the scout meetings and helped out, even managing some gymnastics, which I had been doing since I was quite young. Walking home in the late evening, I could smell the first frosts of the autumn hanging in the clear crisp air which flowed off Cockfield Fell.

All these activities were so ordinary, and it was their very ordinariness that was their great appeal. I did not want to seek excitement during my leave; I had had quite enough of that over the last few weeks. People talk about 'adrenalin junkies' seeking thrills but, believe me, nothing compares with flying at 20,000 feet through a box barrage of anti-aircraft fire to get the adrenalin flowing. I wanted nothing more than a quiet leave doing the things that I loved the most whilst thanking God that I was still alive to enjoy them.

All too soon, it was the 13th and my leave was over; it was time to return to East Kirby. My father had already gone to work by the time I was ready to catch the bus but I said goodbye to my mother, leaving her standing at the kitchen door desperately trying to hold back her tears. I caught the country bus to Bishop Auckland, changed there to the Durham bus at 11.50 and then caught the through train to Grantham, where I met Bill as we had arranged. We changed here for Boston where we had given ourselves enough time to go to the pictures before returning to the camp.

The weather had not improved from the beginning of the month and two days later, with Brunswick as the target, we were down for ops. However, I had by now developed a cold and was grounded, but in the event, the raid was scrubbed because the weather was so bad. Even slight colds in aircrew were taken very seriously and the Medical Officer would not let anyone suspected of suffering with one fly. Because of the altitude and the violent weaving, banking, corkscrewing, and searching manoeuvres operational flying entailed, congestion of the head and nasal passages could cause the eardrums to burst. This would end an airman's flying and his usefulness as aircrew. To help us keep well, we took four cod liver oil capsules every day and drank plenty of milk. Occasionally, we were even given an orange, which was unheard of for civilians during the war.

When our crew arrived at East Kirkby in July, we were one of three new crews to join the squadron that day. Six weeks later, we were the only one remaining, and on Sunday 17th we all attended a memorial service for those fourteen young men, most of whom were, like us, only teenagers.

Since I had returned from leave, along with everyone else on the station, I had become aware of much increased aerial activity to the south. We had no idea of what was happening, but rumours abounded that something big was being planned. D-Day had been three months earlier, and in Europe, our forces were pushing the Germans ever further east. We no longer bombed great areas of France, and Paris had been liberated on 25th August, so we had no idea what was in the offing. Then, on this Sunday morning we were told that Operation Market Garden, the greatest airborne assault in history, was underway. The plan was to seize the bridges over the Rhine and end the war by Christmas. The veterans of the First World War had heard it all before, though.

The failure of the operation to capture the prized bridge at Arnhem was due to over-enthusiastic planning on the part of the Allies coupled with a certain contempt for the Intelligence reports from the Dutch resistance. On the Germans' part it was good luck, logistical skill and the experience of their commanders. No fault lay with our paratroopers, for the raw, grim determination and outstanding courage of all the Allied troops on the ground, but most especially that of the British 1st Airborne Division in and around Arnhem, has never been surpassed in the history of warfare. During the battle, the Commander of the II Panzer Corps in Arnhem, Generalleutnant Wilhelm Bittrich, a professional soldier and holder of the Knight's Cross, was chided by Generalfeldmarschall Model, the overall German commander in the field, about the failure of the SS to regain control of both ends of the bridge. Bittrich, who had seen action across Europe throughout the war and was battle hardened even by SS standards, replied to Model of the British 1st Airborne Division, "In all my years as a soldier, I have never seen men fight so hard."

Chapter Ten

"It made every square metre of Germany a Front.   For us it was the greatest lost battle of the war."
Albert   Speer,   Hitler's   Armament's   Minister   on   the impact of RAF Bomber Command's campaign

We had the Monday free and so since the weather had picked up and promised another fine day, Jerry, Bill and I went to Skegness to enjoy the late summer sunshine along the promenade.   Although the threat of invasion had long since passed, mines and barbed wire still littered the beach, so we didn't venture onto the sand!   That night back in our billet, I was awoken by the hated sound of a V1 flying bomb approaching.   It sounded low and close, but the engine was still firing.   Then it coughed, spluttered and cut out.   A few seconds later it exploded uncomfortably nearby.

The squadron was awaiting a new replacement aircraft, G for George, and next day we were told that PD317 had been delivered and perhaps we might like to apply for it.   It appealed to us to have our own aircraft so we approached the CO and he agreed that we could have it.   We were so proud and pleased with ourselves, we really felt as though we had come of age; only experienced crews had a dedicated aircraft with its attendant ground crew.   Then we found out why everyone else had stepped aside from this one: G for George was a jinxed call sign on the squadron and no-one else wanted it.

The first chance to fly it operationally was sooner than we might have wished when we appeared on the Battle Order next day for a night op to Mönchengladbach.   We chatted with the ground crew about the aircraft, did our external checks and then climbed aboard.   PD317 was brand spanking new; she even smelled right. Like driving a new car for the first time, Jerry carefully taxied around the perimeter track to the runway.   We had a green from the controller, brakes came off and we started to roll.   The tail lifted, I pushed the throttle levers through the gate and G for George climbed smoothly into the evening sky at 18.55 on 19th

September. We set course for Reading on our first leg to the target. Then Bill tried to switch on his Gee radar navigation set. For the following half an hour he and I tried every possible means to get the set to work, but we had no joy at all. We were really keen that our first op in our own aeroplane should not be a boomerang, and so we decided to join up with another Lancaster.

There was still plenty of daylight in the sky at that height and so the plan was to follow this other aircraft and when it changed course Bill would pinpoint that as Reading. From there on he would use old-style DR navigation to enable us to complete the mission. The plan was sound but, much to our disappointment and irritation, it was foiled by the weather. Long before we reached Reading, the cloud built up and we lost sight of the other Lancaster. We had no alternative now but to descend below the cloud and head due east until we crossed the coast of the North Sea. Once over the water, we continued out to sea for a few miles then turned north. Keeping the East Anglia shoreline in sight to port, we dumped 1,000 gallons of fuel and some of our bombs into the sea to bring us down to our recommended landing weight. This was to be our only boomerang, and a complete waste of nearly two and a half hours' flying was made all the more frustrating because it was a brand-new aircraft; the G for George jinx had struck again.

The Master Bomber for the raid that night was W/C Guy Gibson, who two months earlier had joined a No.630 Squadron crew to attack the V1 site at Criel-sur-Mer. His role in the raid on the Ruhr dams the previous year is already well documented, although the contribution of his deputy Sqn Ldr HM Young, DFC*, is less well recorded; not least the fact that it was Dinghy Young's mine which fatally cracked the Möhne Dam ahead of Dave Maltby's final breaching. Like the rest of us, Gibson was not without his faults, one of which was his tendency for rudeness and condescension towards junior ranks and ground crew. It was a trait which had manifested itself early in his career. In 1942 and still only twenty-three, he was promoted to Wing Commander and appointed CO of No.106 Squadron, then stationed at Coningsby. His attitude to NCOs and ground crew had not improved, earning him the title of 'the Boy Emperor'. Ultimately, it was his intolerance of others which would prove to be his undoing.

In early August 1944 Gibson was posted to No.54 Base, RAF Coningsby, as a staff officer, a role which did not sit comfortably with him. He feared that the war would be over before he could return to operations. Our raid on Mönchengladbach was the secondary target, Bremen being first choice, but with a deterioration in the weather, the switch was made. It is unclear why Gibson was to be the Master Bomber that night as he had no experience in this highly skilled and complex role, nor was he supposed to take a participatory role in operations over enemy territory. It is possible that he had appointed himself to the role whilst Air Commodore Bobby Sharpe was absent.

At Coningsby, there was no serviceable Mosquito available to Gibson, a factor which would prove pivotal to the events which followed. He had no regular navigator and so the Station Navigation Officer, Sqn Ldr JB Warwick, DFC, was ultimately selected to fly with him. They were driven to Woodhall Spa where a No.627 Squadron Mosquito was made ready for him.

Over the target, a number of mishaps led to confused marking of the aiming points and the raid was a failure. Gibson's Mosquito crashed in the Netherlands at around 22.30 on its way home. Since both men were killed, no-one knows for certain what happened. At the time of his death, Gibson was the most highly decorated serviceman in Britain and someone who could genuinely be described as a 'celebrity', and with good cause; not famous for being famous, but famous for having demonstrated great courage and leadership. As a result, his loss was kept from the press, although not the Prime Minister, until 29th November; but on the squadron we knew by the next morning that he was missing as the entry in my diary shows, "…*Wing Commander Gibson (Dam Buster) missing.*"

Over the years, many theories about the crash have been put forward. The Luftwaffe did not claim to have shot down any Mosquitoes that night. A No.61 Squadron rear gunner, Sgt Bernard McCormack, believed that he had shot the aircraft down, mistaking the Mosquito for a Ju88. However, when the wreckage was excavated in 1985 no firepower damage was evident. It is more likely that the aircraft which McCormack fired at was that of fighter ace Kurt Welter, who had been in the area at the time.

After the war, Dutch witnesses to the crash talked of seeing a low-flying Mosquito with a light showing in the cockpit and confirmed that the aircraft was not on fire and that there was no German flak activity, all of which suggests that Gibson and Warwick ran out of fuel. Some years ago, I was told the following story by another former Bomber Command veteran. On that September afternoon in 1944, Woodhall Spa received a telephone call from Coningsby requiring No.627 Squadron to prepare its reserve Canadian-built Mosquito with TI [target indicator] marker flares to be used by W/C Gibson as Master Bomber for the raid that night.

When Gibson and Jim Warwick arrived, Gibson rejected the reserve aircraft which had been made ready for him and insisted upon using the Mk BXX, KB267 AZ-E instead, much to everyone's irritation because the armourers then had to swap over the bomb loads. The regular pilot of KB267 was Flt Lt Peter Mallender, DFC, but that evening he was told by his CO, W/C Elliott, that Gibson and Warwick would fly the aircraft, and because the squadron flew Canadian-built Mosquitoes which differed from British-made ones in certain aspects, he was to acquaint the two officers with those differences. Standing beside his aircraft, Mallender attempted to do so but Gibson dismissed him with an imperious wave, saying he had flown Mosquitoes before. Gibson and Warwick climbed in and took off at 19.51 to catch up with the bomber stream already on its way to Mönchengladbach; and that was the last that Peter Mallender ever saw of his aircraft or the two airmen.

Next day, when he heard that the men were missing, he knew exactly what had happened; they had run out of fuel. The fuel tank change-over cocks on British models were located behind the pilot's seat where the navigator could easily operate them and, if necessary, the pilot could also reach them. On the Canadian version they were in a different place altogether and since Jim Warwick had never flown in one, he would have no idea where they were located. Had Peter Mallender not been waved away, he would have shown the cocks to Warwick and the aircraft would almost certainly have returned home safely. Wing Commander Guy P Gibson, VC, DSO*, DFC*, and Squadron Leader James B Warwick, DFC, are buried in Steenbergen cemetery close to where they crashed.

We are all flawed in some way, Guy Gibson no less so, and many saw him as an accident waiting to happen, but he was undoubtedly an outstanding officer and bomber pilot. He had luck but he also had a purpose of mind. Perhaps the war came at the right time for him, allowing him to fulfil a potential that he could never have done in peacetime. A complicated man with a troubled childhood, had he survived the war, he might well not have survived the peace; in that he would not have been alone.

We were not involved with any ops the day after the Mönchengladbach raid as our aircraft's Gee radar was still being repaired. The day did bring a very pleasant surprise, though, when I met up with Bill Burr and Ambrose. I hadn't seen Bill, who had put me and my bed outside the Waafery, since we had left Syerston and it was good to see him and catch up. They had been posted to East Kirkby from Metheringham awaiting the re-forming of No.227 Squadron at Bardney, which was due to take effect on 7th October.

The weather had turned in and there was no flying. I managed to catch up with my letters home, to Lord Barnard, to Tom and Jack, and to friends in the scouts. Mess parties and dances must have been difficult to organise because of operational pressures but they were held regularly to keep morale up, and the CO tried to have a station dance every month, and so, with no flying on Friday night, this was a good opportunity. The station WAAFs came, some of the local girls from the surrounding villages came and other girls were bussed in from Boston and Skegness. I remember there always seemed to be a plentiful supply of food so perhaps the station was allocated extra rations for these events. Bill and Ambrose joined our little group and for a few hours of drinking and dancing, we were almost able to forget the war.

Our Gee navigation set had now been repaired and we were on the Battle Order for Saturday's operation. There were three major targets that night, the docks at Neuss, the infamous Dortmund-Ems Canal, and the Münster/Handorf night-fighter aerodrome, which was our allotted destination. We were airborne at 18.45 but when we got to Münster there was a delay in bombing and we were thirty-three minutes over the target, which, since it was a night-fighter base, was a very unhealthy predicament to be in. The controllers must have put up all of their fighters because there were

179

so many flying around. However, despite that, we bombed the aerodrome successfully and lost only one Lancaster from our group. The wave which went to the Dortmund-Ems inevitably suffered much heavier losses. Throughout the war, the Germans defended this vital stretch of industrial waterway with resolute tenacity and extracted a terrible price in Bomber Command lives for our attempts to breach the vulnerable aqueducts.

By 00.30 our ground crew were guiding G for George into the dispersal pan and were preparing to take back control of their aircraft, happy to see it returned from the mission in one piece. The weather continued to take its toll on the operational ability of the Command. The next day we managed a short period of air-to-sea firing with Lt Reynolds, RN, in attendance before the driving rain made any further test impossible. Although I had now done a total of twelve sorties, as a crew we had completed ten and so were due our ten sortie check with Flt Lt Schofield of the Base staff. The idea was to make sure that we were not becoming complacent, that we had adopted all the latest techniques and were operating well as a crew. He was happy with our performance, which was a big improvement from our uncertain start with Flt Lt Walters.

Some of the crew with LE-G for George. That's me on the right

We were on the Battle Order for 25th, but as the weather deteriorated once again, the night's operation was scrubbed. Needing to unwind and let the adrenalin settle after the anticipation of another mission, a whole bunch of us went to the camp cinema to relax, oblivious of the disaster that had unfolded in Arnhem. The storms and heavy rain which had kept us grounded that night provided critical cover for Major-General Roy Urquhart to withdraw what remained of the British 1st Airborne Division across the Rhine, leaving the wreckage of the Arnhem Bridge in German hands. Operation Market Garden may have been over but the Dutch civilians who remained in Arnhem would continue to suffer retribution, displacement and starvation for another six months.

We had only postponed the inevitable, and the following night we once more kitted up and were transported out to our waiting aircraft. The target this time was Karlsruhe in southern Germany, close to the point where the Rhine forms the border with France. We approached across northern France and the Vogues Forest. Ahead, the city's ring of searchlights sprang into life, lighting up the sky. I was always surprised how wide the beam seemed at whatever height we flew at.

The Mosquitoes had been in and marked the aiming points, but now those weaving shafts of light played across our path like accusing fingers of death. Then it started. Perfidious white balls flicked up and innocent-looking puffs of grey-black smoke pock-marked the illuminated sky. The air in the cockpit became heavy with the stench of cordite, the Lancaster bucked with each near miss, explosions which created a squeaky grating sound audible even above the engine roar, while the spent fragments of shrapnel rattled down the aircraft sides. With stomachs knotted tight in fear, we pressed on into the gathering barrage, hoping, praying, to get through, no longer in control of our destiny.

Ahead and to starboard the inner port engine of another Lancaster suddenly burst into flames. I watched as the fire flared up, died down a little and then grew quickly, spreading over the wing and back along the fuselage. Slowly the aircraft began to dip to port, tip forwards and start to fall away, the flames engulfing the whole structure before it was lost to my view somewhere beneath us.

We had been able to come straight in on our bombing run without having to orbit the target. Then, with photograph taken, we were out on the other side, but there was no flak here and as the Lancaster turned for home, we knew that the Nachtjager had arrived. Jerry started to 'bank and search' to give our gunners every opportunity to see if anyone was trying to creep up underneath us. This manoeuvre involved banking the aircraft 90 degrees port then over to starboard in a yawing motion to let the gunners spot fighters under our blind spot. Weaving was a gentler variation of this manoeuvre. If there was any doubt about a fighter being near us, we would carry out the more violent corkscrew.

As well as helping us see, these actions would let any fighter pilot nearby know that we were very definitely awake and alert, so leave us alone. Since that first flight at East Kirkby with Flt Lt Walters, we had taken his warning very seriously and had worked hard to perfect these manoeuvres. They weren't popular with the crew because it was a horrible sensation, sometimes inducing airsickness, but as Jerry reminded everyone, it was preferable to being shot down! Karlsruhe had been a pretty hot trip and when we touched down again at 07.00 in the morning light, the relief was written on all our faces.

It was Kaiserslautern, also in southern Germany, the following night. We bombed from 4,000 feet and the raid, which was the Command's only one on the city during the war, was highly successful. We had taken off at 22.08 and were back just before 05.30. In stark contrast to the raid on Karlsruhe the night before, I saw no fighters and we were met with only light flak.

After my bacon-and-eggs breakfast I had a good sleep, got up during the afternoon and went down to the Intelligence Room. Following our unsuccessful attack at Darmstadt on 25th August, the Command had revisited the target on the night of 11th/12th September and in clear weather conditions had accurately and devastatingly destroyed almost the entire city of 120,000 people. I was so struck by the Intelligence report and assessment information from the second raid that I made a note of it in my diary that same day, Thursday 28th September, to the effect that the bombing had been so accurate it had killed 33,000 workers. It is now generally accepted from German records made in the days after the attack that the actual figure was 12,300 dead and over 70,000 made homeless. It was still an appalling loss of life and demonstrated how effective Bomber Command had become when all the pieces fell into place.

In their seminal work *The Bomber Command War Diaries*, Martin Middlebrook and Chris Everitt record that this second raid on the city remains a sensitive issue because of the lack of any major industry there. The bombing caused an intense fire which swept through the streets causing most of the casualties and property destruction. I was still on leave at the time of the raid but conclude that the Command strategists still believed that what today we would term weapons of mass destruction were being created at Darmstadt. In retrospect, I can understand why the German population viewed us as *terror Fliegers*; however, for the crews flying out that night, it would simply have been just another target. We were young men doing the job that the successful prosecution of the war demanded of us.

By now I had been promoted to Flight Sergeant. On the Kaiserslautern raid the Command had lost a Mosquito and a Lancaster over France, so on Friday I flew down to RAF Rackheath to collect three of the Lancaster crew who had bailed out and been picked up by American ground forces before being flown back. The USAAF 467th Bombardment Group (Heavy) which flew B-24 Liberators was based at Rackheath and it was an interesting visit, not least because nothing seemed to be in short supply.

Whatever failings our American cousins may have had, a lack of generosity was certainly not one of them. Jerry and Len were taken to the officers' mess whilst the rest of us went to the sergeants' mess. We were given a large cup of freshly ground coffee and after a few minutes chatting were invited to join them for lunch. I don't think that I had ever seen so much food before. The stewards just kept bringing in the dishes, including steak, of course, to which we helped ourselves. All good things come to an end and it was time to return to base, whereupon the duty officer arranged for the ten of us to be transported out to our aircraft. As we made our way around the aerodrome, I casually commented to Jerry, "Well, I didn't expect a wizard meal like that."

The comment was meant rhetorically but it galvanised Jerry, who sat bolt upright and demanded, "What meal?"

So we told him, but that only made matters worse since it seems he and Len had enjoyed nothing more substantial than a cup of coffee.

The flight to Rackheath was the start of what turned out to be a rather good period as the squadron was not involved in operations again until 11th October and it gave us chance for a rest and some relaxation. On Saturday evening I went to the Gliderdrome where the local bands always produced excellent versions of the popular dance tunes by people like Artie Shaw, Benny Goodman, Glenn Miller, and Tommy Dorsey, along with the British bands of Ray Noble, Carroll Gibbons and his Savoy Orpheans, Geraldo and Roy Fox, to name but a few. As usual, the place was packed but it was still a very enjoyable evening.

Sunday mornings brought a special treat at East Kirkby; by practice or tradition, we cared not which, aircrew breakfast on the Sabbath was bacon and two eggs even if not on ops. After that start, we took off for a couple of hours' air-to-sea gunnery practice and then high-level bombing. Whilst we were airborne, I spent some time in the rear turret firing at the sea target, took over the navigation duties and then piloted the aircraft, this time Lancaster ND412 LE-H, on two of the bombing runs. It was all part of the philosophy that everyone in the crew should be able to do some or all of the other jobs so that at times of crisis, if one or more crew were injured but the aircraft remained stable, it could still function as a fighting machine and hopefully bring the crew home safely. Alternatively, if the pilot were killed, the FE could keep the aircraft in the air until over friendly territory to allow the rest of the crew to bail out. Most of us could do some basic navigation, everyone could fire the guns and the pilot could release the bombs should the bomb aimer be injured.

On Monday night, the camp cinema was showing *Manpower*, starring Marlene Dietrich, Edward G Robinson and George Raft, so I wandered across to watch it. It had a somewhat predictable storyline but was enjoyable enough and we didn't have to pay on the camp. The next day, on a twenty-four-hour pass, I went into Boston and stayed the night. In the morning, I looked around

Boston cathedral and tower before meeting up with Jock and Len to go and see *Road to Zanzibar*. This was the second of the *Road ...* films and starred Dorothy Lamour, Bob Hope and Bing Crosby. It was very funny and it felt good to laugh at the carefree innocence of it all after our recent experiences.

Back at the camp it was another session in the Link Trainer. We used this at every opportunity when not flying to hone our skills. That evening I was back in Boston dancing at the Gliderdrome. On Sunday, I was detailed for the raid on the dams at Walcheren Island but the bad weather forced it to be abandoned, which gave me the happy opportunity to go to the station dance instead, and a much more enjoyable evening followed.

We should never have had to bomb Walcheren Island. In the weeks before Market Garden, in their haste to get to Germany, the Allied commanders in the field and in London made a catastrophic mistake, which would ultimately cost them success in the operation and with it the chance of ending the war by Christmas, if such a chance had ever existed. All the supplies for the Allied forces had to come ashore in Normandy and then be transported to the front since the Channel ports remained in enemy hands. As the Germans fell back towards their homeland and their supply line shortened, so the Allies' supply line grew inexorably longer until it became stretched to breaking point.

The British had captured the port of Antwerp intact but did not control the waterway from the port to the North Sea. Our presence in Antwerp had almost cut off General Gustav van Zangen's Fifteenth Army in the area to the west on Walcheren Island, caught between the advancing forces and the sea. Almost, but not quite; a small sliver of land offered a way out and at SHAEF [Supreme Headquarters Allied Expeditionary Force] in London and in Belgium commanders were so preoccupied with finding a way into Germany that they missed it, allowing van Zangen's men to escape.

In an immense oversight, no-one capitalised upon the outstanding success of Major-General George Roberts' 11th Armoured Division in reaching Antwerp and capturing the massive port before the Germans could destroy it. A handful of tanks and eighteen more

185

miles of unopposed advance would have sealed off the two-mile-wide isthmus and locked the Fifteenth Army on Walcheren Island. Instead it left a holding force behind whilst65,000 men, their 225 guns, 750 trucks and 1,000 horses slipped away under the cover of darkness along the single-track road across South Beveland to Zeeland and thence back into the German lines just in time to fight along the vital sixty-four-mile corridor of Dutch towns, villages and countryside that led to Arnhem. Their role was to prove as critical in the battle as was the fateful decision of Generalfeldmarschall Model to choose the area around the sleepy town of Arnhem, that quiet Dutch town in a *"peaceful sector where nothing was happening"*, as the place to rest Bittrich's Panzer troops.

The Walcheren raid was back on for Wednesday in a daylight op. We were part of a force of sixty-one Lancasters and two Mosquitoes with a Spitfire escort detailed to attack the sea walls on the island from 6,000 feet. The purpose of trying to breach the sea walls was to quite literally flush out the defending troops who were still able to exercise control over the Scheldt seaway and prevent us using Antwerp to supply our advancing troops. It is hard to fully convey the sense of security and relief that those Spitfires gave to us. The fact that we saw no enemy fighters would undoubtedly be due to their presence. The Luftwaffe was running short of aircraft, pilots and fuel oil, and to send fighters up to attack such a small heavily escorted bomber force would have been a futile gesture.

Jerry opened the bomb doors as Len guided him in on the run. With the target squarely in his sights, Len pressed the 'tit'. Nothing. Quickly he pressed it again; still the bombs stayed firmly in the aircraft. I looked through the inspection window but could see no obvious reason why they would not release. However, we now had a much bigger and more urgent problem. Our cargo was primed ready to go with delayed-action fuses; if we did not get rid of them soon, they would get rid of us. Whilst Len tried to get them to go, I carefully watched the time because we couldn't hang about here much longer. If they didn't go soon we needed to head for East Anglia where we could bail out and leave the Lancaster to crash into the sea. Finally, Len managed to jettison all but one in the area of the dykes, with the last one eventually slipping out and falling into the sea. We had left East Kirkby at 13.05 and were still back by 16.20, just in time for tea.

The plan for the following night was to attack Munich from the south. We were due to fly over the Alps into Italian airspace, passing around Switzerland and then turning north across Austria to Munich. Security was always very tight around operations, but there was a breach somewhere and the enemy were tipped off about our planned route. The mission was scrubbed, as too was the one for the next day, Friday 13th October, the day on which Air Chief Marshal Harris received the directive for Operation Hurricane. It is a popular misconception, especially amongst the many critics of Bomber Command's role during the war, that Arthur Harris and his team of officers determined the policy, developed the strategy and selected the targets which the aircrews then attacked. This is simply untrue, but for now, suffice it to say that the instructions for this record-breaking but little-remembered operation which took place over the twenty-four hours of 14th/15th October came from the top of the Air Ministry.

The political message was clear; the operation should, *"...demonstrate to the enemy in Germany generally the overwhelming superiority of the Allied Air Forces in this theatre...the intention is to apply within the shortest practical period the maximum effort of the Royal Air Force Bomber Command and the VIIIth United States Bomber Command[sic] against objectives in the densely populated Ruhr...cause mass panic and disorganisation in the Ruhr, disrupt frontline communications and demonstrate the futility of resistance."* It seemed that Harris had been given only a couple of days' notice of what was required of his crews, which was why my next mission had been scrubbed, and why no Bomber Command heavies flew during the forty-eight hours preceding the operation.

In the run-up to the D-Day landings and for the weeks afterwards, SHAEF had taken de facto control of Bomber Command, but following the breakout from Normandy, the Command had been returned to the Air Ministry. On 25th September the Ministry had directed Harris that the first priority for his force was to attack the enemy's synthetic oil production plants, with the joint second priorities of German rail and waterway networks, and tank and motor vehicle production. These were perceived to have the greatest impact upon the course of the war at this time. [**Directive reproduced in British Official History Vol. IV pp 172-173**].

It wasn't long before the Air Ministry seemed to grow impatient for tangible results arising from the directive. Knowing that we now enjoyed immense air superiority over Europe, the Ministry called for a huge display of that power by both the RAF and the USAAF in a round-the-clock bombing mission. Thus Operation Hurricane, a politically motivated, conceived, and ordered mission, was born. Certainly Harris was, and always had been, an enthusiastic advocate of the area-bombing strategy developed during the 1930s, but whilst there was arguably some limited military objective to this operation, I am doubtful that he would, of his own volition, have devoted so much concentrated effort to pulverising Duisburg and Brunswick at this stage of the war.

Long before Arthur Harris took charge of the Command, the political agenda for the use of the bomber force had been established by the War Cabinet and reinforced by the Air Ministry. In July 1940, Winston Churchill wrote privately, *"When I look round to see how we can win this war there is only one sure path… and that is an absolutely devastating, exterminating attack by very heavy bombers from this country upon the Nazi homeland."* Following the end of the Battle of Britain, he had told the Cabinet, *"The Navy can lose us the war, but only the RAF can win it. Therefore our supreme effort must be to gain overwhelming mastery of the air. The fighters are our salvation but the bombers alone provide the means of victory."*

Shortly afterwards, on 25th October 1940, Sir Charles Portal, the C-in-C Bomber Command since 4th April, was appointed Chief of the Air Staff; his replacement was Air Marshal Sir Richard Peirse. Five days later, the Air Ministry issued Peirse with a new directive, *"Regular concentrated attacks should be made on objectives in large towns and centres of industry, with the primary aim of causing very heavy material destruction which will demonstrate to the enemy the power and severity of air bombardment and the hardship and dislocation which will result from this."*

Britain's adoption of a policy to visit upon the enemy what today is known as 'shock and awe' was firmly established by the War Cabinet in 1940 and it was Bomber Command that was ordered to carry it out. When Arthur Harris succeeded Peirse as C-in-C in 1942 the tactic of area bombing in fulfilment of the ordered directive was well established, even if at that stage its true effectiveness was debatable.

I sat in the briefing room that Saturday and listened to the details of the plan for the attack on Brunswick, the routes in and out, the times, the turning points, the weather forecast, the Intelligence reports, the TI colours and so on. Brunswick and Duisburg were just two more targets for us.

So it was that just after first light on 14th October, 1,013 Lancasters, Halifaxes and Mosquitoes, accompanied by an overwhelming fighter escort, took off for Duisburg to drop 3,574 tons of high explosive and 820 tons of incendiaries on the city. The Lancaster squadrons formed the early waves and consequently took the greater losses, with thirteen of the fourteen bombers lost shot down by flak before the defences became overwhelmed in the enormity of the attack. Simultaneously, the USAAF supplied a further 1,251 bombers escorted by 749 fighters to the overall operation, of which more than a thousand attacked Cologne.

As darkness fell, another 1,005 heavy bombers and Mosquitoes attacked Duisburg in two waves, two hours apart. Whilst the Command had plenty of aircraft, it was short of crews, and in order to achieve two consecutive thousand-bomber raids within twenty-four hours, some crews carried out back-to-back trips.

The second target that night was Brunswick, which is where I was bound. Part of the rationale for the second target was to demonstrate the scale of the Command's power, that it could send a thousand bombers to one target and still have enough in reserve to mount a major attack on another city.

It was 22.48 when we had the green light from the controller and set off down the runway heading for the heart of Germany. Eight hours later we were safely back at East Kirkby and returning G for George to the ground crew. It had been a long flight and I was very grateful for the steaming mug of tea and tot of rum that were thrust into my hands when we got to the debriefing room.

The Intelligence Officers receiving our reports must have reflected upon the immense difference which the last six months and D-Day in particular had brought. Instead of reporting heavy sustained flak and numerous fighters with the consequent losses of bombers, on this raid we had encountered very little flak and had not seen any fighters at all, which was hardly surprising since we had been given a fighter escort. My main concern from the sortie was that Len, our bomb aimer, had managed to get his hands crushed between the front guns and the turret mounting. Not a laughing matter under any circumstances, but at the sub-zero temperatures of 20,000 feet it was particularly serious. Thanks to the protection of his gloves, the injury was not too bad and soon healed.

Over the twenty-four hours that Operation Hurricane was effective, RAF Bomber Command and the USAAF Eighth Air Force would fly more than 3,800 sorties to Duisburg and Brunswick. From the Command's point of view, the raid was entirely successful. There was no creep-back and we had systematically and totally destroyed Brunswick, displacing 80,000 people. Consequently, the Command had no need to visit the city again in any numbers during the war. The fire storm which our incendiaries had created swept through the streets and destroyed or seriously damaged almost all the buildings. Like a Promethean messenger, I had looked down from the heavens upon the conflagration beneath to witness my work. The orange mist of fire had spread out as the angel of death had stolen upon Egypt's first-born; insatiable, irresistible, indelible. It is the image that I have carried from the raid to this day.

For those that had not left the city before we arrived, only the underground air-raid shelters offered any hope of survival, but the intensity of the fires that raged in the streets above their heads trapped more than 23,000 people in eight huge underground shelters. Several hours later, the local firemen fought their way through to the shelters and, in what must have seemed like a miracle, were able to rescue almost everybody safely.

There were several diversionary raids taking place at the same time, including one by No.9 Squadron to the Sorpe Dam, which had been the third target on No.617 Squadron's famous raid in May the previous year. Bomber Command's effort in Operation Hurricane, which excludes the American sorties, broke all records for the war and would never be exceeded. During those twenty-four hours we dropped around 10,210 tons of high explosives and incendiaries and flew 2,589 sorties.

There was of course an appalling human cost to all this. More than 3,000 people were killed on the ground in the raids. We lost 156 airmen from twenty-four aircraft, and the Americans lost around a further fifty crewmen. We were, though, engaged in total war, fighting for our survival and for the values that we as a nation believed in.

In his book *Prodromo*, written in 1670, Jesuit mathematician and aeronautics pioneer Father Francesco Lana de Terzi published his concept and calculations for a 'flying ship'. Often described as 'the father of aeronautics', he also recognised the capabilities of his design as a weapon of war with which to attack cities from the air. However, he believed that his idea would never progress beyond theory and wrote with some regret, "*God will never allow man to construct such a machine, since it would create many disturbances in the civil and political governments of mankind. Where is the man who can fail to see that no city would be proof against surprise, when the ship could at any time be steered over its squares, or even over the courtyards of dwelling-houses, and brought to earth for the landing of its crew?...Iron weights could be hurled to wreck ships at sea, or they could be set on fire by fireballs and bombs; nor ships alone, but houses, fortresses and cities could be thus destroyed, with the certainty that the airship could come to no harm as the missiles could be hurled from a vast height.*"

On 6th August 1914, German Imperial Army Zeppelin Z VI flew over Liège and dropped thirteen bombs, killing nine civilians. It was the first known dedicated aerial bombing raid in history, thus both fulfilling and vindicating the vision and scientific faith of de Terzi. From that August day onwards, the European powers sought to develop the potential of the aeroplane as a means by which to attack the enemy at home; his military forces, industrial heartlands, communication systems, and general populations: in short, his ability to wage war. The mantra was '*The bomber will always get through*'.

Perhaps the responsibilities of Empire gave the British a particular penchant for playing fair and by the rules, for being 'a jolly good egg' in competition, and war no less. Consequently, in the early part of the war, Bomber Command was scrupulous in its adherence to attacking only military targets. Playing fair was going to lose the war. It was that realisation which persuaded the politically mixed War Cabinet to agree to Churchill's desire to bomb Germany into submission. But it was not a new strategy or even a British initiative. By the time we came to adopt it, the Germans were already proficient exponents, having tested it to great effect at Guernica during the Spanish Civil War and then with devastating results on the civilian populations of Warsaw, Katowice, Teschen, Krakow, Rotterdam, Coventry, Clydeside, Plymouth, Southampton, London, Hull, and so many more.

We were going on a daytime training flight and these two ground crew lads had been preparing the aircraft

Chapter Eleven

"O for that warning voice, which he who saw
The Apocalypse heard cry in heaven aloud,
Then when the Dragon, put to second rout,
Came furious down to be reveng'd on men,
Woe to the inhabitants on earth!"
Paradise Lost, Book IV – John Milton

A combination of poor weather and cancelled missions kept us grounded until the 19th. At the briefing that afternoon there was a palpable intake of breath by the assembled crews when the cloth was drawn aside from the large map of Europe on the wall and we saw that the red line led to Nuremberg. It would be the first time that the Command had returned to the city since the catastrophe of 30th/31st March. Nuremberg, the spiritual home of the Nazis, the venue for their great pre-war rallies, the city that had cost Bomber Command so dear, would ultimately become the nemesis of the party leadership when the post-war trials began.

The briefing was as thorough as always, but the great difference this time was that D-Day had happened and the Germans had been pushed out of France, losing their night-fighter bases there. We on the other hand had the use of those aerodromes and so most, if not all of Germany, lay within range of our fighter cover. Nevertheless, Nuremberg, barely fifty miles from the Czech border and a long way into the Nazi lair, remained well defended.

One of Bomber Command's many great contributions to the war was to force Hitler to devote almost a million men and 55,000 anti-aircraft guns to the home defence of Germany; men and guns that would otherwise have been available to repel the Allied forces on D-Day. Our attacks on Luftwaffe aerodromes and the synthetic oil plants, the Royal Navy's blockade of German ports, and our access to fighter escorts all conspired to deny Hitler the means to maximise his air power. The Luftwaffe, and the Nachtjager force in particular, was still formidable, but its ability to shoot down large numbers of bombers as it had done seven months earlier had ebbed away. The flak batteries, on the other hand, were as fearsome as ever. Linked to the central radar-controlled searchlight, flak, and especially box barrages, had become our greatest foe. As enemy forces shrank back from two fronts into their homeland, so they became more concentrated.

It was 17.05 when G for George was given the signal to take off. We headed out into the evening sunshine, gaining height and enjoying the illusion that the sun was rising in the west. Importantly, though, it gave us daylight to form up into the loose bomber stream that crossed the English Channel. There were no problems flying across France now, but once we reached the border, the flak opened up on us all the way to Nuremberg. As the Intelligence Officer had reported, the city was heavily defended and the flak was intense but, as it had been in March, the city was covered with cloud. We were given the bombing code Wanganui, which meant that the TIs would be dropped above the clouds and we would bomb through them. The bombing fell almost entirely in the industrial areas of the city to the south.

We turned away at the end of our run and I looked back down across our path. From far below, the seeping orange glow of fire reached up through the cloud, but it was not alone, for with it came an intense bombardment of flak. The Lancaster bucked through the disturbed air, shrapnel pinged along its sides, cordite filled every corner of the fuselage and the noise became overpowering. Leaving the burning city behind, Bill plotted the course for home, hoping we could avoid the intensity of flak we had experienced on the way in.

From out of the blackness, two Fw190s flashed by in quick succession just above the cockpit. Our two gunners, Jock in the mid-upper and Jim in the tail turret, uttered appropriate Gaelic and Anglo-Saxon oaths at them but kept their fingers off the triggers. The Fw190 was the most feared of their fighters and not one to be trifled with. If there was the slightest chance that these two had not seen us or were not intent upon us, then discretion was the better part of valour.

It may also have been the case that the pilots had seen one of our Mosquitoes. We had seven of these wonderful aircraft with us on the raid and whilst they were certainly not invincible, they undoubtedly put the fear of God into the Nachtjager crews. Most Mosquitoes carried air-to-air radar in the nose, but some also carried it in the tail pointing rearwards, enabling the crew to lure in a would-be attacker before slipping around behind; the hunter becoming the hunted.

Despite our best hopes, we had to run the flak gauntlet all the way back to the French border. From there on, our flight home was uneventful other than being diverted to one of our satellites, Strubby. The next morning we were joined by our ground crew, who flew back to East Kirkby with us just to give them a bit of a joy ride. So often the ground crew did all the work on the aircraft out in the open and often in appalling weather conditions but never got to fly. There was always a very good relationship between aircrew and ground crew; they each depended on the other, although in truth, our lives depended on the skill of the ground crew, whereas if we wrecked their aeroplane, the RAF would give them another one.

That night there was a mess dance and party which I noted in my diary was exceptionally good; I must have met a pretty WAAF. When we weren't flying operations, most of our daytime was filled with a variety of training or maintenance activities around the base. The aircraft engines were run up each day, Intelligence reports were available to be read, lectures on radar or the latest development of secret equipment were to be attended, whilst night flying tests, bombing practice, fighter affiliation, and navigation practice all took us into the skies. The evenings were generally our own, which afforded time to write home, do a little bit of sewing, or occasionally some kit cleaning; mostly, though, we went to the cinema, a dance or a mess party.

After the previous evening's entertainment and enjoyment, Monday morning brought a return to business; I was on the Battle Order for that afternoon. The raid was another one on Walcheren Island. We were one of 112 No.5 Group Lancasters to attack a large gun battery at Flushing. No.3 Group had tried to silence the battery over the weekend but without success; now it was our turn. The guns were the last major obstacle preventing the navy from sailing into Antwerp and using the harbour facilities there. Once again, the failure of commanders to cut the isthmus to the island in September was coming back to bite them. Our troops holding part of Holland and trying to push towards Germany desperately needed these port facilities. Take-off for us was 15.15, but when we arrived at the target the sea mist had rolled over and visibility was poor, consequently the bombing became scattered. However, the defending flak was not scattered. It was heavy and accurate and the force lost four aircraft that afternoon.

Our leave came through next day and I travelled to the north-east with Bill, whose home was in Newcastle upon Tyne. We drew our leave passes and hitch-hiked to Grantham. In our RAF uniforms it wasn't long before we were given a lift, but there was a delay on the train to Darlington, so we went to the pictures to pass the time. Once again, the pleasure of leave was in doing the ordinary things I would have done had there been no war, visiting the scouts and cubs, going to dances, cycling, and meeting up with friends who were also home on leave or in reserved occupations. Towards the end I went to the Cockfield dance, which turned out to be a particularly enjoyable evening. It was half-term for the schools and so the next day I organised a wide game for the scouts, starting on the Fell and finishing up in Lord Barnard's woods at Raby Castle.

Then it was over. I packed my kit and headed back, meeting up with Bill on the way. We arrived at East Kirby in time for the Friday night dance!

When I went to breakfast next morning, it was to find my name down for ops. The target this time turned out to be the Dortmund-Ems Canal. It was to be the first of five visits that I would pay to it. No other place in Germany received a greater concentration of bombs than did this canal, and the Ladbergen Aqueduct in particular. Although the broad description of the target is usually given as the Dortmund-Ems Canal, the actual aiming point was almost always the Ladbergen Aqueduct between Münster and Osnabrück.

When it was opened by Kaiser Wilhelm II on 11th August 1914, this arterial waterway was 266km long and held twenty locks. After the Nazis came to power in the 1930s and war was likely, they realised how vulnerable the Ladbergen Aqueduct was. Consequently, they built a second parallel channel and fitted it with safety gates at each end, which could be dropped down vertically to seal the canal and prevent the wholesale loss of water should the aqueduct walls be breached.

The canal was a principal artery in our enemy's industrial heart, feeding his factories with raw materials. The immense Hermann Göring steelworks at Salzgitter, which employed some 800,000 people, produced 1.5 million tons of steel each year, all of which was transported along the Mittelland Canal and then the Dortmund-Ems on its way south to destinations such as the mighty Krupp armaments works at Essen in the industrial Ruhr. In the opposite direction, the canal carried many of the materials and weapons produced in the Ruhr through to the Baltic. Thus almost everything carried on the canal had to pass over the Ladbergen Aqueduct. From 1940, Bomber Command attacked the Dortmund-Ems no fewer than thirty times and the Mittelland a further six times. Of the twenty-two Victoria Crosses awarded to the Command during the war, the Ladbergen Aqueduct produced two.

Germany knew that the canals were vulnerable to attack and defended them with a formidable array of several hundred anti-aircraft guns, and the aqueduct at Ladbergen especially so. Early in the war, high-level bombing on such a narrow linear target was not really practical, so low-level attacks were the only option. That, though, required the attacking Hampdens to fly at between 100 feet and 150 feet along the line of the canal and through the alleyway of lethal flak which the defenders put up. They used a combination of 20mm cannons through to the massive 105mm calibre anti-aircraft guns, which were arranged in groupings on the ground whilst the smaller weapons were mounted on flak towers disguised as windmills, all protecting the line of the canal.

The heavy 105mm flak batteries, which could reach 20,000 feet and which were usually used to defend cities, were set out in a quadrilateral with a command post in the centre. These guns were in turn protected from low-level attacks by three troops of 20mm flak. When an aircraft was detected, the heavy guns were fired in salvos designed to burst within a defined spread of around 50 metres. Our crews, blinded by searchlights, had to fly straight and level through this terrifyingly intimidating hail of fire where survival was entirely a matter of luck.

Part of a quadrilateral of 105mm flak guns protecting the Dortmund-Ems Canal at Ladbergen that we faced on each attack [photo: by kind permission of Malcolm Brooke – Bomber History]

The last raid on Ladbergen in 1940 was on the night of 28th/29th September, with no further raids during the next two years. To guard the Ladbergen Aqueduct, there were originally two 105mm battery locations, each location containing two batteries of four guns apiece, thus a total of sixteen 105mm guns; by 1943, these batteries had been increased to five guns each, an indication of just how important Ladbergen was to both sides. Building on the success of the dams raid, on 15th/16th September 1943 eight Lancasters of No.617 Squadron carried out a low-level attack on the aqueduct. Many of those who had survived the dams raid perished here that night when five crews failed to return.

It was another year before the Command returned to Ladbergen. With better marking and aiming techniques to enable bombing from a greater height, and despite 7/10 cloud, faulty radios, some confusion over marking the twin channels of the canal, and the misgivings of the crews, the aqueduct walls were breached, probably by 617 Squadron's Tallboy bombs. The attack had caught the safety gates in the open position and the canal water drained away, leaving more than eighteen miles of marooned barges. The price, another fourteen aircraft lost, mostly to flak and fighters over Holland.

By the beginning of November, the German workforce had repaired much of the damaged banking and another raid was needed, and that was why I was sitting in the briefing room listening to the details of the raid for that night, all too aware of the fearsome reputation of the canal and the dreadful toll that its defenders had already taken upon Command crews.

Having left East Kirkby at 17.35, we arrived over the canal at around 19.00. The marking was good and the canal was breached again. Once more it was out of use. The flak was not as bad as I had expected but we were troubled by fighters both ways, and Jerry had to bank and weave a great deal. Keeping this going for long periods, especially when fully laden, put a huge strain on both aircraft and pilot, but our lives depended on it and we were young and strong. I think that the average age of our crew was twenty; I was nineteen. None of us could drive a car yet, but here we were flying this huge and powerful Lancaster bomber.

Two days later we were back. This time the aiming point was the aqueduct that carried the Mittelland Canal over the River Aa close to where the Mittelland joined the Dortmund-Ems at Gravenhorst. This was a very small aqueduct, albeit it an important one, and the marking crews had great difficulty in finding it. The exception was No.627 Squadron Mosquito pilot Flt Lt LCE De Vigne and his navigator, Sqn Ldr FW Boyle, who located and marked the aqueduct from low level with such outstanding accuracy that their TI fell into the canal water and promptly went out! No-one else was able to mark the target and the Master Bomber called off the raid.

We dropped two bombs in the sea to bring our weight down to landing tolerance and returned home. This entirely abortive raid was not without cost; ten aircraft lost, seventy men killed or taken prisoner.

The following Sunday, 12th November, thirty Lancasters of Nos.9 and 617 Squadrons carrying Barnes Wallis's 12,000 Tallboy bombs, accompanied by cameramen in a No.463 Squadron Lancaster, took off from Lossiemouth on the east coast of Scotland; their target, the *Tirpitz* lying at anchor in Tromsö Fjord. Sister ship of the *Bismarck*, she was the second of Hitler's immense 42,000-ton battleships. As the attack began, desperate telephone calls were made from the ship and shore batteries to the Bardufoss Luftwaffe airfield for fighter cover but none took off, leaving the ship's defences to be solely provided by flak. She was hit by at least two Tallboys, after which her magazines exploded, ripping her apart from inside. After that explosion, *Tirpitz* was doomed and quickly turned over; her threat to our merchant ships and escorts on the Russian convoys ended.

All our aircraft returned to Lossiemouth bar one which had been badly damaged by flak, although it did manage to land in Sweden with an intact crew. However, for the local population of Tromsö the sinking of *Tirpitz* was a bittersweet day. It later transpired that at the time of the attack there had been a dance on board and most of the girls from the surrounding area were at it. Inevitably, many of them were amongst the casualties.

For the next fortnight or so, No.5 Group was given some rest and had very little involvement in operations. There were a couple of occasions when our crew was detailed for ops but the missions were scrubbed and we were stood down. This rest gave us a lot of free time and we enjoyed the relaxation of the regular dances, both on and off the station, and the cinema in Boston and the camp.

Later in the week we held one of our customary rifle shooting contests, a friendly competition between pilots and their flight engineers using .303 service rifles. Brought up a country lad, I was a better shot than Jerry so he often tried to cheat by firing low on my target when I was shooting. It was all good fun, boys at play, but another necessary break from the emotional and physical stresses which operational flying put upon us.

Autumn was well and truly in air that was becoming increasingly colder by the day, but that didn't stop me relaxing when I was off-duty. The day after the shooting contest, I went into Boston to see *The Story of Dr Wassell*, which had been released in Britain a few weeks earlier. Set around the true events and actions of Corydon Wassell, it would become one of the most popular films of the 1940s around the world. As the Japanese swept through the East Indies in 1942, Dr Wassell escaped from Java under the noses of the invaders and took with him a dozen wounded sailors from the cruiser USS *Marblehead*.

In real life, Wassell had been born in Little Rock, Arkansas, in 1884. A medical doctor and reservist in the US Navy, he held the rank of Lieutenant-Commander. With the coming of the war, he served in the Far East, and whilst at a Dutch hospital on Java, he took charge of the twelve most seriously wounded sailors from *Marblehead* and brought them to safety in Southampton, following which he was awarded the US Navy Cross for his actions. In a radio broadcast connected to Wassell's award, President Roosevelt made much of the story. This ultimately led to the making of the film which, incidentally, held a small part for the classically trained Danish pianist Victor Borge, who had escaped from the Nazis and would after the war go on to entertain audiences worldwide most notably with his hilarious phonetic punctuation.

201

I sometimes wonder about the Britain I see around me today and regret the passing of many things, especially National Service. Had we retained it, I am sure we would have a more respectful and valued society and a much less selfish and aggressive one. For instance, when families struggle to make ends meet, why do hooligans waste eggs by throwing them at people, houses and cars? During the war, eggs were a valued luxury. The standard ration for everybody was one egg per week which is why the egg-and-bacon meal before and after a mission for operational aircrew was such a treat. Understandably, aerodromes close to farms were popular postings as farmers were usually very willing to give an egg or two to an airman who had helped out with some task or had 'acquired' a needed item for him. This bounty was carefully taken into the mess at breakfast time when the bearer would ask one of the WAAF cooks to boil or fry it for him.

Tuesday brought the dreadful news that my good friend Bill Burr was missing from the operation to the Rhenania-Ossag oil refinery at Harburg three nights earlier. I put a note in my diary that I hoped he had been able to bail out; but it proved to be a forlorn hope. I was greatly saddened when, sometime later, it was confirmed that Bill had definitely been killed; he was a good sort. His No.227 Squadron Lancaster PB643 9J-S captained by Flying Officer TD Hooper took off from RAF Balderton near Newark at 16.41 and so far as I can find out, it seems that it may have been in collision with another Lancaster, LL939 DX-H of No.57 Squadron piloted by F/O S Bowden from our base at East Kirkby. No-one from Bill's aircraft survived the crash and they are all buried in Becklingen War Cemetery.

It was very hard not to dwell on the loss of a close friend. The traditional custom of raising a glass in the mess and then move on didn't work so well with friends like Bill; their loss cut much deeper. But the job still had to be done and so the private grief was put into the box; it would keep for another time. When the war was over, the memories of people like Bill came flooding back and the pain of their loss was renewed. For years after the war, sleep did not often come easily nor, when it did, was it peaceful. Long after I was no longer a young man, I would still see their faces in my dreams and nightmares. They were the faces as I remembered them, some still only teenagers. It is very true; they do not grow old as we that are left grow old.

Then the Group's rest was over. We were detailed to attack the U-boat pens at Trondheim. This would be almost as long as my first trip to Königsberg, the longest mission that I undertook and, like that one, was at the limit of our range. We took off at 15.50 in the fading light of a cold Wednesday afternoon, flew up the North Sea and then turned in towards the Norwegian coast. The further north we flew, the clearer the air and the sky became. Nearing Norway, I could easily see the mountains ahead, already covered with snow. Soon we were flying over the peaks and, despite the absence of moonlight, their corried and plunging faces were laid out beneath us on a monochrome canvas of snow and rock.

Looking up through the cockpit canopy into the heavens, a million tiny pinpoints of light winked back at me out of a darkness the intensity of which I had rarely seen. My eyes began to sting from the strain of searching around us for other aircraft; a collision here could have no happy ending. Too many aircrew like Bill had been lost in collisions and we did not want to be among them. It was the telltale clues that I was looking for; a larger star or small group that suddenly disappeared as an aircraft passed in front, or an exhaust flame that had escaped from under the cover and would show up in an otherwise seemingly empty void. Occasionally, our own kite would warn us as it reared and bucked, caught in the backwash from an unseen companion too close in front.

At last we reached the target but there were no TIs and no order to bomb from the Master Bomber. The whole area of Trondheim, including where the U-boat pens were, was completely obliterated by a smoke screen. The Mosquitoes of the illuminating and marker force flew back and forth trying to locate the actual target, the bomber stream circled above, and all the while the anti-aircraft guns peppered the sky with flak. Finally, the raid was called off; the risk to the civilian population was too great. There would be another day to come back. Reluctantly, like disappointed hounds who had lost the fox, we turned for the long flight back across the North Sea.

Once well clear of the Norwegian mountains, with the fjords receding, I sat down and watched the various pressure and fuel gauges, occasionally looking out through the cockpit Perspex into the night. Outside, the darkness was intense. The Merlin engines throbbed with their steady, hypnotic rhythm, the warm air wafted up from the wireless operator's position, and I felt my eyes becoming very heavy. I was looking at the gauges but not seeing them. My head fell forwards and my eyes closed; the bliss of sleep had claimed me. I awoke with a start, unsure how much time had passed, and looked at Jerry. His head was slumped forward too; he was fast asleep. The strain of operations and the constant state of readiness was grinding us down. I woke him up and then Bill gave us a change of course. At 03.00, after eleven hours and ten minutes in the air, we landed back at East Kirkby, tired, cold, and hungry.

The tea and rum warmed us up while we reported to the Intelligence Officer. It had been such a long sortie that after the eggs-and-bacon breakfast, for once I didn't need any rocking. We were on stand-down for the rest of the day and that evening I went to the pictures in Boston to see *Home in Indiana*, a rather sugary film starring Walter Brennan. Also showing that night was *No Greater Love*, which was an interesting Russian film about a woman who led a band of guerrillas fighting the Nazis at the time of Operation Barbarossa in the winter of 1941/42. It was pure propaganda, of course, but was certainly not fiction and echoed many of the experiences of our own courageous women SOE agents.

November was the first anniversary of the formation of the Squadron and the CO had arranged a big celebration party on the 25th with a one-off bus trip into Boston for everyone. With all the aircrew and the ground crew gathered together, it was naturally a very boozy do. Although there was a mess party every month, this was something special and everyone from the CO to the lowliest AC2 had a memorable night. After that, all further celebrations off camp were held in the Red Lion, East Kirkby's only pub.

The next morning, along with many others on the station, I had a sore head and was not enthralled to see my name down for ops that night. After breakfast, I cycled out to the aircraft and made use of the oxygen supply to clear my head, after which I felt much better. The target turned out to be Munich, the birthplace of the Nazi Party. The Nationalsozialistische Deutsche Arbeiterpartei had been formed on 24th February 1920, not by Adolf Hitler but by Anton Drexler. Originally no more than a small fringe group of extremists, the Nazis and their rise still hold lessons for us today. From 1920 to 1933, they used the proper democratic process of parliamentary elections to gradually build their power base; once having taken control, they abolished democracy. Now Bomber Command was working around the clock to restore it.

This would be my third attempt at Munich. I had originally been detailed for this raid on 12th October, when it was cancelled because the enemy discovered our planned route over the Alps. I was kitted up and ready for the next raid on 18th November, but it was scrubbed once more. So this time I had every expectation of being stood down again, but instead we left East Kirby with full fuel tanks at 23.40. The attacking force that night was made up of 270 Lancasters and eight Mosquitoes. We flew down to Reading, crossed the coast at Selsey and then passed to the west of Paris. At Lyon, we turned east and gradually began to climb, threading our way through the Alps to pass between Milan and the Swiss border and then turn north towards Austria, all the time keeping in the radar shadow of the mountains.

It was all very different from the Trondheim mission; tonight a three-quarter moon shone so brightly it was as if someone had pulled down the stars. Around me I could see the squadron codes on the closest aircraft, whilst the canopies and turrets of those further away winked and sparkled through the crisp air. Close to the moon, the sky was almost azure, gradually darkening through the shades of blue from pale to midnight at the furthest reach. The mountains lay covered with snow so deep and smooth they seemed like a gigantic bowl of cream whipped up into towering peaks. Looking down, I could see the shadows of aircraft sliding across the snowy slopes with effortless ease. Deep in valley bottoms, water glistened and glinted in the moonlight whilst little groups of darkened houses clung to their sides, trembling at the thunder of our approach.

The moon cast an ethereal spell over the landscape. I was surrounded by such immense beauty and physical majesty in every sense. I had never seen anything like it before and it became increasingly difficult to keep in mind the purpose of the mission. Barely three miles away to port, I could see the domed mass of Mont Blanc, standing out proudly above all the other Alpine peaks. We continued to track close to the Swiss border and then the unmistakable image of the world's most perfect natural pyramid came into view: the Matterhorn. Standing high above all around, even at ten miles' distance, it was truly impressive. However, like benefit and burden, beauty and danger pass together; for all its imposing magnificence, conquering the Matterhorn has come at a dreadful cost and it remains one of the deadliest mountains on earth.

For another hour we shared the company of these giants of nature that had challenged and divided Europe's northern and southern nations. Then it was all behind us and Munich lay ahead; reality replaced the dream. Searchlights sprang into life, seeking us out, weaving around the blue pencils of radar light, and the flak started, but there were no fighters to be seen. The moon had set at 04.45, giving us the cover of darkness for our approach. Fifteen minutes later, we bombed the railway and industrial centres with great accuracy and effect. With our bombs gone, Jerry turned us to the west and home, leaving the rail centre to burn and the flak shells to burst in an empty sky. By the time we were flying across France it was daylight and I had a clear view of the landscape around Normandy, so badly scarred by the fighting and our bombing in the days and weeks after D-Day. It reminded me of the pictures I had seen from the First World War battlefields at the Somme, Ypres and Passchendaele. From the air, the bocage, all those hills, hollows, subtle undulations, small woods, hedges and sunken tracks which had been so difficult and costly for the invading ground troops to seize during the Battle of Normandy became a flat two-dimensional board.

By 10.00 we were handing the aircraft back to the ground crew. I felt so very tired. Munich had been my twenty-second operation; we were now a senior crew on the squadron and the strain was biting deep. There was no novelty in anything anymore; it was just a slog until the war finished.

The rest of the month was taken up with routine lectures and activities on the camp. December began with the squadron crews gathered to watch two instructional films. The first was a regular update on bombing tactics, but the second was quite unnerving. It showed us German practices for the interrogation of POWs, and whilst it did not deal with the physical torture we knew some airmen had been subjected to, it did deal with the more subtle aspects of what we could expect. These included suggestions that we would be handed over to the Gestapo if we didn't tell them what they wanted to know; that other members of our crew had spilled the beans so we may as well do likewise; the interplay between the hard interrogator and the kind one, the 'good cop, bad cop' method; sleep, food and water deprivation; being blindfolded during questioning or alternatively blinded by bright lights; solitary confinement in a dark, dank, reeking cell; being moved around by car every few hours, or at least being given that impression, often whilst blindfolded. In fact the car would usually be driven around for half an hour and then the prisoner brought back to the same building to be interrogated by different people; and so on and so forth. It was all designed to help to prepare us for what we could expect if captured.

That evening, I went into Boston and finished off the day with a much more enjoyable film, *Gone With the Wind*. After church parade on Sunday, there was an instructional film about 'careless talk' followed by another helping of POW interrogation techniques. At the camp dance that evening, I met a WAAF named Nora Richardson. She hadn't been on the station long and worked in the accounts department. She came from Middleton-in-Teesdale, a village about twelve miles from Cockfield. It was really good to chat with someone from home and we often enjoyed each other's company at station dances. Nora was a lovely girl who was engaged to a soldier, so we simply stayed friends. That was probably just as well since I had decided not to get involved with anyone whilst I was on ops; I'd had to deliver that awful message to a waiting girl more than once.

Monday morning brought our leave passes and so I quickly packed and headed home for a week of normality and rest. As usual I went to the local scout meetings and, on the last night of my leave, had a long talk with the patrol leaders and then a sing-song afterwards. When I left Cockfield next morning, a thick fog hung over the east coast. Throughout the day, the fog got steadily thicker while the trains got steadily slower. When I arrived at Grantham, I had missed my connection to Boston by four minutes.

I got up next morning to the news that I had lost yet another really good friend. Vin Taylor had flown with our crew as second engineer for a month at Swinderby, notching up fifty hours on Stirlings with us before joining his permanent crew. At the end of our training we had been posted to East Kirkby together, he to No.57 Squadron, me to No.630, and I was truly saddened at his death.

Vin Taylor with our crew
Front row L-R – Vin Taylor, Bill Whenray,
Middle Row – Len Knowles, Jim Kenealy, Jerry Monk, Ted Watson
Back row – Joe Baldwin, Jock Gillespie.

Vin had been killed in a daytime raid on the Urft Dam. When opened in 1905, it had made the largest reservoir in Europe. This had been the second raid on the dam within a week, and although several hits were scored, the wall remained solid and held back the water. A flight engineer from another No.57 crew told me that he had seen Vin's Lancaster just blow up over the target even though there was no flak at the dam. It was the only aircraft lost.

I had an oral examination with the Staff Engineer the following afternoon, and in the evening Bill Whenray and I went to the camp pictures. I needed something to take my mind off Vin's death. The weather over the weekend was terrible and there was no flying; I just passed the time scrounging around the station, all of which only served to deepen the feeling of despondency which had come over me.

The new week brought a change in the weather and an operation to the distant Polish port of Gdynia, where the main targets were quayside installations and the pocket battleships KMS *Lutsow* and KMS *Admiral Scheer*, which were anchored in the harbour. Our outward route took us once more through the neutral skies of Sweden where their searchlights still shone in static vertical poise, their flak still aimed at some phantom force off our beam and the lights in their houses and streets glittered like scattered gold dust. It was a very different reception approaching Gdynia, where the flak was intense. The two warships, whose fighting days on the high seas were now over, nevertheless added to the general mass of firepower that was ranged against us, creating a dense envelope of exploding shells in the sky above the city.

The harbour area had been well marked and was brightly lit by our white, red and green flares, the orange flames of the first fires and the numerous searchlights. We could see industrial and defence installations along the quayside as well as the two pocket battleships and other vessels at anchor. I didn't see any fighters, and with such intensity of flak, did not really expect any, but the time had now come for us to make our bombing run, which meant flying straight and level through that barrage for about two minutes whilst Len picked up the aiming point, released our bombs and waited for the photograph. I could feel my heart beating faster as the moments passed; the Lancaster bucked with

209

each close shell burst and the cockpit reeked of cordite. Then, with the photograph taken, we could get ourselves out of this mess and start the long haul down the Baltic, over Denmark and across the North Sea. There would be no danger of any of us falling asleep tonight.

With no bomb load and having used nearly half our fuel, the Lancaster was much lighter now. Covering the icy Baltic water at over 200mph, we sped on our way home, leaving Gdynia far behind. On a route that would take us over the Danish islands and its mainland, we had come down low to avoid radar detection and fighters. In quick succession, a familiar sequence of water, land, water, land rushed by beneath us as we made our dash towards the North Sea. Jerry weaved and dodged the Lancaster this way and that to avoid the shafts from sporadic searchlights that sprang into life probing the night for returning aircraft. Then in a moment of déjà vu, reminiscent of our second Königsberg raid, a light anti-aircraft battery found us. The white balls of flak shells snaked up to us before zipping by, and pale orange flashes pierced the night. From the rear turret Jim's guns chuttered in reply like a football rattle. The battery fell silent. Not that Jim hit anything; it was simply that we'd gone, lost to the night.

Ahead, there seemed nothing but an enveloping, intense inky darkness. The expanse of the moonless sky was evident only by the stars that shone from it. No hint of our progress came from the land beneath save the dull glow from some small lake, river or canal that lay under our path. When we reached the sea, it was discernible from the land solely by the ragged ranks of surf that crashed upon the shoreline. Growing in confidence, we made some height and flew on across that expanse of uninviting water, its black, formless presence betrayed only by tumbling wave tops.

A call from Jim in the rear turret made me look back over the top of the aircraft in time to see a bright luminous vapour trail rising up and arching high into the sky over our heads. Higher and higher it went until eventually lost to my sight. It was a V2 rocket on its way to London via the stratosphere and was the first of several that I would see.

Not long afterwards, we were diverted to the emergency landing ground at RAF Woodbridge near to Ipswich because Lincolnshire's notorious fog had rolled in off the sea and closed the county's aerodromes. We had taken off at 16.50, giving a valedictory wave to the last retreating fingers of light as they slipped beneath the rim of the western sky. It was eleven hours later that we taxied around the peri-track to our allocated parking slot at Woodbridge.

The fog persisted and a return to East Kirkby was out of the question. We were given breakfast and then the time was our own. In the afternoon I went into Ipswich, booked a bed at the YMCA and then went to a dance with the rest of the crew. The next day brought no fairer weather so Jim and I strolled around Ipswich before going to the pictures. Once more the YMCA provided us with shelter since there was no accommodation for visiting crews at Woodbridge. We were still fogbound on Thursday and so headed for the dance at Woodbridge Village Hall, where we slept on the floor afterwards. East Kirkby remained closed but on Saturday we were able to leave Woodbridge, although only for as far as Swinderby, where we were at least given a bed.

I awoke to more fog. It was Christmas Eve. Whilst scrounging around after breakfast, I bumped into a Scots lad named Jock. I had been 2nd Engineer to him whilst here at Swinderby on our Heavy Conversion Unit. That seemed such a long time ago now; I had aged a lot since then. Later, I went with Ginger from another No.630 crew to the pictures and then to a dance at Morton Hall, where we had a brilliant time.

In front of an earlier Just Jane at East Kirkby

Part of my view from the starboard side of the cockpit

Chapter Twelve

Christmas Day 1944. With no prospect of flying back to East Kirkby, the CO sent some transport to pick us up along with the other marooned squadron crews. We piled into the back of the 3-tonner and set off at a frenetic pace, with our driver obviously anxious not to miss the festivities and his Christmas dinner. The lorry lurched left and right around the bends while we clung tightly to the canopy supports. Predictably, we crashed. There was a huge bang, the lorry left the road, ploughed through a hedge and hit a tree. Inside, we were catapulted simultaneously forwards and sideways.

Everyone was badly shaken up, with various cuts and bruises; all except one, that is. Blood poured down the man's face from a vicious-looking gash on his head. The crash had happened not far from RAF Cranwell and help was soon at hand. We had given the lad some First Aid by the time the ambulance arrived. He was really quite badly injured and would not be flying again for some time, if at all. Another Cranwell vehicle pulled the 3-tonner out of the hedge and we inspected the damage, which was for the most part superficial. A now much subdued airman climbed in behind the wheel to resume his duties, this time supervised by one of the officers in the passenger seat. A formal charge followed later.

It had taken us a full week to get back to East Kirkby from Woodbridge, which ought to have qualified us for the Late Arrivals' Club. We were just in time for Christmas dinner followed later by a jolly good station dance.

Boxing Day was business as usual. The weather had cleared, ops were on and at last Bomber Command could take part in the Ardennes fighting, the Battle of the Bulge. Our own aircraft was still at Swinderby, so just after lunch we took off in PB894 LE-N. The raid, which involved 294 aircraft from all groups of the Command except 100 Group, was an army cooperation mission and our target was the enemy troop concentrations around the town of St. Vith, on the Belgian/German border just north of Luxembourg at the heart of the Axis offensive. Their advance had stalled and our job was to prevent it restarting.

The enemy had launched what would be its last counteroffensive on 16th December through the densely forested Ardennes. Codenamed *Unternehmen Wacht am Rhein*, Operation Watch on the Rhine, the Allies referred to it as the Ardennes Counteroffensive; to those doing the fighting it was the Battle of the Bulge, a name which has remained. Planned to coincide with heavy overcast weather conditions, it caught the Allies completely by surprise and the thin line of American forces in the area took the full onslaught. The same winter low-pressure system which had grounded us at Woodbridge and Swinderby prevented the wider Allied air forces giving support to our ground troops, which is exactly what the German commanders had intended, although they were unlikely to have known that the conditions would last so long.

Only two aircraft from East Kirkby, our own and one from No.57 Squadron, were detailed to join the main force for the daylight attack on St. Vith. We had been briefed about the importance and urgency of our mission to the beleaguered ground troops, and as we flew east, we hoped that the clear weather would hold. We had a trouble-free trip until we approached the target. The enemy knew the wind strength, our direction, and our height. Bombing accuracy was essential and therefore we were not flying particularly high. In favourable conditions, their gunners put up an intense predictive flak box barrage along the whole of the twenty miles that we flew on our approach to St. Vith. It was one of the heaviest barrages that I had experienced and there was a point when I really thought that we could not possibly survive.

The Lancaster began to buck and yaw with the intensity of the explosions so close to it. Then a shell exploded just in front of us. Pieces of shrapnel clattered and bounced off the cockpit Perspex as we entered the hanging thick black plume of smoke, leaving us momentarily unable to see a thing, the air rich with cordite. Then we were out, all the time knowing that another shell was on its way to explode in the same position. It did, but we had moved on and the explosion rolled us forward. The next one came ahead and just to starboard, this time the wing slicing through the thick pall of smoke. Looking back to the starboard wing, I could see the surface scarred with shrapnel damage.

By now we were close to the target, the bomb doors were open and Len's voice was in our headsets giving Jerry final approach instructions, "left, left, steady, steady." At that moment I glanced up and looked straight into the massive open bomb bay of a Halifax, not thirty feet above our heads, their bomb aimer ready to press the tit and drop his entire load on us. I felt my throat dry up, my stomach contract and my whole body turn ice-cold with the sweat that bubbled from my skin. I was, quite literally, gazing into the jaws of death. I grabbed Jerry's arm and pointed upwards whilst at the same time pulling the throttle levers back. Our engine note changed, the Lancaster's nose dipped a little, and we slowed just enough. Barely had the Halifax edged ahead when 13,000lb of high explosives slipped out of its belly and hurtled through the air in front of our nose. Jerry turned to look at me, his eyes staring wide. He too knew how close it had been. An oath on the crew was uttered from the mid-upper turret but our guardian angel had once again protected us.

Unperturbed by all the activity, lying in his 'bubble', Len continued to line us up on the target and renewed his instructions to Jerry. It was always a relief to hear Len say, "Bombs gone", rarely more so than on this occasion. The flak continued to pepper the sky, but much less so as we banked away from St. Vith, leaving behind the carnage we had wrought. It was clear from our perspective on the scene that the bombing had been accurate and concentrated. We had done our job well and helped our ground forces.

By the time we were approaching the French coast on our return journey, fog once more covered much of England and so we were diverted to St. Eval near Newquay in Cornwall where FIDO was installed. Fog Intensive Dispersal Operation was a system installed on some Bomber Command aerodromes and a few others such as St. Eval to help returning aircraft land in these conditions. It consisted of two pipelines, one each side of the runway, which were filled with petrol and then lit. The intense heat from the flames evaporated the water droplets forming the fog to about 100 feet, enough to allow pilots to see the runway and land safely.

That was the theory, and in practice it worked very well. However, from a crew point of view, to put down a large four-engine bomber in the narrow space between two channels containing blazing highly volatile petrol was an unnerving experience, to say the least.

Although the fog had cleared next day, the weather was still duff, and so Bill, Jim and I went into Newquay. It was the first time that I had been to Cornwall and I was bowled over by the scenery and the views, especially from the cliff tops. Happily, it wasn't going to take us another week to get back to base, as the next day we were cleared to fly, which we did in formation with another Lancaster and a Typhoon.

On balance, I preferred daylight raids. Night sorties engendered a feeling of isolation, that as a crew we were completely on our own, huddled in our aeroplane bereft of company and support. But then, when nearing the target area, other aircraft would momentarily appear like phantoms in the flashes of flak bursts, whilst further on over the target their darkened bellies and sides would flicker and dance in the Dantesque glow that reached up from the burning city below.

Daylight missions placed an extra strain upon the flight engineers, who acted as 'throttle jockeys'. This meant that we had to operate the throttle levers most of the time to keep a safe distance from the other aircraft around us in the bomber stream, whereas at night we couldn't see them anyway. Despite this, I still preferred daylight ops.

It was always a comforting sight to see our massed fighters providing cover against the enemy. Although the Luftwaffe was numerically inferior to its earlier days, its technology had kept it a potent fighter force. The condensation trails in the sky above us betrayed the presence of Messerschmitt Me262 jet fighters and the Me163 Komet, which was actually a rocket-propelled aircraft and the first piloted aeroplane to reach 1,000 km/h [621mph]. These short-duration fighters would climb well above the bomber stream, which was then silhouetted against the earth below. They would dive down, attack an aircraft and then climb away to repeat the tactic. Their combat window, however, was very short before they had to land and refuel.

Whilst target marking was in progress, six experienced wind-finder crews would check the wind speed and direction. This information was radioed back to No.5 Group HQ, which used the information to establish the two averages which were then radioed back to the bomber stream so that bomb aimers could factor it into the bomb sight mechanical equipment. On the run-in to the target, the control of the aircraft passed to the bomb aimer. The pilot was required to fly straight and level to enable his bomb aimer to give him minute directional changes to line up the bomb-sight graticule with the target indicator that had been dropped by the marker crews of the Pathfinder force. Only when the bombs had been released and the aiming-point photograph taken did the pilot resume full control of the aircraft. Meanwhile, German controllers had been busy trying to anticipate the target and our route into it so that they could put up their fighters and a heavy barrage of predictive flak on the bombing-run approach.

Like so much of the war, the last few days of the year contained horror, fun, and sadness, each one following on the heels of the other in quick succession. Pleasure had to be squeezed out of every opportunity for no-one knew what awaited them around the next corner. The weather continued to be unkind, but even so, operations were planned for that night. In the late afternoon, an American B17G Flying Fortress, UX-L the *Belle of Liberty*, called up to make an emergency landing. It had been badly damaged on a daylight raid against the Bullay railway bridge at Koblenz and was clearly in trouble and trying to come in on one engine. We saw it overshoot the runway at the first attempt and then, with the throttles open wide, it rejoined the circuit to try again. This time the pilot approached over much higher ground and we watched in helpless horror as the Fortress struck the hill, its remaining engine unable to maintain height. There were no survivors from the nine crew.

East Kirkby personnel mounted a guard on the crash site until the next day. In the morning, a Liberator flew in and our station CO provided the crew and other airmen with transport to visit the site. Afterwards, they recovered the nine bodies back to their Liberator and then on to their own base.

In the early hours of New Year's Eve, our squadron put up twelve aircraft for the army cooperation raid on a Wehrmacht troop and supply bottleneck at Houffalize on the Belgium/Luxembourg border just behind the Ardennes Front. On the ground, the soldiers of opposing sides must have felt panic, relief, frustration, and disappointment, according to their viewpoint. Although cloud covered the target area, the German troops must have been quaking at the thunderous roar made by the 640 Merlin engines of 154 Lancasters and twelve Mosquitoes as they circled above for fifteen minutes looking for a hole in the cloud base. None was found and, with great reluctance, we turned away and returned home rather than risk bombing our own troops by mistake. There were no fighters and very little flak to trouble us.

After breakfast, I went to bed and slept for the rest of the day. My stomach woke me, reminding me that it was time for tea, and then in the evening I went to the mess New Year's Eve dance. It was a long time since I had enjoyed myself so much. The band was very good, playing all the popular dance tunes, the beer flowed freely, and morale was high; the squadron had lost only one crew since 18th August. I danced with Nora Richardson and many other WAAFs and local girls there. For a few hours I forgot about the war, about how tired I was and all the destruction I had witnessed. I did, though, spare a thought for P/O Ted Thomas, who had drawn the short straw and was part of a force of sixteen Halifaxes and ten Lancasters laying mines in the Kattegat that night whilst we all partied.

In September, we had had a change of CO. Wing Commander John E Grindon, DFC, had taken over and, like his predecessors, he knew the importance of maintaining morale on the squadron. The weekly mess party and monthly station dance were designed to help us relax, to forget what we did and saw for a few hours. But these were superficial pleasures and afterwards the job was still there to be done. We tried to live each day to the full, whatever it brought.

I had enjoyed myself immensely at the mess dance and drank more than I would have done had I known that I was to be on ops next morning. I seemed to have only just gone to sleep when at 04.00 we were called out and briefed for a raid. The target was the

Dortmund-Ems Canal at Ladbergen once more. The squadron put up ten aircraft for the raid, which involved 102 Lancasters and two Mosquitoes. After an early breakfast, we left East Kirkby at 07.50 that morning and headed east, climbing towards a brilliant clear blue sky.

The canal was, as usual, heavily defended. The forced labourers had just finished repairing the embankments after the last raid, and in these crystal-clear conditions we had no difficulty pranging the target all over again. However, the clear conditions also helped the defending gunners and they put up a concentrated and lethal flak barrage. They were not going to let us undo their hard work without a fight. Explosions, shrapnel, smoke, cordite, noise, all filled the air, but we succeeded, and as Jerry banked away from the canal, I looked back to see water pouring through the breaches into the fields alongside. Many of the bombs we dropped had delayed-action fuses and would continue to disrupt and frustrate the repairs for days to come.

Below me, bathed in the first morning's sunshine of the new year, I could see the little village of Ladbergen, which lay about half a mile to the east of the canal and slightly away from the immense camp that housed some 4,000 forced labourers. The thousands of bomb craters left by our many attacks on the aqueduct over the years had pock-marked the fields around the village to such an extent that it looked like the surface of the moon. Living in one of Ladbergen's houses were the relatives of Friedrich Wilhelm Kötter, who had emigrated to America in 1864. Every day Friedrich's relatives picked their way through that intensely cratered moonscape, unaware that one day twenty-four years in the future, his great-grandson Neil Armstrong would become the first man to truly walk on the cratered surface of the moon.

Apart from the occasional appearance of the Me262 and Me163, we were not generally troubled by fighters on daytime raids, the Allies having gained almost total air supremacy during daylight hours; night-time was still a very different matter. As we flew back from Ladbergen, the winter anticyclone that had brought such ideal bombing conditions now gave me a clear window onto the devastation and destruction that five years of war had brought to the industrial cities of the Ruhr. I didn't feel jubilation at what I saw or even satisfaction, but nor did I feel any guilt. This destruction was not of our bidding. What I saw beneath me was the inevitable consequence of the failed ambitions of the Third Reich. It was a deep sadness at the necessity of it all that filled me.

The New Year brought nothing that was new. The joy and pleasure of the night before were tainted by sadness; I had lost another friend. After the debrief, it had become clear that Ted Thomas's aircraft had not returned from his mine-laying sortie and there was no news of his whereabouts at another airfield. Ted had only just received his commission and been promoted to Pilot Officer. He hadn't even had a chance to celebrate. His crew was the second that the squadron had lost in December and it left a bitter taste at the end of the year. Neither they nor their aircraft were ever found. In addition to Ted, there was Bill Marshall, Bernard Phillips, the two Glamorgan boys, Joe and David Jones, Rex Boden and Eric Leese. All are remembered on the Runnymede Memorial and now here too.

Despite the beautiful day and the real possibility that 1945 would be the year that the war would end, my despondency persisted. I was reconciled to the fact that very soon I too would be killed. Enemy action, a collision, an engine failure, bad weather, bad luck, bad judgement, bombed from above, mistaken identity, out of fuel; the possibilities were many and varied. Out there, they were all waiting for me; I just didn't know which one would get me.

I finished my lunch and went to the library. Wearily, I sat down at one of the tables, took my diary from my pocket and wrote the following words to try to express the inner turmoil that I was feeling:

'I have learnt much during the last year; how to kill men, women, and children; how to let Hell loose over the world. I have seen many things, cities and towns bombed and devastated, men blown to bits in the skies, men plunging down to earth in burning aircraft. How long will this last and how long will I last? Every day I wonder, surely I can't carry on like this forever? But then death doesn't seem to be much to me now, just an everyday occurrence and so all I can do is to just carry on and leave everything to fate.' - I was nineteen.

It was about this time that I realised I had developed a nervous twitch after landing back at base from those operations where we had nearly bought it. Today, my mental well-being, my physical feelings and my emotional condition would be recognised as PTSD. But during the war, such conditions were not seen in the same way. We were given home leave on a regular basis and good COs would stand down for a short while a crew who he thought were showing signs of too much strain. It was better to keep a tired crew on the ground for a week than to send them to certain death on the next mission.

We were all volunteers and could leave the Command at any time, but such a departure was accompanied by the utmost ignominy. An airman drained of his emotional and psychological stamina, who could take no more and refused to fly, was classed as LMF, lack of moral fibre. He was immediately stripped of all rank and, together with his kit, was removed to the guardroom. The next morning he would be taken from the station to a special remand centre. I do remember that this happened on a couple of occasions. We all knew what these men were experiencing and felt very sorry for them; they had simply come to the end of their endurance. In the First World War, they would most probably have been shot; at least we didn't do that anymore.

The New Year's Day raid produced the second Victoria Cross of the Dortmund-Ems Canal. Flak could be very persistent and concentrated, especially over small targets such as aqueducts, and none more so than at Ladbergen. F/O Denton was the pilot of No.9 Squadron Lancaster PD377, his wireless operator was Flt Sgt George Thompson. A Scot, born at Trinity Gask in Perthshire, the twenty-four-year-old had first served as a ground wireless operator in Iraq before volunteering for aircrew. Moments after releasing his bombs, a flak shell exploded inside Denton's aircraft just forward of the mid-upper turret, leaving a gaping hole in the Lancaster's floor and putting in chain an astounding sequence of events and courage.

The cockpit crew were momentarily stunned by the suddenness and the noise, as shrapnel, pieces of Lancaster, and bits of broken equipment hurtled around their heads. The ammunition in the channels of the mid-upper turret began exploding as fire and smoke quickly engulfed the fuselage.   Then, a second shell exploded on the nose of the Lancaster, shattering most of the Perspex, opening several gaping holes and setting fire to one of the engines.   The inrush of air, though, cleared the smoke and Thompson quickly realised that amongst all the chaos the mid-upper gunner, Sgt Ernie Potts, was trapped and on fire.   Sliding over the wing spar and ignoring his own safety, he squeezed into the turret, undid Potts' harness and, though his own clothes were now burning, carried the unconscious gunner around the hole in the floor to where he could lay him down safely.   Despite the worsening burns to his own hands, face and legs, Thompson used his bare hands to beat out the rampant flames on Potts' clothing.

Barely had he succeeded, when he saw that the rear turret was also on fire.   Once more ignoring his own safety and injuries, he worked around the hole in the floor and, fighting his way through the narrow, blazing tunnel of the fuselage to the rear turret, he pulled the gunner, now overcome by the flames and fumes, out of his seat and into the body of the aircraft, where he again used his burnt bare hands to save his comrade.

All this time, Denton and his flight engineer were fighting to keep the crippled aircraft in the air and get as far away from the flak as possible; the aircraft could not sustain another hit.   The fire inside the wrecked fuselage had gone out and Thompson had saved the two gunners.   His next duty was to report the situation to his captain, but when he did, he was in such an appalling condition and so badly burned that his skipper failed to recognise him.

There was almost no possibility of them being able to get back to England but they did manage to fly for another forty minutes before crash-landing near Eindhoven.   The rear gunner made a full recovery but Ernie Potts was too badly burned and died the following day.   George Thompson was taken to a hospital in Brussels where he began to make a recovery but then developed pneumonia as a complication of his severe burns.   He died on 23rd January.   The award of his Victoria Cross was gazetted on 20th February and his medals are on display at the National War Museum of Scotland in Edinburgh.

There are many similarities in the circumstances of George Thompson's action and that of fellow Scot John Hannah, VC, who in 1940 also sustained severe burns to save the life of a comrade. Their actions and those of many others serve to underline what Sqn Ldr Tony Iveson of No.617 Squadron meant when he said,

"There is nothing more close than a bomber crew. You had to have confidence in each other. Each one had to know his job thoroughly…you depended on each other. No matter what difference in rank, as a crew you were a unit and the closer you were, the more confidence you had, the better you were."

Flight Sergeant George Thompson, VC
[photograph: Crown public domain]

Enjoying some free time in the sunshine with the black & white checked Controller's wagon behind us

RAF East Kirby Watch Tower

Chapter Thirteen

"Out of the night that covers me,
Black as the pit from pole to pole,
I thank whatever gods may be
For my unconquerable soul."
Invictus – William Ernest Henley [1888]

Although the year had not started well, I was determined that I would see the job through, come what may, for however long I was needed or survived. I would also enjoy myself at every opportunity because I had no idea how many more I would have.

The Battle Order was up for the next day and we were on it. We learned from the ground crew that it was a full-tank trip, which meant one far into eastern Germany or to Poland. In the end it was scrubbed, thank goodness, and so Bill, Joe and I went to the camp cinema to see *Four Jills in a Jeep*. Starring Kay Francis, Carole Landis, Martha Raye and Mitzi Mayfair, it was an enjoyable autobiographical film telling the story of their time in 1942/43 as entertainers with the USO, the American equivalent of our own ENSA, the Entertainment National Services Association, affectionately known as Every Night Something Awful. Amongst others, the film also featured Dick Haymes, Carmen Miranda and Betty Grable, with the music courtesy of Jimmy Dorsey and his Orchestra.

The station entertainments officer certainly did a good job for us as most of the films shown were recent releases and were very popular, especially when operations, time or a lack of transport prevented us getting into Boston.

Operations continued relentlessly with a night op to the French town of Royan at the mouth of the River Garonne on the Bay of Biscay. The town was occupied by an enemy garrison that was holding out against De Gaulle's Free French Resistance fighters. We were told at the briefing that the only civilian occupants of the town were quislings and therefore legitimate targets.

We were back in PD317 and left East Kirkby at 01.30 on Friday morning. At Reading we turned south to fly over Normandy and then on to Royan. The raid was carried out in two waves an hour apart. We were in the second wave and could see the fires burning in the streets of the town long before we arrived. There was no compunction about bombing a town filled with military personnel and collaborators; that is what our ground troops had been doing for months and what the Free French Resistance had been doing for years.

Although the Luftwaffe did not trouble us, the defenders certainly made a fight of it, and for a small garrison, they put up a far more intense flak barrage than we had been told to expect. The sky seemed full of exploding shells, smoke and shrapnel. "Bombs gone", as our 4,000lb cookie and incendiaries slipped out into the night, and the aircraft rose, once more relieved to unload the weight.

Jerry banked the Lancaster away from the town and out over the waters of the Bay of Biscay. Sitting on the starboard side of the cockpit, I had good view of Royan. It seemed as though the whole town was burning. The flames reached up high into the night and even at our height I could see the orange glow reflecting on the water, dancing on the gentle swell as it rolled in off the Atlantic. It was nearly 04.00 as we set course for home. The aircraft was performing well; all the gauges read normal, the engines sounded sweet, the revolutions steady; the rhythm became hypnotic. Warm air from the port inner wafted up into the cockpit, I felt my eyes getting heavy and beginning to close. My head dropped with a jolt and woke me up; I looked at Jerry, his head firmly down on his chest. I knew he was fast asleep. This was my twenty-seventh mission; it was no wonder that we were all exhausted. I leaned across and punched his arm to wake him. He just looked at me and then put his thumb up. He would stay awake now.

As a bombing raid, the operation was highly successful, but as a mission, it was a disaster; there were 2,000 French civilians trapped in Royan, more than a third of whom were killed that night. Far from being occupied only by quislings and the enemy, most of the resident population had remained, even though, anticipating a raid, the German commander had earlier given them the opportunity to leave.

Bomber Command had not chosen Royan as a target; that decision had been made by SHAEF. Not for the first or last time, Air Chief Marshal Harris had been given a direct order to attack a specific target. The finer details of what led to this attack are open to some dispute by those involved, but it does appear that during the previous December there was a meeting in nearby Cognac involving some Free French officers, an American Air Force officer, a meal and a lot of brandy. The outcome seems to have been that, after having been told the only French citizens in Royan were collaborators, the American suggested bombing the German garrison there. The idea was passed to SHAEF, who gave the job to Bomber Command, no doubt confident that the RAF was more experienced in precision bombing than were the Americans. Thus the order was given to ACM Harris, and then passed down to the squadron crews.

At the eleventh hour and fifty-ninth minute, SHAEF lost confidence in the information it had been given about the lack of French civilians and called the raid off, but it was too late, our bombs were already falling. In the normal course of attacking a French target, we would have taken great care to avoid civilian casualties, sometimes at the cost of aircrew lives. We would not have plastered it as we did Royan; that is where the consequences of the Intelligence failure became so tragic. When the full scale of the disaster was reported back to SHAEF from the French Resistance in the field, the recriminations were far and wide. Bomber Command was completely and immediately exonerated. We had done what we had been ordered to do by a higher authority and we had done it well; there was no blame to be attached to us for that, either collectively or as individuals. We could not possibly have known that the civilians had remained in the town.

I am grateful to Martin Middlebrook and Chris Everitt for providing this insight into the raid, all of which was completely closed to us at the time. However, looking back, I am just so glad that on the squadron we did not know about it. Those of us who had been operational for some months were already racked with a conflict of conscience, an overload of experiences we can never forget and a weariness which transcended ordinary tiredness; I just don't know what effect this news might have had on me or the other crews on the raid.

It is difficult to convey just how draining operational flying was. The physical, emotional and psychological stress was immense. Combating the effects of disrupted and irregular sleeping and eating patterns was a constant drain. Regular practice, both in the air and in the Link Trainer, was essential but tiring. Then the operations themselves sapped emotional and physical strength. From the moment of entering the aircraft until leaving it, the risks were high. An engine failure or tyre burst on take-off or landing, a collision, equipment failure, fuel loss, bomb load explosion, bad weather or fog were usually fatal events. And then landing was never straightforward. Had the aircraft been damaged, was the undercarriage locked down, are there enemy intruders lurking? And that was without the strain of flying for hours over enemy territory being shot at. Nerves quickly became shredded. It is no wonder that aircrew drank, danced, and partied at every opportunity; we had a lot to blot out.

After the Royan raid, I had been debriefed, had breakfast and was in bed trying to sleep by 10.00. Later that afternoon I was called out for another raid; we were to have another go at the enemy troop and armour concentrations at Houffalize. Our own Lancaster was in for a major service and was not operational for this raid, so just after midnight we took off in ND338 J for Johnnie, and a little more than two hours later were over the Ardennes. Nearing Houffalize, the heavy flak started. The troops and armour were still squeezed into a bottleneck outside the town and presented a congested target which was heavily defended; it made for a hellishly hot reception at 10,000 feet on the receiving end of all that fire power.

In the same way that the German troops were concentrated on the ground, so the bomber stream was concentrated into the narrow air corridor above to ensure that all the bombs fell on the enemy and didn't creep out. The clear weather provided perfect conditions even at night, but with 131 Lancasters flying so close together, the risk of collision was extremely high. From the cockpit, I kept a sharp lookout for other aircraft, while Joe Baldwin, our wireless operator, was watching from the astrodome.

Even so, on our run-in our Lancaster suddenly bucked and kicked as we were caught in the backwash of the aircraft in front. I could faintly see the exhaust flares flicking back inside their covers but couldn't judge the distance, only that it must be very close. Then a shell exploded just above and in front of us, and for a few moments the other Lancaster was lit up. I throttled back a fraction and the turbulence eased.

The bombing run was very often the most nerve-racking part of the whole mission as Len brought us in on the TIs. Flying straight and level through dense flak in the illuminated target area was asking for trouble, but it was what we had to do to get the bombs on target and then take the photograph for the Intelligence chaps. Each time we did it, it became harder to do, not easier; we knew that our luck was not boundless and it had already served us well.

This night, the Mosquitoes had nailed the aiming point and the main force bombed with great accuracy, which alleviated much of the pressure on the hard-pressed American forces on the ground. The German counteroffensive through the Ardennes was spent.

Fog had again rolled in across Lincolnshire and we were diverted to Middleton St. George. It was a message that I greeted with great pleasure, as the aerodrome, which is now the Durham Tees Valley International Airport, was only about fifteen miles from Cockfield. We touched down at 05.50. After the debrief, Joe Baldwin complained of headaches and hearing difficulties, whereupon the MO declared him unfit to fly. Since the fog at East Kirkby prevented our return to base, I managed to get home for a few hours that evening and enjoy a small family celebration for my forthcoming birthday.

By 11.00 next morning the fog had lifted and so the remaining six of us left Joe behind and flew J for Johnnie back to base, only to find that we were on ops again that night. The service on our aircraft was now complete and G for George was back from the Maintenance Unit. Jerry reported to the squadron CO, W/C John Grindon, that we were an incomplete crew as we had left our wireless operator in the Middleton St. George Military Hospital. The CO knew that we had had a difficult few weeks and agreed to stand us down and let F/O George Billings and crew, who had just returned from leave, take our aircraft. Billings, though, was without a bomb aimer and so providing that Len would volunteer to fly the mission, the rest of us could have the night off. The target was Munich.

As I had done many times before, I joined the group of well-wishers at the head of the runway to wave the boys God speed on the mission. Len had gone off in PD317 at 16.45, one of the last to leave. Bill and I decided to have a night out in Boston, and whilst we were waiting for the bus to pick us up just before 18.00 we heard a Lancaster circling the aerodrome and coming in to land in the fading evening light. The engines didn't sound right to me and I knew that the aircraft was in some trouble. Then there was a huge explosion and a great cloud of black smoke slowly billowed up into the sky. The bus pulled up and we climbed in.
"Some poor sods have had it," remarked Bill in a matter of fact way as we dropped into our seats.

We had a good time in Boston but when we arrived back at the sergeants' mess later that evening, Jerry was waiting for us. Those poor sods were George Billings and his crew, including our bomb aimer, Len Knowles. Our aircraft was a write-off; two of the crew, F/Sgt Hobson and Sgt Holloway, had been killed, F/O Billings was seriously injured and had lost an arm. Len had been thrown fifty yards from the wreckage by the force of the explosion and, like the other three, the Australian F/Sgt Todd and Sgts Harris and Duncan, was alive but badly burned. We stood there stunned. We had come so very far as a crew, we had been through so much together, and now we had lost one. The seal of unity that bound the knot was broken.

Then the realisation began to sink in, that had it not been for Joe's illness, we would all have been in that crash. It was the day before my twentieth birthday and I might never have seen it. That night as I lay in bed, the vulnerability of my mortality weighed upon me more heavily than ever before.

It seemed that just after take-off at 16.45 there was a complete failure of the port inner engine. The crew realised that they could not continue to fly the mission on three and so headed out to sea where they dumped fuel and part of the bomb load to bring the aircraft weight below 55,000lb, the maximum for landing. Then, returning to East Kirkby, in the last moments of the final approach, the port outer engine also failed. The aircraft dropped, hit the runway, bounced, and as Billings opened the throttles to try to go round again, the wing dipped, struck the ground and PD317 cart-wheeled, burst into flames and exploded.

We were never sure, and never have been sure, that this crash was not caused by sabotage. It was something that we were often warned to guard against and was one of the reasons for carrying out NFTs before a mission. The aircraft had just been to the Maintenance Unit for a major overhaul and service and had been sent back to us in a completely unflyable condition. Although no-one else on the squadron had wanted her, PD317 had been a good aircraft to us, had served us well and we had great affection for her. We had completed thirteen missions in her, she had taken a fair amount of battle damage and had got us out of some tight scrapes, but now she was gone. We were angry at her loss and at the needless loss of life and injuries suffered by our friends.

Since the inception of No.630 Squadron six aircraft coded LE-G had been held on unit charge, the last of which had been PD317. All six had been lost in quick succession over an eight-month period. The code letter did indeed appear jinxed and that was why no-one else had wanted this aircraft when it was offered to us back in September. It seemed that without us to protect her, she had fallen victim to the jinx too. Whatever the reasons, it marked the end of this letter on the squadron when the CO refused to register the replacement aircraft as LE-G and the squadron flew the rest of the war without one.

I got up for breakfast the next morning, 8th January 1945, and hardly noticed that this was my twentieth birthday; I didn't feel like celebrating any more. We had news that Len was responding to his treatment and was slightly better, but his injuries had ended his operational flying days and he would be medically discharged from the RAF at some point. Which is indeed what happened and we didn't see him again until squadron reunions after the war. Jerry and Joe were both engaged to be married, but after the shock of Len's crash, their respective fiancées didn't want to wait until the boys were tour expired so decided to press on with plans for their wartime weddings. The two lads, who were both from London, were each other's best man, although sadly the other four of us didn't make either occasion.

Back on the base, it had stared snowing in the afternoon and slowly became heavier with the accumulations mounting up around the aerodrome. When we woke next morning, it was to a changed landscape. It had snowed all night and showed no sign of easing. Across the airfield it was impossible to discern any feature through the relentless cascade of white flakes that drifted, tumbled, and swirled silently to the earth, intent upon covering the brutality of our purpose with a blanket of virginal purity.

Louis Sullivan, often described as the 'father of skyscrapers', espoused the view that the first rule of modernist architecture is that form follows function, an idea whose origins lay two thousand years earlier with the Roman architect Marcus Vitruvius Pollio. The function of an aerodrome is to provide a flat, wide-open, uninterrupted space to enable aircraft to take-off and land, and that is the form it takes. An inevitable consequence of that form is that it makes an aerodrome a hostage to unfavourable weather, be it wind, rain, snow or ice. Overnight, the airfields of Lincolnshire and south Yorkshire were transformed into an Arctic landscape. With our runways several inches deep in snow, flying was brought to an abrupt halt. But this was war and this was an operational station, so East Kirkby's CO, Group Captain Bernard Casey, ordered everyone on the base to snow-clearing duties. With whatever equipment was available, from snowploughs to shovels, we set about the task of clearing the main runway.

In the evening, the camp cinema showed *The Desert Song*, which, given the weather outside, was an amusing choice, although the film was actually quite good. Next morning, John Grindon, our squadron CO, decided to parade all aircrew before we continued our snow-clearing duties. The Wing Commander complained about our lack of smartness and decided to take us on a route march through the snow around the peri-track. Halfway round we unexpectedly met up with No.57 Squadron approaching from the opposite direction, also on a route march for the same reason. The inevitability of what followed came as no surprise, for what else would some three hundred high-spirited young men do in such circumstances other than have an almighty and much enjoyed snowball fight! I rather suspect that the two squadron COs had hatched this little plan to excuse their crews from the Group Captain's order for snow-clearing duties.

The cold snowy weather continued for much of the week, and on Friday night the cinema showed Errol Flynn's *Uncertain Glory*. Saturday brought a break in the conditions and with it a return to operations.

With Len's loss, we were now a permanently incomplete crew and would finish our tour as such. Joe remained unfit to fly, which made us two down, so that night I flew with F/O McGuffis to Politz, just north of Stettin to attack the oil plant installations there. It was to be another long-duration raid at the limit of the Lancaster's range. The Met boys had predicted heavy cloud over Politz, which meant Wanganui bombing, aiming on the TIs above the cloud.

Fully kitted up, we clambered into the back of the truck to join the three other crews already there waiting to go out to their aircraft. At dispersal, McGuffis and I chatted to the ground crew corporal in charge for a few minutes and then, leaving the pilot to sign for NG123 LE-U, I went through my external checks. In the quiet before the engines started came the sounds of someone being violently sick at a nearby dispersal. The waiting out here was often a very difficult time, even for experienced crews. It was time in which to think about the horrors and dangers that were waiting for us out there. It was better to keep busy. Everyone preparing for ops was frightened; it was then that we had to draw deeply upon our courage to keep flying the missions. As each sortie came along, the odds mounted against a crew's survival. Greater was the courage that was demanded and the harder it became to find it; but we did, until we survived or perished. It was not unusual to see or hear people vomiting. We were all so damned young and none of us wanted to die.

The planned route to the target was over the North Sea to Sweden, down its west coast, then, to keep the defenders guessing, just before reaching Copenhagen we dog-legged south-east to cross the Baltic before turning in to Politz. Closing upon the Swedish coast, the thrill of seeing the pinpoints of light shining in the little fishing villages and then Gothenburg all lit up was just as great as the first time I had been there back in August.

Germany's synthetic oil plants were critical to its ability to continue with the war. Increasingly denied access to crude oil, without the synthetic substitute, its war machine would literally grind to a halt. Consequently, the plants were very heavily defended with searchlights and dozens of anti-aircraft guns. It was into this cauldron that we flew. When the Mosquito markers arrived ahead of the main force, they found that the visibility had greatly improved, and so the order came through for Paramatta, visual aiming.

Weaving between the shafts of searchlight beams, our Mosquitoes had clearly marked the plant for the main force of No.5 Group's 218 Lancasters. The whole area of the refinery quickly became a mass of different-coloured lights. White phosphorus flares glowed brilliantly as they floated down over the plant, then the marker leader dropped the red TIs for us to aim at on the command from the Master Bomber. In the light from the flares and the defenders' searchlight beams, I could see the first bombs falling from the lead aircraft. A few seconds later, blast followed blast on the ground in a gathering inferno as high explosives and volatile liquid mixed up a deadly cocktail. One after the other, oil storage tanks exploded, raising arms of angry flames high into the sky as if reaching up to try and pull us down. The sky had turned a deep orange glow, reflecting the mayhem on the ground. From outside the plant, the defenders continued to fire 88mm shells into the sky, which had become a heaving mass of aircraft, searchlights, and explosions.

With aircraft in front, behind, above, below and on both sides, we started our run on the target, which was clearly visible and lit up like a fairground. "Right, right, right. We've overshot; we'll need to go round again." And so we peeled off as soon as we could and with everybody watching in all directions, we found a gap and rejoined the stream. For a second time we endured the searchlights and the flak sent up to snare us. At any moment the bomb load might be hit; a scarecrow hanging in the sky, slowly drifting with the wind, would be all that remained of the aircraft and her gallant crew.

"Left, left, left, left. We've overshot." The bomb aimer's voice remained flat, steady, calm. There was nothing to do but go round again. Not for the first time could I feel sweat running down my back and into my eyes, the salt stinging them. I glanced at McGuffis. He lifted his goggles and pushed a gloved hand over his face; the tension in the man's body plain to see. As he brought the aircraft round and back into the bomber stream, I worked the throttles so that he could keep both hands on the column.

Steadily we came in for a third time. There were fewer aeroplanes over the target now; we were amongst the tail-enders. Shrapnel zinged and clattered off the cockpit, sides and wings. I held my breath waiting for the words we all longed to hear. "Bombs gone." At last. The relief in the aircraft was audible. With the picture taken, we turned away and headed back across the Baltic to the vertical searchlights and 'friendly' fighters of the Swedish air force.

Exhausted from more than eleven hours in the air and the strain of having to go over the target three times, it was an immense relief when we landed back at East Kirkby at 03.30 on Sunday morning. I thanked the young WAAF who had volunteered to stay up all night to serve us steaming hot tea and rum on our return, and never had I meant it more sincerely. I recognised her from one of the dances and promised to buy her a drink at the next one.

Whilst being debriefed, I looked over at the returns board; Taffy Thomas's aircraft was not yet back. Like me, he had been flying as a replacement engineer with another crew. I began to feel that familiar ache which accompanied the loss of another friend. Bill Burr had gone in November, then Vin Taylor just before Christmas, and now Taffy; three very good friends in six weeks. After the Politz raid, I increasingly felt that very soon it had to be my turn. I no longer believed that I could continue to defy the odds. I was so tired.

The report next day from the photo reconnaissance flight was that the whole oil factory was a shambles. Ops were on again that night, but the MO had stood me down for two days. Jerry was on the Battle Order with a fill-in FE and bomb aimer for a diversionary raid so I went out to the runway to wave them off. Being Sunday, there was a station dance on. The WAAF was there, so I fulfilled my promise and had several dances with her too. I'm glad that I went because I actually had a jolly good time. It was like that, living on adrenalin, everything was experienced in extremis; fear, fun, sadness, and pleasure rolling in one on the other.

I was woken up next morning by the sound of stereo snoring, but this time I didn't mind; the boys had returned safely from their raid and were sleeping soundly. I crept quietly out of the billet and went for breakfast feeling better than I had for some time. During the week, I managed several sessions on the Link Trainer and attended the Wingco's talk on Marking and Bombing Procedure. Regular training and practising our skills when not on ops were essential parts of what we did and helped to keep us efficient and alive.

Thursday brought good news for once. My friend Taffy was safe. His aircraft had crash-landed in Sweden and everyone had got out alive, although it transpired that the mid-upper had later died in hospital. For the time being, Taffy and the others would be interned, as was the duty of a neutral country. No-one knew when the war was going to end, but we all felt that it could not go on too much longer, and in due course the crew were returned to England.

We were due some leave and next afternoon left the camp to go to our various homes. Bill and I hitch-hiked to Grantham station where we caught the 18.10 train to Darlington, arriving there at 21.15. Bill stayed with the train going on to his home in Newcastle whilst I caught the Workmen's Bus to Bishop Auckland from where I walked home. Next night, before going to a dance, I went to the pictures to see *Wing and a Prayer*, the title having been inspired by the 1943 American No.1 hit by the Song Spinners, "Comin' in on a Wing and a Prayer", which was covered here in Britain by Anne Shelton.

The week quickly flitted by, helping out at scouts, cycling, dancing, cinema going and catching up on some much-needed sleep. My mother never asked me what it was like on operations; I don't think she wanted to think about it. I was no longer the fresh-faced teenager who had left home eighteen months earlier; I had aged, I looked and felt ten years older. Other people, though, would sometimes ask me. How could I possibly explain what it was really like to know that I had blown women and children to pieces, to have seen friends plunge to their deaths, trapped in burning aircraft, the utter exhaustion of it all, the fear of sitting on 12,000lb of high explosives while flying through a predictive flak barrage? How could I put that into words when I was still doing it? I would change the subject.

I returned to East Kirkby just as the weather closed in again. January ended with another snowstorm and we spent two days helping the ground crews keep the weight of snow off the aircraft. By 1st February, the snow had stopped and we had cleared the runways. Ops were on, the target, the railway yards at Siegen in North Rhine Westphalia. The wind was blowing hard across the aerodrome when we left East Kirkby, and Jerry had to work hard to hold the Lancaster straight as we raced down the runway. By the time we reached Siegen it had increased, causing many of the TIs to blow off the target. The defences were much heavier than we thought and the night-fighter controller had guessed our intentions correctly; he had his force waiting for us.

Before we had reached the railway yards, the searchlights ahead were sweeping the sky in their radar-controlled pattern, but the flak was light, which meant fighters. It had been some time since we had encountered such a heavy Nachtjager force and they didn't take long to make their presence felt. Out of the darkness not far ahead, a bright yellow gash rent the night apart. It quickly grew until the shape of an aircraft could be seen attached to it. By now the aeroplane was no longer flying but plunging earthwards in a spiralling final descent from which there could be no escape, either for it or the airmen inside. Those precious early seconds which might afford an opportunity to bail out had long gone; anyone still inside would be trapped by the G forces.

This was not like Hollywood; there would be no chance of crawling up the floor to reach the escape hatch and, in a dramatic last effort, slip out of the burning aircraft and float down to safety. Once the pilot had lost effective control of his stricken aircraft, the window of opportunity to escape quickly closed and the obstacles to a safe exit were many and varied. They included fire, smoke, loss of oxygen supply, injury, bits of equipment littering the fuselage floor, hatchway damage, the aircraft's angle and rate of descent, the desperate needs of other crew members, time, courage, fear and bad luck, to name but a few.

Our relief bomb aimer did a good job and guided Jerry in first time. Then as we turned away from the fires below, I saw another Lancaster going down, flames streaking from one of its engines. I told Jerry it was time to open the throttles and get away from here and head for home as quickly as possible. He needed no urging. The Intelligence reports later showed that the raid had not been particularly successful because of the wind and the decoy fires lit by the defenders, which had drawn some of the bombing away from the town and the yards.

The squadron put up nineteen aircraft for a raid on the railway yards and factories of Karlsruhe the next night. It was one of three towns that the Command attacked that night and was my second visit to this border town, although the reception was no friendlier than on the first occasion! When we arrived above what we thought were the railway yards, the cloud was so deep that even the Mosquitoes couldn't find a way through it to mark the target accurately. We bombed on the TIs from 15,000 feet on a pitch-dark moonless night. As usual, I kept a good lookout for aircraft above with their bomb doors open, which was all but impossible in that darkness, made worse by the fact that there was no reflected glow from the fires beneath. There weren't any fires because we had missed the targets.

I hated these conditions. Below me, I could see the pallid grey mantle of clouds faintly lit from beneath by the searchlights that played across its lower surface, turning the whole mass translucent and betraying each bomber that crossed. As we flew the treacherous route, the two aircraft in front of us succumbed in quick succession, possibly to fighter pilots working together. Fire streamed from the engines and wings as each one stumbled and fell away into oblivion, swallowed by the clouds. For a few moments, their burning glow could be seen as a pool of colour in the grey abyss beneath, before fading and disappearing, gone as if never existing.

The thick cloud was to prove a problem for all the night's targets. For our raid, it was so bad that it turned into a complete failure; all the bombs fell in open country, causing no damage to anything.

After a late breakfast, I wrote some letters, one home to my family, one to Lord Barnard, and one each to my friends Tom and Jack. We had kept in touch and wrote to each other regularly, but recently Tom's air-mail letters had stopped and I feared the worst. Nevertheless, I hoped otherwise, and since Jack had no news of his fate, I continued to write.

That evening, too tired to make the trip into Boston, Joe and I decided on the camp cinema, where we thoroughly enjoyed watching MGM's *Thousands Cheer*, starring Gene Kelly and Kathryn Grayson supported by a whole host of well-known names from Judy Garland and June Allyson to Lena Horne and Lucille Ball, from Red Skelton to Kay Kyser. The weekend was nicely rounded off with a really marvellous station dance on Sunday night.

In the morning I went out to our aircraft and found the petrol bowser crews filling the fuel tanks to capacity, which meant that another target deep into Germany was going to be on the map. Later, the weather closed in and the op was scrubbed, thank goodness.

The bad weather hung around for forty-eight hours before clearing and opening the way for operations to resume. We stood to attention as Wing Commander Grindon entered the briefing room and went to the still-covered wall map which concealed our destination.
"Thank you, gentlemen. Please sit down. You will be pleased to know that your target for tonight is the Dortmund-Ems Canal at Ladbergen."
"Not again," was the collective groan around the room.

The plan was to lay all delayed-action bombs to cause the maximum disruption to repairs. We took a second dickie with us, and it turned into quite a baptism of fire. Following the New Year's Day attack, the Wehrmacht had further strengthened its defences around the canal and we flew into a veritable cauldron of fire. The whole area was lit up like daytime by the dazzling white of searchlights and flares. The flak bursts seemed to literally fill the sky and were so heavy and concentrated that it prevented us hitting the canal. Almost all the bombs fell into fields beside the canal and would prove a much greater problem after the war.

The intense fire power of the 105mm flak guns defending the Ladbergen Aqueduct on the Dortmund-Ems Canal [photo: by kind permission of Malcolm Brooke – Bomber History]

The fire power coming up at us was as intense as anything I had experienced. Just as we banked away from the canal, the searchlights coned the Lancaster ahead and almost immediately, in a bright orange flash, its port wing was blown off, the propeller blades still turning as it tumbled away. A few moments later, a second aircraft seemed to be surrounded by shell bursts until, almost inevitably, the flames started to pour from the fuselage, streaking back along its length, turning it into a flying torch. Fourteen lives lost in just those few moments of absolute terror. I looked at the second dickie and could tell that he was badly shaken by what he had seen. I flicked my intercom on and told him that it was all right to be frightened, that we were all frightened, but it would be okay. I think I was trying to convince myself as much as him.

Doing a wide sweep, we left the canal with its weaving searchlights and still-firing ack-ack behind and headed for home. Then amongst all that mayhem, four or five large explosions occurred close to the canal in quick succession. They were bombs going off as some of the shorter delayed-action fuses had started to activate.

But we were not out of the woods yet as we still had to fly around the top of Happy Valley, the Ruhr, before we could think about reaching the relative safety of southern Holland. The darkness closed in around us and with it came the feeling of isolation, loneliness, exposure, that we were the only RAF aircraft in the sky and the whole Luftwaffe was looking for us. Far over to starboard, a small yellow ball appeared out of the darkness, dimmed, then grew and fell to earth, ending in a larger orange ball that glowed until I lost sight of it. Remote though it seemed, it told its own story; a crew whose luck had just run out. But it also told the rest of us that there were fighters about.

Against the inky darkness of the moonless sky, I hadn't seen another Lancaster that must have been flying close to our starboard side and a little below us. I could see it now, though. Flames licked out of its starboard outer engine and spread back across the wing. They must have activated the fire extinguishers because it died down a little before flaring up again. Then from the front escape hatch one, two, the tiny figures appeared, dropping down, tumbling over like pine needles. The off-white parachutes fluttered, billowed, blossomed to carry them safely back to earth, like dandelion seeds in the wind, to land God knows where.

I turned my gaze back to the Lancaster and watched as, almost in slow motion, it peeled away to starboard. I looked hard for other parachutes but saw none. The fire had spread all along the wing, the aircraft doomed. Before it hit the ground, it was lost to my gaze beneath our own wing. That could so easily have been us.

Had they not been flying just there alongside us, the fighter might have picked us out instead. It didn't do to dwell, but I would be more relieved than ever to reach East Kirkby tonight. And so it was.

Winter snow on the runway, most of which had to be cleared by hand

Kitted up ready for another mission: I'm 2nd from right

Chapter Fourteen

"Home is when the props stop spinning."
No.630 Squadron axiom

Inches above my head, the sudden whiplash crack of rending metal broke my concentration. I looked up just in time to see the top of the cockpit disappear into the darkness and felt the blast of freezing night air that rushed in from the front turret. Having just taken off and still gaining height, we were vulnerable to everything from engine failure and collision to marauding intruders. In that moment, I was sure we had been shot up. Jerry looked as startled as me but kept the aircraft climbing whilst I held onto the throttles. Urgently I looked around in the failing light of the evening sky where the other thirteen aircraft that the squadron had put up for this raid were steadily climbing with us. There was no indication of intruders.

Over the intercom, the two gunners bluntly asked what had just dropped off. The three other crew remained silent, seemingly unaware that anything untoward had happened. Simultaneously, the wind began to howl and swirl around the cockpit, quickly chilling Jerry and me. I now realised that the ditching escape hatch in the cockpit roof canopy had blown off and vanished into the gathering dusk. It would have already floated down to earth and landed in a field or garden, waiting to be claimed as a war trophy by some lucky schoolboy. Ground crews regularly used these escape hatches whilst refuelling or doing maintenance checks as a short cut from the cockpit area onto the wings, and whoever was last to use it had clearly not secured it properly.

Facing us now was a serious problem and an even bigger dilemma. Already en route to the target, the aircraft fully fuelled with an all-up weight of 67,000lb, of which 10,160lb was our bomb load, Jerry as captain had to decide whether to press on and complete the mission or return to base. Every part of what we did had elements of danger attached to it, including the moments of a fully laden take-off. Thus having got safely into the air, crews understandably hated to boomerang and take the risk of landing with bombs and a substantial fuel load on board unless it was absolutely necessary.

We had also taken our wakey-wakey pills, so there would be no sleep for any of us tonight even if we did elect to return. The problem with losing this hatch was that for the rest of the trip the freezing cold night air would drive in through the front turret, swirl around my legs and feet and Jerry's arms and hands before being sucked out through the canopy roof. In short, we would have to fly the aircraft whilst engulfed in a 100mph Arctic gale. Our target was the oil refinery at Rositz near Leipzig and so we could expect outside temperatures at this time of year to be as low as -30°C at our cruising height of 12,000 feet. In the pilot's seat, Jerry would be slightly less exposed than me, but we were both in for a very unpleasant and bitterly cold ten-hour flight if we pressed on.

Jerry called up the rest of the crew and shared our predicament with them; unsurprisingly, no-one wanted to boomerang and so we decided to press on. As we climbed to our cruising height, the air blowing through the cockpit became appreciably colder and then even more so as we passed over central Europe to Rositz. Despite the lambswool lining of my flying boots and several pairs of socks, my feet had long since lost all sensation. At first, the intense cold had made them feel wet, but before we had ventured very far over enemy territory, not only my feet but my legs as well had become so completely numb that I was having difficulty moving about in the tight confines of the cockpit area. It did cross my mind that this would not be a good time to have to bail out.

Characteristically, the refinery was heavily defended and, in the absence of any fighters, the flak barrage was intense. We successfully bombed the southern portion of the plant from 8,000 feet and got away quickly. The Command lost four aircraft on this raid, although I only saw one of them hit by the flak.

Not far away and off to port, surrounded by flashes of exploding shells, I saw the first yellow streaks of fire begin to flick out from the wing of the stricken aircraft. The flames subsided a little before suddenly bursting into a furious blaze. Seconds later, the Lancaster seemed to simply break up as the wing fell off and the whole jumbled mass tumbled earthwards in a shower of fire, sparks and exploding ammunition.

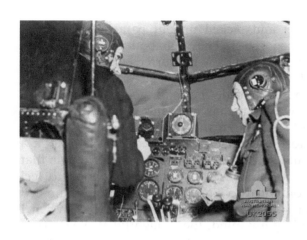

[Top] Pilot [left] and flight engineer. [Above] Flight engineer at work.
The escape hatch that went AWOL is just above our heads
[photographs: public domain – Crown & AWM]

After nearly ten hours in that freezing wind tunnel of a cockpit, we landed back at East Kirkby. I was so cold I could hardly move. I now understood the true meaning of the expression chilled to the bone; Jerry was no warmer. Even through five layers of gloves, his hands were so devoid of feeling it was a wonder that he had been able to land the aircraft at all and was a tribute to his flying skill. Barely able to hold the pen to sign the aircraft back to the ground crew, he had some choice words for the corporal in charge.

Jim Kenealy came over and picked up our parachutes to carry them to the waiting transport. He knew all about being cold. Our rear gunner sat for hours on end in his turret, a position which resembled a seat on the end of a telegraph pole, located as it was, to all intents and purposes, outside the main body of the aircraft. In the debrief room it was with shaking hands that I accepted the tot of rum and mug of steaming tea from the WAAF. I downed the navy-strength liquor in a single swallow, coughed and took a sip of tea. The hot liquid burned all the way down with a pain that was as luxurious as it was intense. It was just so good to feel something again. I continued to sip the hot tea through numbed lips, allowing the rising steam to slowly thaw my face. When I had finished, as if reading my mind, the thoughtful WAAF thrust a second mug of tea into my hands, but sadly there was no more rum.

The hot breakfast of bacon and fried egg with more tea made me feel much better, but my feet still remained numb. Time for some therapy; I found a Nissen hut with an empty bath, filled it with steaming hot water to a lot more than the regulation five inches, and lay in it until the feeling returned to my pedal extremities, as the incomparable Fats Waller had described feet. Notwithstanding that Jerry was also the senior officer on board, as the captain of the aircraft, the decision to continue or abort the mission had been his alone. However, since we had to share the icy wind, we had agreed it together, but we could never have known the implications our decision would have many years later.

By the afternoon, the aircraft of South African Lt GR Lacey had not returned from Rositz. Among his crew was F/O Robert Proudley from South Shields, whose father was a captain in the Merchant Navy. Although I didn't know him well, since we were both from the north-east we did tend to chat to one another. I will never know whether it was his Lancaster that I saw breaking up, but as I had watched it I had imagined the crew fighting to get out and the horrors of their last moments. It was one of many images which would haunt my dreams for years to come.

Saturday 17th brought the encouraging news that Len had been discharged from hospital. By Monday I had well and truly thawed out. The raid that night was on the Böhlen oil refinery, a well-defended installation located in a deep quarry. Scheduled for a late take-off, at 23.30 we set out in the dark, once more heading to south-east Germany, just south of Leipzig. The flak was heavy, there were barrage balloons up to 9,000 feet, and in the beam of the weaving searchlights I twice caught sight of an Me110 fighter. The raid was a complete failure. The Mosquito of Master Bomber Wing Commander EA Benjamin, DFC*, was hit by flak at the outset, which left the bomber stream coming in above the balloons at 9,200 feet without any detailed target direction, and only superficial damage was caused to the refinery. We would have to come back another time.

By contrast with Monday, take-off for ops on Wednesday was teatime. We were one of the first crews to our aircraft, which for that night was to be ME739 LE-F for Freddie. Out at dispersals, before the engines fired up, a quiet calm reigned for a short while. Above me, the darkening eastern night sky was winning the battle with the retreating day. The deep navy blue which soon would wrap its cloak of secrecy around us was stealing across the heavens, inexorably capturing the azure remnants of daylight. In the west, the vermillion sun slipped slowly beneath the rim whilst the fading rubescence that filled the distant horizon turned the land to purple. In the hedgerows around the airfield, the birds that had spent the day optimistically preparing for the approaching spring sensed another frost in the air. Settling down in whatever cover they could find, one by one they fell silent until only a last sentinel blackbird could be heard singing a valediction to the departing day.

The evening reminded me of so many like it that I had enjoyed at Cockfield. For those who survived tonight's operation, tomorrow held the promise of another lovely late-winter day. Would I see it? I wondered. I felt a pang of homesickness and frustration at a war that never seemed to end. Their cause was lost. Why didn't they just throw the towel in and have done with all this killing?

The spluttered firing of a distant Merlin engine jolted me back to the present; I had details to check, a job to be done. I climbed the short ladder into the Lancaster's fuselage and picked my way through the multitude of equipment that we carried, swung over the main spar and settled to my tasks in the cockpit.

247

Our target was the Mittelland Canal at Gravenhorst. No.5 Group had flown to attack it the night before but the Master Bomber had called off the raid as the canal area was completely covered in cloud. The squadron had sent eleven aircraft on that raid; tonight it was sending thirteen to be part of the overall force. The aiming point was to be the short Düker aqueduct which allowed the small river Hörsteler Aa to flow under the canal. From 10,000 feet it presented a minuscule target. When we arrived at Gravenhorst, we were greeted by only searchlights and very light flak.

At our bombing height, we were too high for the dreaded four-barrelled 20mm Flakvierling 38 which fired upwards of 800 rounds per minute, but we were within range of their 37mm Flakzwilling 43. However, the fire rate put up against us was not as great as we had previously experienced at the canals, and it may well be that previous concentrated bombing had overwhelmed the defences. This time we were successful. The aqueduct and canal were completely destroyed and remained out of use for the rest of the war. It was time to go home.

The brilliant moonlight that had helped us to destroy the aqueduct was now a perfidious companion which followed our progress as the spotlight follows an actor across the stage. Hunted from the dark ground below, we were silhouetted against the lighter sky. The bright cream light shone upon wings, glinted on Perspex, glowed on con trails. It wasn't long before the first aircraft fell victim, long tongues of yellow flames licking out from its engines as it plunged to earth for the last time. Within a few minutes, flames started to splutter from another aircraft, on our other side this time.

Jerry started to corkscrew as a precaution. The atmosphere in the aircraft became ever more tense. Joe sat transfixed to the cathode ray tube of his MONICA radar set, watching for the telltale blip of an enemy. Bill, secluded behind his curtain, pored over his maps, plotting, calculating, and refining our homeward course as best he could with the aircraft diving, turning and climbing in successive moves. With eyes that burned from strain behind our goggles, everyone else in the crew scoured the sky for signs of fighters.

We continued to corkscrew until nearly over the North Sea and the coast of East Anglia coming up. It was such a relief to end that relentless motion but to none more so than Jim Kenealy stuck out in the rear turret. As the Lancaster's nose dropped and turned to port, so the tail would rise up, tipping Jim onto his back with a view straight up to the stars. Then, when Jerry came to the bottom of the dive, pulled the nose up and banked to starboard, the tail would whip down and round, throwing Jim forward to gaze down at the earth with nothing but his harness and guns to hold him into his turret. Rear gunners suffered the most from the corkscrew, which often induced violent airsickness. It was not unknown for them to be simultaneously vomiting and firing at an attacking fighter. They were the unsung stalwarts of a crew.

Once more it was a huge relief to get safely back to East Kirkby. The fighters had made it one of our worst trips. Later in the day we heard that the No.83 Squadron Lancaster flown by Group Captain Anthony Evans-Evans, DFC, the CO of RAF Coningsby, had failed to return. Intelligence confirmed that it was one of thirteen aircraft lost on the raid. At forty-three, the Group Captain, whose younger brother had been killed four months earlier, was one of the oldest senior officers to be lost on operations. Amongst his crew was Scotsman Sqn Ldr William Wishart, DSO, DFC*, from Keith in Banffshire, who at twenty-two was one of the youngest squadron leaders to be killed.

Saturday brought another attack on the Dortmund-Ems Canal; once more the Ladbergen Aqueduct was the target and this time we were to have a go at it in daylight. We climbed to 18,000 feet and flew more or less in formation, but when we arrived over the canal it was covered by cloud. On the ground, though unable to see us, the defending gunners would have heard the circling bombers clearly enough, and they sent up a predictably formidable barrage of heavy flak. With no hole in the cloud through which to pinpoint the aqueduct, the raid was abandoned and all aircraft returned to their bases safely.

Not all the danger we faced came from the enemy. On 1st March, we were involved in a night flying high-level bombing and fighter affiliation exercise over Ruskington Fen. Little more than an hour after we had landed, there was a mid-air collision over the Fen between two Lancasters, one from No.57 and the other from No.207 Squadron, with the loss of all fourteen crew plus a ground maintenance crew airman in each aircraft. Flying was a very dangerous activity, even amongst friends.

Yours truly in the driving seat – it was essential that we could all do a bit of everything

A week after the previous attack came the inevitable return to the Dortmund-Ems Canal on what was the two thousandth night of the war. This would be the fifth time I had attacked Ladbergen, more than any other target during my tour, together with another two missions to the Gravenhorst canal. The squadron had been to the canals so often that when John Grindon unveiled it as the target at the briefing, he knew what was coming and waited patiently for the groans around the room to die down.

Ideally, the best results when attacking this target were achieved by dropping 14,000lb of explosives in three sections. This was done by flying down the direction of the canal and releasing a third of the bombs on the embankment at the start of the aqueduct, a third on the centre of the structure and the remainder on the embankment at the far end. It was much easier in theory than in practice. The enemy knew the wind strength, together with our direction of flight and height, and so put up a box barrage across our route. When we approached Ladbergen on that Saturday night, everything was waiting for us. There were fighters in the outer defences and both the 50mm and 105mm batteries seemed to be firing constantly. After our demolition of the Düker aqueduct, the defenders here were determined to save their charge from a similar fate.

The whole battle area was lit with sky flares, target-marker flares, exploding bombs and flak-shell bursts. The flak batteries concentrated their fire at the aircraft on their bombing runs whilst the fighters went for those on the way in or coming out at the other end. The closer we came to our run, the more the Lancaster bucked and shook; it was like riding a rollercoaster and dodgem at the same time. Then ahead, I saw the first aircraft go down, flames streaming from one of its engines. Within a few minutes, another one followed, the flames adding to the light which seemed to cover the whole area with a deep orange hue, including our condensation trails.

In all, I saw six of the seven Lancasters that were lost that night go down. It is an appalling sight to see aircraft that contain colleagues and friends being blown up or on fire and falling out of control before your very eyes. Perhaps it was a good job that I had so much to do in the cockpit and was kept busy, denying me too much time to think about it.

Away from the brightly lit target area, the darkness wrapped its welcome shawl of cover around us as we droned our way westward towards home, Jerry steadily weaving the aircraft from side to side.

One of the greatest worries we had when returning from ops was that enemy intruders would follow us back under the cover of darkness. Usually it was the twin-engine Ju88, which was a formidable fighter/bomber used extensively by the Luftwaffe as a night-attack aircraft. Although not in the same class as a Mosquito, it still had the speed, manoeuvrability and range to slip into the returning stream of Lancasters and Halifaxes. When the squadrons reached their home aerodromes they stacked in the circuit, and with navigation and runway lights now lit, the ground controllers needed to get the aircraft down as quickly as possible to minimise their exposure to intruders. Once an aircraft was into its final approach to the runway and no longer able to take evasive action, it became an easy target for an intruder.

Nearing East Kirkby on our return from Ladbergen, we received the radio message we had dreaded. Several aircraft had already been attacked in the circuit, and in all the Command lost another eight aircraft to intruders that night. There was a frantic effort to get our two squadrons' Lancasters safely down and the runway lights switched off. That done and the aerodrome once more plunged into complete darkness, we were debriefed. Then suddenly, without any warning, we heard the unmistakable sound of a German aircraft approaching, flying fast and low over the airfield. With its machine guns clattering, the Ju88 roared by and sent us all diving for whatever inadequate cover there was in the room. The sounds of splintering wood and shattering glass followed in its wake and then a series of explosions as it dropped 50lb-bombs.

The attack missed the building I was in, but not everyone was so lucky, with several personnel being wounded. Later we learned that six intruders had been brought down, including one that had crashed after hitting telephone wires and trees. There was perhaps an element of poetic justice in that event. At around 01.30 a JunkersJu88 piloted by Feldwebel Heinrich Conze of 7/NJG5 had attacked and shot down the No.460 Squadron Lancaster of F/O WB Warren and crew. Conze then saw a car on the Welton to Spridlington road near to RAF Scampton and dived upon the hapless vehicle and its single occupant as his gunners opened fire. The driver, Mr JP Kelway, an observer with the ROC, was killed. Flying lower for this attack than he might have realised, Conze struck the telephone wires and trees before ploughing into the ground. The Junkers completely broke up, killing all four crew and spreading debris over a wide area. The airmen are buried at the front on the right-hand side of the little village church in Scampton, which also has a neatly kept rose garden dedicated to John Hannah, VC.

A few minutes after Conze had crashed, at 01.51, Ju88G-6 D5+AX became the last enemy aircraft to crash on British soil during the war. In his attack on RAF Elvington, the pilot, Hauptman J Dreher, became confused by car headlights and hit a tree, killing himself and his crew of three. This intruder raid had been carefully planned by the Luftwaffe. Code-named Unternehmen Gisela, it involved around 190 Ju88s which infiltrated the bomber stream. It was, though, a costly operation as these were just two of around twenty-five intruder aircraft that were either shot down or crashed, some on their return.

Later on Sunday, the petrol bowsers were again at the aircraft for another full-tank trip deep into Germany or Poland, but the bad weather put a stop to it.

Monday 5th March 1945 turned out to be my last operational mission, although as I sat listening to the briefing for the raid that would give us another crack at the Böhlen synthetic oil refinery, I didn't know that; nor did I know that it would very nearly be my last of everything. Pilot Officer Duggan accompanied us as second dickie on his pre-operational raid to gain an idea of the sort of conditions he and his crew could expect.

Because of 10/10 cloud cover across most of Germany with a ceiling of 10,000 feet, the operating height for the 248 Lancasters on the raid was to be 12,000 feet. Our take-off time was 17.00 hours, but the ten Mosquitoes whose job it was to mark the target would leave their aerodromes much later and, flying at twice our speed, would catch us up nearer Böhlen. The late-afternoon light gave us the chance to be well on our way before darkness fell, and as we crossed the coastline of the continent, I was once more treated to that strange illusion of flying by both day and night at the same time. Below, the earth was dark and it was only the white threads of surf snaking along the Dunkirk beaches that betrayed the meeting of sea and land. Above me, the crepuscular sky still held on to the pastel shades of the fading day. We pressed on across Belgium and into Germany on a course that would take us to the south of the Ruhr, and as we did so, 2,000 feet below, the covering of cloud promised by the Met boys began to slip beneath us, veiling the dark earth.

Relentlessly, the bomber stream headed towards Böhlen, incorporating turning points in our game of cat and mouse with the German controllers, trying to conceal our destination for as long as possible. The rising moon lifted the cloak of pitch black to give a hint of light. It played tricks with the eyes as vague shapes of other aircraft emerged from the gloom then just faded away again, making judging their distance from each other, and more importantly from us, very difficult.

Suddenly, some way ahead and slightly above, there was a blinding flash. As the glare subsided, I could see the flaming mass split in two halves and fall away from each other burning fiercely. Then in quick succession, the bomb loads of the two doomed Lancasters exploded, sending a cascade of burning aircraft fragments tumbling to the earth. At the turning point, a crew had turned too soon and flown across the stream. Fourteen young lives wiped out.

"My God." The words were gasped more than spoken. It was P/O Duggan; I had forgotten all about him standing quietly at the back of the cockpit. I had no words of consolation for him; he would just have to get used to it.

Nearing Böhlen, the Master Bomber on the raid, Wing Commander Stubbs, had called in the Mosquitoes to mark the target and then instructed Wanganui bombing from Bandwagon, code for the bomber stream, on the green TIs that floated down into the clouds. Weaving shafts of white searchlights illuminated the clouds against which we would yet again be silhouetted, while the exploding flak shells created starbursts of violent orange and black to add to the colour palette. Far beneath us, successive explosions, one following upon another, were interspersed by larger ones whenever an oil tank was hit and blew up, sending towering plumes of livid orange-yellow flames and great billowing columns of thick black smoke skywards, filling the cockpit with an acrid smell. The coloured mist we had created spread through the clouds, mingling with the weaving searchlights and clothing our deeds in a warmth that belied their truth.

At the beginning of the raid the flak guns were silent as the fighters tried to pick off aircraft on their bombing run, but by the time we arrived, the defenders had changed tactics and we had to run the terrifying gauntlet of the flak barrage against which we had no defence but good luck. The smell in the cockpit of cordite mixed with burning oil was so overpowering that it seemed to foretell disaster. At last, our run over the target complete, bombs released and photograph taken, we climbed away, glad to leave the burning refinery behind shrouded beneath its glowing misty cloak.

The engines of ME739 beat with a reassuring rhythm; the gauges all read normal. Gently weaving, we sped through the sky like a returning homing pigeon. From above, Selene's three-quarter globe cast a silver-parchment mantle upon the strange formation of clouds that lay several thousand feet below. Bubbling folds of whipped cream churned and spilled one upon the other, stretching out on each side for as far as I could see. Hidden behind his navigator's curtain, Bill quietly plotted our course. Steadily, we flew on, finally passing over the edge of the cold front and leaving behind the wallowing clouds. A contented, vigilant calm had settled upon the aircraft and the eight young men that she held tightly in her bosom.

The searchlight flooded the cockpit with a blinding whiteness that was as startling in its intensity as it was unexpected. Even as Jerry began to dive and turn the aircraft, another two lights locked on; we were coned. The flak gunners poured shells into the air, intent upon bringing us crashing out of the sky. Every muscle in Jerry's body was stretched taut as he used all his strength on the controls of the Lancaster to twist and turn, dive and climb like never before. The aircraft trembled in the shock waves of exploding shells; the fuselage pinged, rattled and thudded at the cascade of shrapnel, much of which came straight through, and the wings groaned under the strain of the pilot's demands for ever more violent manoeuvres. For eight interminable minutes we battled on, wriggling this way and that in desperate moves to escape the web of light that held us trapped in its unrelenting grip and the intense hail of fire that was directed at us.

Whilst I worked the throttles, the aircraft rose, fell, banked and twisted like a leaf in a storm, but all to no avail. No matter what we did, there was no escape from the deadly grip of the lights. We had already taken too much shrapnel damage. We knew we had ridden our luck to the very end. At any moment, the final blow would fall, the fateful shell would burst upon us. Below, the ack-

ack gunners were determined that we should not escape, that we should be made to pay for our night's work at Böhlen. Already frustrated that we had evaded them for so long, they seemed to redouble their efforts. In the cockpit, Jerry and I instinctively knew that time had run out, that we had only one last chance, just one more card to play. It all came down to this: if it worked, we would escape; if it didn't, all eight of us would die in the next few moments.

I pushed the throttle levers forward and through the gate as Jerry dropped the Lancaster's nose and banked her hard to port for one last desperate dive. The engines drove the aircraft down towards the earth, quickly reaching 300mph. I kept the power on as ME739 spiralled through the hail of flak and cannon fire that was coming up towards us. We passed 360mph, knowing that at this speed the wings were very likely to be ripped off. I kept my hand hard on the throttles as down the blinding shaft of light we plunged. The engines screamed in protest, the airframe vibrated in sympathy, and the buildings rushed up towards us. If the lights held us now we would either hit the ground or be blown out of the sky. I don't think anyone drew breath in those moments. It was now or never. I eased the throttles back, Jerry pulled the Lancaster out of the dive and we flashed across the rooftops at an unimaginable speed. Then suddenly everything was dark again; we were out.

Even through his goggles, I could see that Duggan's eyes were staring wide. He was no different from the rest of us; we had all thought that we were going to die, but gradually we settled down again, and then Bill astounded us all by revealing that in the end our dive had reached an astonishing speed of over 400mph.

Our luck had held, after all; just. But we had taken a lot of battle damage and were in serious trouble. Home was still far away and reaching it had never been less certain. Jerry asked for an injury and damage report from each of the crew, and whilst no-one was seriously hurt, the aircraft had been hit several times by both 20mm cannon shells and shrapnel, and we had lost our oxygen supply, which now forced us to fly much lower than was wise across Germany. Tense minutes ticked by as we followed Bill's shortest and safest route out avoiding the Ruhr and seeking the sanctuary of friendly airspace.

To make matters even worse, we had come upon another blanket of cloud and, unable to climb above it, were forced to fly through it, which caused the Lancaster's wings to start icing up in the bitterly cold night air. We needed to get to France and find an RAF emergency landing ground with a long enough runway. In the turbulent air of the clouds, the icing added to Jerry's difficulties controlling the aircraft. We both realised that the aircraft had taken so much punishment that it would probably not stay in the air long enough to get us home and Jerry warned the crew to be prepared to bail out.

In all our missions, many of which had tested both men and Lancaster to the limits, we had never before contemplated abandoning our aircraft. We had had very little parachute training and had never actually jumped out of an aeroplane. If we were to go out tonight, it would be the first time for everyone. Each man in turn anxiously clipped on his parachute until only Jerry's remained in its holder. Unable to take his hands off the controls, I clipped his parachute on for him and then confirmed our position with Bill before checking the fuel levels. We had used more than I would have expected, although it was too soon to know whether we had a leak.

Cracking and clattering against the fuselage, lumps of ice began to break off from the wings and sail away into the night. Once sure that we were well inside French air space, we dropped below the cloud base to find a suitable aerodrome, but try as we may, there was no response to our calls. Left with no attractive alternative, we pressed on in the hope that we would reach England before our fuel ran out or the aircraft broke up.

In the liberated French villages and farms beneath us, slumbering citizens turned over in their beds, briefly disturbed by the thunderous roar above their rooftops of a passing solitary Lancaster. Then at last, the English Channel ahead lay. It was decision time. Without our oxygen supply, the journey had become increasingly tiring, but none of us wanted a forced landing in France and even less so one in the sea. I felt sure that we had enough fuel to get across the Channel providing nothing went wrong, and so on we flew, leaving the surf to pound upon the shores around Le Tréport.

We had left the clouds behind and flew under a flawless sky from which the dim light of a thousand stars reflected in the sparkling phosphorescent wave crests that toppled and jostled above the inky watery troughs of the sea a few hundred feet below us.

Twenty-five minutes later we crossed the English coast west of Hastings, flew between the High Weald and the South Downs, turned at Reading, just scraped over the Chilterns and headed for home. By the time we approached East Kirkby we had been in the air for almost ten and a half hours, and in reply to Joe's message, we were cleared for an emergency landing. The fire tender and ambulance at the side of the runway was a reassuring sight, although we didn't need their services, and an anxious ground crew had dutifully stayed out at dispersal to await our return. Even in the dark it was plain to see that the aircraft had suffered significant battle damage. However, the very fact that she had got us home and had survived that dive was a remarkable testimony to Roy Chadwick, the Lancaster's designer, and the women who had built her at the Woodford Avro factory.

Rarely had I been more pleased to see the smiling young WAAF holding out my mugs of steaming hot tea and rum, and rarely more pleased to be able to drink them. I gladly accepted her offering and thanked her. As I slumped into a waiting chair at the Intelligence Officer's table, utterly exhausted, I looked around at the faces of my crew and knew that they all felt the same. The whole trip had been a complete nightmare and a baptism of fire for young Duggan, but I also knew that he would cope with anything after that; and he did for he survived the war.

The report included details of being coned and our escape dive, which was met with equal astonishment by all who heard about it. After that, we shed our kit, devoured breakfast and turned in for some much-needed sleep. Later that day Jerry and I had to report to our Flight Commander, Sqn Ldr Chelenmere, DFC. Thinking that, like our second Königsberg trip, an explanation would be required of us, we were surprised when he told us that he and the CO had been considering our future and this last mission had made up their minds; we had done more than enough on the squadron and we had come to the end; we were being stood down, our tour was over.

The implications of Chelenmere's unexpected words began to break through to my conscious thought. A feeling of immense relief washed over me. Against a formidable enemy I had survived a total of thirty-seven missions, and now it was all over. No more staring into the abyss of Hell as ack-ack exploded around me. No more long hours waiting for the thudding vibration of cannon shells to rip into our aircraft, no more watching for flames to lick from the engines, no more contemplating the fleeting seconds between life and death. It was done. But unlike Bill Burr, Vin Taylor and so many more, I would after all, have a life to live.

But my relief was tainted with disappointment. Along with the engulfing fear, the shredded nerves, the loss of friends, and the self-doubts, had been the adrenalin-fuelled life, the operational atmosphere, the fun, the parties, the dances, and above all, the immense exhilaration of it all. The bonds of friendship in the face of death had been so strong, the wider camaraderie of the station so powerful, the relief of each return so intense, and the engagement upon the common purpose so worthwhile. Even as we stood in the spring sunshine chatting to Chelenmere, I already knew that the page had turned on a chapter of my life which would see no equal. Never again would I experience anything remotely like the last seven months.

Jerry gathered his crew and broke the news. It was received without fuss or outward emotion. We were all exhausted and, without Len, the anticlimax seemed even greater. We decided on a rather quiet and solemn celebration to mark the end of our tour, choosing to go to the NAAFI for a cup of tea and a wad. Inevitably, we indulged in a little reminiscing. One such reflection was that by a strange coincidence, the aircraft we had flown on our final mission, ME739 F for Freddie, the aircraft that had held together at over 400mph, was the very same one we had flown right at the beginning on that first occasion when Flight Lieutenant Walters had demonstrated how poor we were and had shown us what we needed to do to survive. We had come a long way and owed our lives to his blunt assessment of our performance that day.

Earlier in our tour, around the time we had completed twenty-something ops and were full of confidence, as a crew we had considered volunteering for one of the Pathfinder squadrons at Coningsby. Then it was rumoured that our CO and his crew were going to be posted to Woodhall Spa to take over command of the Dambusters squadron there, and we thought of applying to go with him to No.617. Losing Len from the crew had changed all that and we had to forget such possibilities. In the event, the CO didn't go to No.617 but was offered an even more attractive posting, that of the King's Royal Flight. For us, we had seen out the rest of the tour using any spare bod available as bomb aimer, but it wasn't the same any more. Deep down, we knew that the CO's decision to end our tour was the right one.

That evening I went to the pictures in Boston and then on to the Gliderdrome. With the weight of ops lifted from me, I had an absolutely wizard time, more than on any other occasion and I had had some bang-on evenings! I spent the next day clearing my stuff out, packing most of my kit and getting ready to leave. In the evening, I cycled out to the head of the runway to watch the boys leave for the raid on Harburg, from which they all thankfully returned. As the last aircraft climbed away into the evening sky, the group of well-wishers beside me drifted away. The deafening thunderous roar of the Merlins that had lifted each heavily laden Lancaster into the air slowly faded until a strange quiet spread over the aerodrome. From a hedgerow, a blackbird gave voice to his approval of the renewed stillness. Standing alone listening to his song, I thought of home and how much I would have missed had I been killed.

On Friday 9th March, having said goodbye to W/C Grindon, Sqn Ldr Chelenmere and our friends in other crews, we finally left East Kirkby on one of the crew buses which took us to Lincoln station. The six of us and our twelve kitbags stood round in a small group in front of the platforms; Bill, Jock and I were to travel north, Jerry, Joe and Jim, south. It seemed no time at all since we had first got together as a crew at Swinderby, and now it was all over. Reluctantly, we shook hands, said we would keep in touch, and parted, destined at first for three weeks' end-of-tour leave and then to our disparate instructors' postings. I managed to catch a little sleep on the train and arrived home that evening. I gratefully ate the supper my mother had cooked and then went for a walk through the village and along the dark lanes to breathe in the cool fresh air blowing off Cockfield Fell. It was good to be home again, and yet I was filled with a strange emptiness.

We had reached the end of our tour, but we missed Len

I was promoted to Warrant Officer a few days after this photo

Lancaster bomber at East Kirkby

Chapter Fifteen

" We saw young men put against the wall and shot, and they'd close the street and then open it and you could pass by again...Don't discount anything awful you hear or read about the Nazis. It's worse than you could ever imagine."

Audrey Hepburn [1929 - 1993] who lived in Arnhem from 1939 to 1945

Dresden, capital city of Saxony, 13th February 1945. During the war it was a military and communications centre. By this stage, the war was won but it was not over; Hitler would not surrender. British and American politicians were looking for ways to force the Nazi leadership to sue for peace. Drawing upon the experiences of operations Gomorrah and Hurricane, the Air Ministry had for some time been contemplating the effective timing of further intensive raids on German cities in order to bring about a total collapse of civil administration and so pushing the over-stretched military machine to seek an early end to the war.

Berlin, Leipzig, Chemnitz and Dresden, all of which lay just behind the Eastern Front, were each considered to be suitable and legitimate targets. They were significant and vital supply and communication centres for moving men and equipment up to the Front to repel the rapidly advancing Russians. The destruction of the buildings and infrastructure of these cities would greatly assist the Red Army advance whilst denying them to the retreating forces. Finally, all these cities were close to being overwhelmed by refugees fleeing the fighting in the east, and so the Air Ministry concluded that the impact upon civilian morale would be even greater.

During the conflict, the Nazis had reduced the Jewish population of Dresden from over six thousand to forty-one; almost all of those lost had been murdered one way or another. A further 1,100 men, women and children had been classed as Jews, just in case they were. Additionally, more than 1,300 people had been executed at the city's Münchner Platz, the courthouse. These included labour leaders, resistance fighters, so-called undesirables and anyone caught listening to foreign radio stations.

At the end of January, the Air Ministry issued Bomber Command with a directive ordering the raids to be undertaken in what was to be known as Operation Thunderclap. It was, as the Official History discloses, an operation that the Prime Minister had a direct hand in planning **[Vol. IV, pp 112-113]**. Just as SHAEF had ordered the attack on Royan, the Air Ministry now selected Dresden, Chemnitz and Leipzig as targets and directed ACM Harris to bomb them.

The possibility of the raids was discussed at the Yalta Conference in early February, when Stalin specifically asked Churchill and Roosevelt for them to take place soon to relieve the pressure on his troops. The Germans considered Dresden a 'safe' city and had moved much of their civil and military administration there together with armament production. Entrained American POWs shunted into a siding the night before the attack, later spoke of thousands of German troops and hundreds of tanks and artillery pieces passing along the railway through Dresden heading for the Russian Front.

At around 22.30 on the 13th,, the air-raid sirens of the city wailed their warning of the approaching RAF bombers, although few people took any notice at first because of earlier false alarms. As the bombs and incendiaries poured out of the sky, panic-stricken men, women and children ran for cover amongst the tumbling and burning buildings. The bombing was carried out in two waves and created an immense firestorm which sucked the air out of the old city centre. The following morning, 311 B-17s of the USAAF bombed the city again, particularly the railway yards, whilst its Mustang escort fighter pilots were ordered to strafe the streets.

For some four thousand prisoners, the raid came just in time; they had been busy digging an immense mass grave into which they were shortly to be marched and then shot. Much has been written about the Dresden raid, in particular about the scale of the death toll. It has always been difficult to accurately quantify this because no-one really knows how many refugees were in the city. At the time, the Nazis claimed the casualty figure was 200,000. Since the war, politically or ideologically motivated estimates have suggested it was in excess of 500,000. In 2010, after five years of research, the Dresden Historians' Commission made up of thirteen prominent German historians concluded that the total casualties numbered between 18,000 and 25,000.

Few people would argue that this was anything but an appalling loss of life, second only to Hamburg in the European theatre. Ultimately some ninety percent of the city centre was destroyed, but when nations engage in total war it tends to lead to total destruction. For the young men who sat in the RAF squadron briefing rooms of the various bases that Tuesday afternoon, there was nothing to suggest that this would be any different from any other large raid or that it would have the result it did. It was just another raid.

I didn't fly to Dresden that night as I was duty engineer, ready to advise other crews should they have any engineering problems. Another function I had was to join any crew whose FE was not able to fly. In the event, I was not needed to fill in and so rested in the briefing room until the crews returned, when I would be available to help at the debriefings.

Those who accuse Bomber Command of war crimes, usually people who have never risked their lives for anybody, should instead get down on their knees and thank God, because without us, they would not have the freedom to make such baseless accusations. I can certainly understand that those on the receiving end of our bombs might feel embittered, just as I did when the Luftwaffe bombed Coventry and our other cities and even more so when it was very nearly my own home. But I find it deeply offensive that anyone who was not involved, who was not old enough to be in the war, accuses Bomber Command of a war crime, especially so when they ignore the further death toll of the Eastern Front had Dresden not been bombed.

Winston Churchill, the great advocate of area bombing, whose War Cabinet and Air Ministry had adopted and introduced the policy in 1941, who had publicly stated his belief that only the bombers could deliver victory, quickly sought to distance himself from the Dresden raid when the public and the press became uneasy as details began to emerge. Others followed and left Harris and Bomber Command to carry the blame of what our political masters had ordered us to do. Shooting the messenger is always a futile gesture.

From Dunkirk to D-Day, RAF Bomber Command was the only major force able to consistently take the war to the enemy and particularly to the German people. Had it not done so, the war might well have been lost long before the Americans arrived in 1942, who, but for our bombing campaign, might well have focused entirely upon the Pacific and left Britain to its fate.

When war came in 1939 it was a struggle for survival and it involved everybody. We had soon learned at immense cost to our forces that this was not a conflict to be fought by the Marquess of Queensbury rules. Working clothes were as much a uniform as any other. Factories, mines and shipyards all helped to produce the tanks, the planes, the ships and subs, the bullets, the bombs, the guns and shells, whilst on the land, another army produced the milk we drank and the food we ate. Every side was the same. The Second World War was like no other for the very reason that every Home Front became a war zone and every house a battle area. That was part of Francesco Lana de Terzi's legacy to the world.

We were serving aircrew tasked with doing the job of saving the country from invasion and occupation. We did not have the luxury of a moral compass to be examined and contemplated whilst sitting in the comfort of an armchair in the free and democratic world won by the efforts of others. I would much rather have stayed in Cockfield than risk my life night and day, but had I and millions like me in the air, on the ground and at sea, not done so, the swastika would very soon have flown from Buckingham Palace and everywhere else in Britain; indeed Hitler had already earmarked the Palace for his personal residence. We are not, and never were, war criminals; we were just young men risking our lives to carry out our orders with no idea whether we would live to eat breakfast next morning, let alone what the wider geo-political and socio-economic implications of our actions would be many years into the future.

Chapter Sixteen

"Here during a period which is too long while it lasts and too short when it is over, we may placidly reflect on the busy world that lies behind and the tumult that is before us."
London to Pretoria – Winston S Churchill [1900]

Just before I left home at the end of my three weeks' end-of-tour leave I received notice that I had been promoted to Warrant Officer with effect from 27th March. I wasn't sure what awaited me, but my posting was to 16 OTU at RAF Upper Heyford in Oxfordshire, between Bicester and Banbury. This Doomsday Book village, then spelled Haiford, and later known as Heyford Warren before the adoption of the modern name about 200 years ago, was about a mile from the airfield. With its pretty stone-built houses, ancient parish church and the Barley Mow pub, the village was always a very pleasant place to escape to from the base. Further afield, Oxford and the surrounding countryside provided a pleasant change of scene from the flat fenlands of Lincolnshire.

The aerodrome had first been used by the Royal Flying Corps in 1916 and had remained a training station. It was from here that in 1938, three Vickers Wellesley monoplanes of the RAF's Long Range Development Flight piloted by Sqn Ldr R Kellet, Flt Lt AN Combe and Flt Lt HAV Hogan took off for Ismailia at the start of their world-record-breaking non-stop flight of 7,162 miles to Darwin, Australia.

As 16 OTU, together with its satellite at Barford St. John to the north-west, RAF Upper Heyford trained Mosquito crews, primarily for the Oboe bombing of Berlin. However, since Mosquitoes have a crew of two, a pilot and a navigator, and I was a flight engineer, I soon realised that I was surplus to requirements. For all that, I did manage a little flying in Oxfords and Mosquitoes during May and June, but most of my time was involved with crews' safety equipment. Albeit a very worthwhile function, after the excitement of the life of an operational squadron, I was bored to tears.

My friend Tom Marton, from whom I had not heard for some time, hailed from Oxford and his parents still lived in the city. Fearing that he might have been killed, which was why my last letters had gone unanswered, I had been reluctant to write to his parents and ask about him, but now that I was so close I felt compelled to visit and find out what had happened.

Whilst we were training at St. Athan, Tom had decided to become a flight engineer on Liberators, which at the time seemed a particularly good choice since he then completed his flying training in the Bahamas, where he joined an otherwise all-Australian crew. At the end of their training, they picked up a brand-new Liberator and flew it to North Africa where they joined an Australian bomber squadron, eventually moving to Foggia in Italy. We had kept in touch and wrote to each other regularly as we did to Jack, who, like me, was on Lancasters, but then suddenly Tom's letters had stopped.

The late April sunshine felt warm on my back as I turned the corner and walked down the quiet suburban avenue. The trees that stood sentry along each side wore their best spring green uniforms as if knowing that the war was almost over. Dappled afternoon sunlight shone lazily through the young leaves onto the neat gardens where rows of vegetables dominated, their owners still diligently digging for victory. With no ineluctable traffic noise to drown them out, the air was full of bird song welcoming the coming season. It was all in stark contrast to my inner turmoil.

Nearing the Martons' house, I saw one or two curtains twitch at neighbours' windows until finally I stood at the front door of the pleasant 1930s semi-detached house. My finger on the bell button, I hesitated. I needed to know; we had been good friends. I pushed the button and heard the faint ringing from somewhere inside.

Tom's mother answered the door; I would have known her anywhere as her son bore a striking resemblance to her. When I told her who I was, she smiled and invited me in. She knew all about me from Tom's letters home and so further explanations were not needed. While the kettle boiled and she made the tea, she chatted about the war and the RAF in a strangely inconsequential way without mentioning Tom. I carried the tray and followed Mrs Marton through to her comfortable but unpretentious sitting room. She poured the tea and asked me about my own tour. I side-stepped most of the questions and told her that I had finished it and was now rather kicking my heels at Upper Heyford, hence being able to call and see her. She gave a wan smile but said nothing; an uncomfortable silence filled the room.

I was struggling to find the words for the right question about Tom. Have you heard from him? is he all right? do you know why he stopped writing? was he shot down? is he a POW? They were all fraught with the likelihood of causing pain.

In the end, Tom's mother put me out of my agony. "I expect you would like to know what has happened to Thomas. Well, we are not very sure at the moment. He is alive and somewhere in Italy." Well, that was good news and I was about to say so when she lifted her hand to stop me. "You see, Edwin, so far as we can tell, he is in a military prison waiting a court martial."

I was dumbstruck. Whatever I had expected her to say, it certainly wasn't that. She went on to explain that Tom's crew and all the other Australians on the squadron had refused to carry out extra missions against a rail viaduct on a major German supply route between France and northern Italy. It appeared that this target had already cost the squadron numerous lives, which is what led to their decision. It sounded horrendous, their version of the Dortmund-Ems Canal which had cost us so dearly. The Australian crews had been sent home to face their court martial while Tom, as the only British airman involved, had been put into custody in Italy to await his fate. Whilst locked up, he was allowed only one letter home per month. His next month's letter would be to his girlfriend and so Mrs Marton was unable to give me any more information.

I felt very sorry for Tom because I knew only too well what he and the crews would have gone through before they got to the point of making that anguished decision, fully aware of the consequences. I had seen so many aircraft shot down, becoming blazing torches with no hope of escape for the men inside, and I understood. I never learned the full outcome as Tom and I didn't manage to renew contact after the war. I would imagine that the court martial found him guilty of LMF, stripped him of his rank, sentenced him to military custody and then imposed a dishonourable discharge. Few doctors understood the impact of repeated trauma and it would be many decades before PTSD was recognised as a medical condition. Jack had completed his tour on Lancasters and had then been posted to the flight engineer training base at St. Athan, which is where I met up with him on a few occasions when I was ferrying, but he knew no more about what happened to Tom than I did.

General Jodl signed the unconditional surrender of all German forces at 02.41 on Monday 7th May, to be effective at 00.01 on the 8th, but to save life, an immediate ceasefire was declared. In the habit of Empire bureaucracy, that morning the Home Office issued a circular instructing the nation how it could celebrate, but in typically British fashion the population acknowledged it with a 'V' sign, for victory of course, and then completely ignored it. After nearly six years of all-out war, where one way or another almost everyone had risked life and limb, we were not about to be told how to party by some stuffy civil servant.

Tuesday 8th May 1945. Victory in Europe Day. The public holiday found me, for part of it at least, in the Barley Mow. At 15.00, Churchill addressed the nation from the Cabinet Room in 10 Downing Street, the same room from which almost six years earlier Neville Chamberlain had broadcast his message to tell us that we were once more at war with Germany. There were celebrations everywhere, with bonfires, street parties and dancing. Perhaps, though, the most striking impact came with the darkness. The blackout had already been eased but it now ended and we enjoyed at least a little lighting in the streets once more. Then at 21.00, the King spoke to his people. There was no television, but the BBC Home Service presenter described the floodlights at Buckingham Palace and the two great searchlights over St. Paul's, creating an immense 'V' for victory image in the sky.

Whilst VE-Day was welcomed by all, not everyone was able to share the joy of the occasion. There were many families for whom it was a time of sad reflection and remembrance of loved ones lost. For others, the uncertainty surrounding the fate of POWs

270

remained, and nor was it the end of the war. In the Far East the Japanese remained undefeated and unwilling to contemplate surrender, determined to fight to the last man.

I was told that No.5 Group was to become the mainstay of the Very Long Range Bomber Force, better known as the Tiger Force, to be sent to the Pacific and based on Okinawa in readiness for the invasion of the Japanese mainland. I missed the excitement of an operational squadron and saw this as a solution. My old squadron was due for disbandment on 18th July, an early casualty of reducing bomber squadrons in what today is called the peace dividend. Consequently, I requested a posting to No.57 Squadron, which was one of those selected to go to the Far East. However, my application was turned down because I still had several months to go of my operational rest period.

A bicycle was an essential form of transport around any airfield

Possibly as a result of my request for the Tiger Force, a short time later I was posted to No.22 Maintenance Unit at Silloth in Cumberland, where newly manufactured Lancasters were being sent for tropicalisation in readiness for the Pacific conflict. I was to be involved in their test flying and then later I would be posted to a Tiger Force Squadron.

On 28th July the Americans gave the Japanese government an ultimatum to surrender. It was completely ignored, and so on 6th August an atomic bomb was exploded over Hiroshima and then three days later a second one over Nagasaki, the British observer to which was Group Captain Leonard Cheshire VC, DSO**,DFC. The Japanese surrendered shortly afterwards and the war was finally over.

There were more celebrations for VJ-Day, Victory over Japan Day, 15th August. But a general election had resulted in a change of government and the world had already moved on. The VE-Day scenes of wild excitement, street parties and universal dancing were not repeated in Britain to the same extent. Our troops in the Far East, our 'Forgotten Army', came home to a much subdued nation and for many young men, especially the POWs who returned in dribs and drabs over many months, there was no welcome, no bunting, no bands, no street parties, nothing; they were simply left to make their own way home from the railway stations.

Those who had been prisoners of the Japanese were in such an appalling physical condition that most were brought home by ship, the long way round via South Africa's Cape of Good Hope, with several stops along the route, including in Australia, in order to have the time and opportunity to begin to put some weight on and start the recovery process, physically at least, from their malnutrition and disease. Some of these men had not seen their wives and families for three or four years and had only been able to keep occasional contact with letters home. For some, their wife was no longer waiting, while for others she was but with a child who was not his. Others still were met by their loving, caring wife, but the daughter or son he had last seen as an infant when he was posted away was now a four- or five-year-old for whom their father was a complete stranger. Even more than their comrades from the

European theatre, immense psychological barriers and challenges lay ahead for these men with almost no support from a government that had a few years earlier been so keen to enlist their services.

The use of nuclear weapons against Japan has remained as controversial as the role of Bomber Command in Europe, but it was just as necessary. Buried in the Japanese psyche was the anathema of surrender, so much so that they intended to fight to the very last soldier for every little island, town and city on the way to the Imperial Palace, and tens of thousands of troops and civilians alike would have died in the process. That is what the atomic bombs avoided.

Even so, it took many years for all the groups of indoctrinated soldiers scattered amongst the myriad of Philippine islands to finally come to terms with their Emperor's acceptance of defeat. The last two soldiers of Emperor Hirohito's Imperial army were not found until 1974 and provide a perfect illustration of the Japanese mindset. Lieutenant Hiroo Onoda and Private Teruo Nakamura were living on different islands and after thirty years were still waging their private war in the belief that the Emperor could not have surrendered. Private Nakamura was finally arrested by the Indonesian army and flown back to his home in Taiwan.

When found, Lt Onoda, who had been born into an ancient Samurai warrior-class family, refused to surrender until ordered to do so by a wartime superior officer. Only when Major Yoshimi Taniguchi, his commanding officer from 1944 but by now a book seller, met him on 9th March 1974 at Lubang Island and formally relieved him of his command and his military orders did he finally relinquish his sword.

My posting to Silloth, located on the edge of the Lake District, was very acceptable. Knowing how beautiful the Cumberland countryside was (it would be designated a National Park on 9th May 1951), on the way there, I stopped off at my home for two days so that I could collect my bicycle and take it with me. Over the next six weeks I spent some very happy hours cycling down the coast, through the beautiful quiet country lanes and around some of the lakes. With so few cars on the roads, it was such a pleasure. One lovely sunny afternoon I rode into the pretty little village of

Gosforth, which, grouped around the small junction in the centre, had two inns and a hotel all facing one another; a most convivial arrangement.

Whilst at home and to save me lugging it all around, I left one of my kitbags and some of the extra flying kit that I wouldn't now need. At Silloth, I became one of the aircrew who, on 15th October founded No.5 Ferry Pool, transferring Lancasters, Halifaxes, Liberators, Stirlings, Yorks, and Douglas C47 Skytrains, known to us as the Dakota from the DC3 version, in an area from Yorkshire to the north of Scotland. Within six weeks, I was posted again, this time to Lichfield to form No.3 Ferry Pool on 30th November. After four months the Pool moved to RAF Polebrook and was classified as a lodger unit with all records and documents being held at No.41 Group Headquarters. Finally, after a further fourteen months, we moved to Henlow where the Pool was eventually disbanded on 10th September 1947.

Aircraft production had continued apace right up to the end of the war but now the government had to decide what to do with all these aircraft. Some of them were brand new whilst others were tired and scarred, but they were all scattered about the country at various RAF stations, many of which themselves were no longer needed and were being closed down. Together with a pilot, I would be taken by air taxi to a factory or aerodrome to pick up an aircraft. Once in the allocated aeroplane, the two of us were supposed to take off, carry out an air test, land, sign the paperwork, take off again and then fly to the delivery airfield. It all took too much time so instead we signed for the aircraft as we got into it and set off. We air tested it on the flight whilst carefully studying the pilots' and flight engineers' notes for that particular type, be it twin or four engine. We navigated by map reading and identifying the features on the ground such as canals, railways, coastlines, river estuaries, and major conurbations.

The work was exciting as well as exhausting, sometimes flying as many as twenty types to four different airfields in a single day. However, the four months that we spent at Lichfield over the winter of 1945/46 were memorable for the thick blankets of smog which spread out from Birmingham. It frustrated our rudimentary navigation but added to the excitement. Smog, which is not often experienced now, was one of the most dangerous weather conditions for flying because once sight of the ground is lost, disaster can quickly follow. For all that, it was still nothing like as dangerous as operations.

The world was changing quickly and already the jet age was upon us. The aircraft which had served us so well throughout the war were rapidly becoming outdated. Newer models or variants were kept operational until the new generation became available, others were mothballed, some were sold to the growing number of private airlines, but most were cannibalised and scrapped. Like the passing of steam engines twenty years later, few people were thinking about preservation. It was the job of the ferry pools to move these aircraft around the country to wherever they were needed or destined. Over the two years that I did ferrying work, I flew in at least eighteen different types of military aircraft and visited more than 120 aerodromes.

The first and foremost duty of any government is to defend the land and its people. After the First World War, the government reduced Britain's military capability in all its forms to such a critical level that, coupled with the Ten Year Rule, we were close to being unable to defend ourselves against the Nazis. In 1945, the country was bankrupt and the government started the process again; one which successive administrations have continued since, and now political expediency has once more compromised our defence capabilities.

I enjoyed flying and did not think that I would easily take to going back to the drawing office at Wilson's when I was demobbed, even if the opportunity existed. The great ocean liners had dominated international travel in the years between the wars, but now, with the advances in aeronautical engineering, flying was set to become the modern way to travel. There were plenty of aircraft available for the expanding air passenger and transport business coupled with an abundance of well-trained aircrew looking for work with these firms. One day in early May 1947 whilst still at RAF Polebrook, I was on Orderly Officer duties when I was called by tannoy to report to the guardroom, where I was introduced to a Dutch civilian, Mr Van de Dykes, who it transpired was a Director of Trans Airlines. He had escaped from the Nazis to the UK, served with the RAF and had made Wing Commander by the time he was demobbed.

No.3 Ferry Pool RAF Polebrook

Around the peri-track of Polebrook aerodrome were stored some transport Stirlings without camouflage colourings and with as little as eighty hours' flying time. Built by Short Brothers in Belfast and converted for transport duties, these were now surplus to the RAF requirements and could be bought for as little as £600 each. Liberators were also £600, although in contrast, the ubiquitous, tried, tested and ever-reliable Dakotas were £2,200 each. Van de Dykes' company was to buy several aircraft and he asked me if he could borrow a spray gun compressor unit to over-spray the RAF roundels and other military markings on one of the Stirling before he flew it back to Shorts to obtain a certificate of airworthiness. I ordered an erk (an AC2, the lowest rank in the RAF) to get him the compressor unit and whilst we waited, we chatted. I told him that I had flown as flight engineer on Stirlings for a few months and he offered me a job on my demob. I met up several times with the air and ground crews of this company, including doing a flying test with Captain Ellington, but having spent so much time ferrying, I didn't consider the job offer further.

My next flying job offer was on the Dakota. This was, and remains, one of the outstanding aircraft of the twentieth century, with many still flying today. The Dakota was the mainstay troop carrier and transport aircraft of the war. It served in every Allied theatre and even today, its swept-back wing profile is unmistakable. The company which offered me the job was Orient Airways based in Calcutta. It was to be a five-year contract and I was very tempted, but my parents reminded me that I had already been away from home for most of the last four years and another five would be too long. Very reluctantly, I turned the job down.

The outstanding ubiquitous Douglas DC-3 Dakota

One day in late August 1947 I was told to report to the CO, Sqn Ldr John Clayton. He told me that my demob date was overdue and that I should get cleared from RAF Henlow before being flown to RAF Burtonwood just outside Warrington. This was all rather sudden and I hadn't had the chance to go back home to collect the kit I had left there, which I explained to the CO. John was a keen fisherman and he agreed to sign off the kit in exchange for my heavy-duty aircrew thigh-length woollen socks, which he considered to be ideal fishing wear!

RAF Burtonwood was built in the run-up to the war, opened on 1st January 1940, and was occupied by No.37 Maintenance Unit. The station acted as a base for servicing, storage and modifying British aircraft. With the arrival of the Americans in 1942, it was transferred to the USAAF and quickly became the largest wartime airfield in Europe. It was from here that I was finally demobbed on 28th August.

A flying job that really did appeal to me came up at Lytham St Annes aerodrome, just south of Blackpool. Skytravel was based there and they flew Bristol Freighters for the Lancashire Air Company. Now freed from the RAF, I travelled to Lytham and made myself known. They told me that they were extremely busy, that I should go home, enjoy the rest of my demob leave for a month and then telephone them. I took the advice and whilst I rested on leave, the company went into liquidation; so that was that. I gradually settled in to life at home once more, although after my experiences on ops and all the flying I had done, I found it very difficult. Not least I started to have real difficulty sleeping at night as my subconscious began to replay some of my ops in a disjointed and irregular pattern. Nightmares of burning aircraft, fighters, searchlights, flak, and the faces of men I had known all haunted my dreams.

Hitching a ride

Meeting the Dakota head on!

279

Two more types that I flew in, the Lockheed Hudson [above] and the Avro Anson

Chapter Seventeen

"Hope! When I mourn with sympathising mind
The wrongs of fate, the woes of human-kind,
Thy blissful omens bid my spirit see
Thy boundless fields of raptures yet to be."
The Pleasures of Hope - Thomas Campbell [1799]

It was time to come to terms with finding a job that didn't involve flying, to consider my options and prospects. As an engineer with practical experience of aircraft, I was much better placed than many lads leaving the services and I started to scan the local papers for suitable jobs. The Labour government was concerned about rising unemployment in the north-east as thousands of men returned home. Women had undertaken almost every kind of job during the war and many who had enjoyed the independence and money which this work had given them were reluctant to go back to the kitchen sink. Those who were able to hung on to their jobs, which resulted in fewer vacancies for the returning men.

In a familiar tale, London and the south-east was the focus of most economic activity, and so in an effort to prevent a return to the devastating levels of pre-war unemployment, the government provided financial assistance, incentives and grants to firms which would relocate to the north. I had considered a couple of jobs but then I saw that Smart & Brown, an engineering company manufacturing machine tools, was moving to the area, attracted from the south by these grants. The company had just moved its R & D department into a former wartime munitions factory at Spennymoor, which was some fifteen miles away on the other side of Bishop Auckland, and was looking to develop electrical and domestic products. In applying for the job, I hoped that my part-served pre-war apprenticeship together with my RAF flight engineer experience would stand me in good stead. They did, and I was offered the post.

Even though it was straight through on the main road, travelling to and from Spennymoor by bus was very time-consuming, so I bought a motor cycle to make it easier and quicker. Not long after

I started, some work colleagues suggested that one weekend we meet up to go and enjoy the night life at the Rink, Spennymoor's dance hall, the area's most popular haunt of the younger generation. The bike helped with my social life, and the Rink, which played host to the celebrated Saturday night '10 'til 2' dance, now became a regular destination. The '10 'til 2' dance was the starting point of many romances; some would last a few weeks, others a lifetime, even if the Rink was not so lucky; it was demolished some years ago to make way for a car park.

It was at the '10 'til 2' that I met Enid. I had asked her for a dance and then another, and after that we just stayed together all night. She lived not far away in the small town of Ferryhill, about three miles from Spennymoor. We arranged to meet at the Rink the following Saturday. I did wonder all week whether she would turn up again, but she did. Enid was a year younger than me and had worked in the Women's Land Army on a farm at Ross-on-Wye during the war. By now I was twenty-three but had seen and experienced so much that I felt much older than my years. I think that was part of what attracted me to Enid; she had worked through the war and knew how tough it had been. We started to step out on a regular basis and our relationship developed.

Most Saturday nights we would go dancing at the '10 'til 2', and then on Sundays go to the pictures in Bishop Auckland or Ferryhill. In the better weather, if I had enough fuel, Enid would ride pillion and we would take a picnic up onto the moors and walk along the tracks through the heather.

All our early courting was restricted to the weekends out of necessity. Petrol was still rationed until 1950 and so after allowing for my fuel to and from work, there wasn't much spare to travel the twenty miles each way between Cockfield and Ferryhill. Then as now, public transport in the rural area was as sparse as hair on an apple. The buses from Bishop Auckland only ran every two hours and the last one back left Ferryhill at 21.00. When travelling to work had used all my petrol allowance, necessity prevailed and we would each catch the bus at weekends and meet in Bishop Auckland to go to the pictures or the Eden Theatre. In time, though, our thoughts turned to marriage. I met Enid's parents, sister and brothers and got on very well with them. However, our two families did not meet until the day of the wedding, which was not unusual then.

The country was still trying to get back on its feet after the war. Rationing continued and for a time was even stricter than it had been during the war years. There was very little of anything except a general determination to make the best of life. Our wedding was not a big affair and even though I was earning quite good money at Smart & Brown's, there wasn't any spare cash for all the trimmings that are splashed out on and seem so important to couples today. We married on Friday 3rd February 1951. It was a perishingly cold day with the wind coming off the North Sea, but we didn't mind, we are used to that in the north-east.

Enid, my lovely bride - Friday 3rd February 1951

We had found a house in Ross Terrace in the Broom area of Ferryhill and had been able to get a mortgage to buy it. We moved in on our wedding night, saving the honeymoon for the summer months in Torquay, although we did have the weekend at Runswick Bay, which lies between Whitby and Staithes in what is now part of the North York Moors National Park. Like its better-known neighbour to the south, Robin Hood's Bay, and many other such picturesque fishing villages along this coast, Runswick Bay nestles into the hillside around the harbour at the end of a roadway off the moors.

Our home needed quite a lot doing to it and so we spent most of our spare time renovating, decorating and working in the garden. We had very little furniture when we started our life together and none at all in the front room. Instead I used the room to strip my motorbike down in, service it and I even carried out a major overhaul of it in there. Garages were just starting to get going again but most people worked on their own bikes and cars to save money. Enid worked in a local drapery shop whilst I had by now moved to a firm at Aycliffe. The factory was about 10 miles away and located on an industrial estate in the former Royal Ordnance powder factory munitions building. Travelling to Aycliffe was much easier, and when the bike was off the road and spread out on the floor of the front room I could catch the bus to and from work.

We had very few holidays in the early years but we did manage one when Enid took me back to the Herefordshire farm where she had worked in the Women's Land Army. We had a wonderful and memorable time and they made us very welcome.

Our daughter Julie was born on 13th February 1957 and our son Stewart eighteen months later on 6th August 1958. Along the way we had acquired a sidecar for the motorbike, but after Stewart's arrival, I thought it better to have a car and so treated us to a brand-new green Ford Cortina. When the children were old enough, I exchanged the Cortina for an estate car and a ridge tent and we became seasoned travellers and campers in England, Scotland, Ireland, France, Italy and Switzerland. Around this time, we moved from Ross Terrace and bought a shop at Ferryhill Station. Enid ran the shop until we took over the general stores in Kelloe, which has remained our family home and where we also had a smallholding complete with our own pig. It was like turning the clock back to the Rose Cottage days of my childhood.

The shared life of marriage inevitably included my nightmares, which continued for many years. I would wake up at night shouting, sweat pouring from me, my heart pounding, having dreamed that our aircraft was being attacked by dozens of fighters as we corkscrewed through the searchlights, or that it was on fire and I was trapped or that everyone else had gone but I couldn't get my parachute on. I still saw the faces of the friends I had known and who had been killed, Bill Burr, Vin Taylor and the others. I was very lucky that Enid was so supportive. She knew something of what I was suffering because she was there beside me in the night, but she never pried, just calmed me down and helped me get back to sleep. The only way that I knew how to deal with this was to work hard, often seven days a week and to just get on with things, to make a future for my family. It was many years before the nightmares became occasional instead of regular.

After joining Smart & Brown, the following four years were interesting and reasonably satisfying as I gained more experience. However, in the way of these things, the early 1950s saw a downturn in the economy nationwide. Costs at Smart's were cut, belts were tightened and the R & D department became a casualty. It was a small staff and we were all offered other jobs within the wider company, but I decided that this was an opportunity to move on and broaden my experience elsewhere, so I took a chance and left.

It was then that I took the job at Aycliffe. Here I became involved in engineering tool-making design and production, working with four different companies during the next three years before joining Darcham Aero, where I stayed for the next twenty-four years. The main focus of the firm was on tool design, manufacture and management for the production of jet pipe insulation blankets and components for the new generation of jet aircraft such as the V bombers, the Comet, the F104 and the amazing TSR-2.

It would take too long to recite the history of this revolutionary strike and reconnaissance aircraft designed and built by BAC, the British Aircraft Corporation. Commissioned by Harold

Macmillan's Conservative government of the late 1950s, TSR-2 was capable of more than twice the speed of sound. It was an outstanding aircraft that set new standards which left the opposition, including the Americans, on the runway. Many obstacles lay in its path, including poor political judgement from successive governments, escalating costs, and inter-service wrangling. The project was cancelled by the Labour government under Harold Wilson on 6th April 1965 and announced that day by Jim Callaghan in his budget speech. As Sir Sydney Camm, the designer of the famous Hawker Hurricane, said of the TSR-2, "*All modern aircraft have four dimensions: span, length, height and politics. TSR-2 simply got the first three right.*" Of the handful made, there remains only one completed example, that of XR220 at the RAF Museum, Cosford, in Shropshire.

My work at Darcham Aero involved me in visits to Rolls Royce, the Bristol Aeroplane Company, and Avions at Charleroi in Belgium. Later, I was involved in a project to design and manufacture a production unit for stainless-steel and other alloy metal pipe fittings for the oil, chemical, nuclear and food processing industries. This plant was to be purchased by a branded stockist and supplier of stainless-steel pipe. It was a successful project with several hundred component parts being manufactured, but the original deal did not go ahead when Darcham decided that it was not sufficiently allied to its normal manufactured products.

However, those of us who had been working on it had great faith in the project and so six of us bought out the plant and transferred it eight miles away to Hartlepool. With a completely new company and factory unit on a new industrial estate, we went into production. I was appointed as the Production Director. Business was good, and since our most important customer was BNFL, we expanded into fabrications for it on another site two or three miles away, where production continued to grow. One project was to design, make and supply 120 flat-bottomed boats powered by hydro-jet thrust engines. These boats were designed to carry a payload of up to seventy passengers or about thirty cattle along the shallow African rivers where standard propeller propulsion engines would be impractical.

The Darcham Aero plant manufacturing jet engine insulation

Another project during the 1970s took me to Singapore, Malaya and many of the islands in the area, where a colleague and I spent a long time selling and installing a similar pipe fittings plant. There is probably nowhere on earth quite like Singapore, the Lion City, a place with a long and colourful history. Founded in 1300 by Sang Nila Utama, Prince of Srivijaya, the Kingdom of Singapura became a trading post for the area until the Portuguese burned it down in 1641. However, shortly after the defeat of the Spanish Armada in 1588, a group of London merchants had already begun to explore the trading potential of the East Indies and had laid the foundations of the Honourable East India Company, which at the height of its success and influence was the largest business in the world, accounting for more than half of global trade. Even in today's contentious global economy, no one company occupies such a position of power. To protect its assets, the East India was supported by its own private militia of some 260,000 men, which was twice the size of the British army at the time.

On 6th February 1819, by an agreed treaty with Sultan Hussein of Johor which afforded exclusive trading rights to the British, Sir Thomas Stamford Raffles established Singapore as a trading centre on behalf of the East India Company. Raffles had chosen the island of Singapura carefully. Its location off the tip of the Malayan peninsula, next to Sumatra and Java and on the sea route through the South China Sea, the Java Sea and into the Indian Ocean, was fundamental to its success. Over the next hundred years, two hospitals and ten schools were established. In 1845, the *Straits Times* newspaper, which still flourishes today, was founded, while on 1st April 1867 Singapore formally became a crown colony of the British Empire. Two years later, the opening of the Suez Canal significantly increased the already booming trade. Singapore continued to grow in importance both as a sea port and as a colonial centre of British influence in the Far East.

By the second half of the 19th century, the British Empire was the greatest the world had ever seen. It had largely been built on trade and thus the use of military power became an adjunct to protecting its commercial interests across the world as opposed to a means of conquest. Britain has unfortunately always been politically resistant towards National Service by its citizens; a policy which twice in twenty-five years very nearly cost us total defeat and subjugation by Germany. However, in the 19th century, British technological and industrial might allowed the government to police the Empire with a surprisingly small professional and well-trained army, whilst at sea, the Royal Navy was unchallenged. There was no air force until 1912. Certainly within other European empires, and Germany in particular, there was much jealousy of Britain's dominant world position, but it would not be seriously threatened until the 20th century, and in the meantime all the industrialised nations grew wealthier from the freedom and security to trade.

Europe became more settled after the Napoleonic Wars, creating peace, stability and wealth, albeit that much of the latter was made from the sweat and graft of populations whose housing, living and working conditions left much to be desired. In this climate of industrialisation, trade and entrepreneurship, wealth was no longer the sole preserve of the aristocracy, and although tourism was not yet an industry, those of the middle classes who could afford to began to travel for pleasure. Singapore had become a symbol of British Imperial power in the Far East and was an important destination of choice for European travellers.

The Armenian Sarkies brothers from Julfa saw the opportunity and on 1st December 1887, Singapore's most famous hotel opened its doors and proudly carried the name of the colony's founder; the Raffles Hotel legend was born. With a reputation for great luxury, the hotel quickly grew and by the end of the century the now-familiar late-Victorian Italianate-style building, the first in Singapore to be fully served by electricity, had replaced the original hotel and had become one of the colony's most recognisable landmarks.

In Edwardian society it was considered most improper for ladies to drink alcohol in public. Ladies staying at the hotel or attending a function there would sit in the rattan chairs at the tables of the veranda and Long Bar sipping fruit juices whilst their male companions enjoyed pink gins or whisky and sodas. In 1915, the Hainanese head barman at Raffles, Ngiam Tong Boon, sought to bring some equality and created a drink which has become synonymous with the hotel and remains one of the most famous cocktails worldwide, the Singapore Sling. Designed to appear no more innocuous than a pink fruit juice, it was served in a long glass with plenty of ice and garnished with fresh pineapple and a cherry. Needless to say, this innocent-looking drink, which broadly contains three parts gin, one part each of cherry brandy, Cointreau, and Bénédictine DOM, mixed with some grenadine syrup, fresh lime, pineapple juice, Angostura Bitters, ice and garnish, became an immediate favourite with the ladies and undoubtedly enlivened many an otherwise dull evening.

Among the great, the good and the aspiring who stayed at Raffles before the Second World War were writers such as Rudyard Kipling, Somerset Maugham, and Noel Coward. The enduring literary tradition of the hotel and its Writers' Bar are legacies of these and others who have stayed at Raffles, written there and woven it into their stories. As Pulitzer prize-winning novelist James Michener put it, "*To have been young and had a room at Raffles was life at its best.*"

In the more permissive atmosphere of the Roaring Twenties, with its focus on pleasure, a ballroom was created and quickly recognised as the finest in the East. Travelling as a tourist to Singapore and Malaya was increasingly popular and the elegant colonial surroundings of Raffles had become the preferred place to stay as well as the venue of formal and informal occasions; it was simply the finest hotel east of Suez.

One had to be affluent to stay at Raffles and it was the rich who were the first casualties of the Wall Street Crash in 1929, which brought about the worldwide depression of the 1930s. The hotel was not immune and the controlling company went into receivership, but like the phoenix, it wasn't long before the hotel rose from the financial ashes. However, worse trouble lay ahead for war was coming down the line. Following the fall of Singapore in February 1942, the Japanese occupied the hotel and renamed it *Syonan Ryokan*, Light of the South Inn, but after Japan's subsequent surrender in August 1945, Raffles emerged once again.

Having been used by the occupying forces as the HQ of the Imperial Army Transport and Supplies Section, it was a mere shadow of its once fine colonial elegance and status. At first the British used it as a transit camp for POWs waiting to return home. As that purpose concluded, the hotel was redecorated, repaired, and improved, slowly regaining something of its former glory. During the 1950s Ava Gardner and Elizabeth Taylor were amongst the many Hollywood personalities who stayed there, and in 1967, Raffles played host to the filming of *Pretty Polly* with Trevor Howard and Hayley Mills.

By the time I reached Singapore in the 1970s, change was in the air again with the town becoming an eclectic mix of the old and the new. In addition to Raffles Hotel, there were still many other impressive colonial buildings, such as the former St. Joseph's Institution, now the Singapore Art Museum, the Clifford Pier, and the smaller but no less fine Orchard Road Post Office.

Lying just one degree north of the equator in the heart of the tropics, Singapore has a climate to match. With very little temperature variation from day to day, almost no dawn or twilight and plenty of rainfall, especially during the monsoon periods, it is always hot and humid. It was the respite afforded by the shade of the palm and frangipani trees, the cool air, heavy with the scent of wild orchids, wafting from the ceiling fans and the temptation of a Singapore Sling that daily lured the pre-war residents and visitors alike to Raffles Hotel. And it was no less so for my colleague and I when, at the end of a tiring day, we would drive down Orchard Road to the hotel.

Stepping out of the bright sunshine and into the shade of the hotel, it took a few moments for our eyes to adjust, but as the cool of the Long Bar wrapped its arms around us, we ordered our Slings and collapsed into the comfort of the rattan chairs. We talked for a while about our day's work, what we had achieved, what remained to be done, and then sat back and soaked up the atmosphere of the place, as seductive as the Sling. The walls resonated with the smatterings of conversation that floated over the room just as they had for a hundred years; the strands of convivial trivialities, business machinations, local gossip, meaningless chatter, contractual anecdotes, domestic intrigues, social scandals, and family tribulations all intertwined like a bowl of spaghetti. I never tired of this ritual during my whole time in Singapore.

Orchard Road, which had been created as the main thoroughfare, had once rung to the clatter of rickshaws and the call of their riders but it now reverberated to the drone and roar of the motor car. Ever-higher anonymous skyscrapers jostled, overpowered, and in some cases replaced, the architectural grandeur of the colonial landmarks. Even the hotel, whose address is No.1 Beach Road, is no longer on the sea front. A land reclamation scheme started since Singapore's independence from Malaysia in 1965 has increased the land area of the sovereign city state by 23 percent.

Singapore has continued to grow and prosper into a global commerce, finance and transport hub. It ranks fifth globally and first in Asia on the United Nations' Human Development Index and has the third highest GDP [at purchasing power parity] per capita on the International Monetary Fund Index. Both organisations rank Singapore's education and health-care systems highly, an undoubted legacy of the vision of Stamford Raffles and others who at the outset focused on establishing schools and hospitals on the island.

By comparison, Britain is ranked sixteenth and twenty-fifth by the UNHDI and IMFI respectively. There is no surprise in that. Since the war, I have seen so many changes in Britain, many of which are not for the better; we seem to have lost our way in the world. At home, society has become overwhelmingly acquisitive, obsessed by a culture of so-called 'celebrities', too many of whom have little or no talent, are merely famous for being famous, and whose meaningful contribution to our society escapes me. In conjunction, education, be it academic or vocational, is no longer truly valued, whilst respect for figures of authority in any form has almost entirely evaporated. Discipline has been dispensed with in exchange for universal rights without responsibility.

Singapore was a marvellous place to work and do business when I was there and it remains so today. The main airport has just introduced a fully automated passenger check-in system where there is no human interaction. The Lion City is not perfect, of course; nowhere is. But for a sovereign state with no natural resources other than its people, it is an example to us of what can be achieved through education and a healthy, motivated workforce.

Julie had been stepping out with David Blake from the village for some time and they were to be married in our local historic church on 6th December 1980, but I was still working in Singapore at that time. However, I was not going to miss this for anything and managed to get back home a couple of weeks beforehand, much to my and everyone else's relief. It was another bitterly cold day and the church doors were kept closed during the ceremony, but when they were opened as Julie and David came back down the aisle, we were met by a dazzling winter wonderland. It had snowed heavily during the service and everywhere was white over. If nothing else it was very beautiful. Four years later, on St. Andrew's Day 1984, Julie gave birth to her twins, Stephanie and James.

As the 1980s dawned, the decline in the UK economy gathered pace and it once more slipped into the doldrums. British Steel was decimated, the mines were closing faster than they had opened, the car industry was a shambles; wherever one looked, the wheels seemed to have come off the four corners of our economy and the political system which was supposed to guide it. Instead of working together to combat foreign competition, there was open warfare between the government and the trade unions. No longer was there any pretence at cooperation for the greater good of the nation. Both sides adopted entrenched positions and had their own agendas, neither of which related to the people they were supposed to represent and serve but which impacted upon all our lives. The country was ridden with strife and discontent. Widespread civil unrest was no more than a heartbeat away.

Oil had become civilisation's most sought-after commodity. Renewed Middle East tensions and fighting brought a crisis in its supply and rationing was once more threatened. The salvation which broke the OPEC embargo came from an unexpected source: Nigeria. Oil flowed from the fields off Africa's west coast and produced not only great wealth for the country but, for a nation starting from such a low economic base, unimaginable opportunities. It now had the money to buy all the things that it needed for a balanced, vibrant economy. Power stations, electric cable and rod mills, cement factories, low-cost housing, pharmaceutical plants, LPG bottling plants, vehicle production and so many more were springing up whilst in Britain the focus was on closing down such industries as the government and the trade unions continued their private war.

Our company saw the opportunity that Nigeria offered and got involved in supplying many of the country's needs for its LPG plants, low-cost housing, and the cable and rod mills. For a while things went very well and our investment seemed to be paying off, but then, along with almost all the other companies trading in Nigeria at that time, we ran into an insurmountable problem that we had simply not encountered before or anticipated: systemic corruption. It is a disease which is endemic in so many of the world's emerging economies, and Nigeria was the worst of them all. Whilst we had to pay our suppliers, our own invoices remained unpaid, and coupled with the necessity to run a slush fund to pay officials to do their job, the company balances drained away.

Consequently, like others, we had to rely on expensive business loans to maintain a cash flow, but eventually the bank put a stop to it and the company that we had worked so hard to build over many years of careful management and innovative developments was forced into liquidation in 1986. It was a bitter moment for us all. I was more fortunate than some because the part of the group I was involved with was purchased by a Birmingham-based company manufacturing the same type of products and so we were able to complement their range along with our sales experience and output.

When I reached sixty-one, I decided that it might be nice to get up into the air again and so that spring I obtained my CAA Class D licence and took up micro-light flying. I bought a Medway Hybrid R twin-seat micro-light G-MX11, and flew it from various local farmers' fields. With nowhere to store my kite fully assembled, I had to keep it at home, which meant that when I wanted to fly, it had to be trailer mounted for transport and then rigged by two people at the take-off point. After the flight, it all had to be done again in reverse to return home. Nevertheless, it was great fun and gave me many hours of enjoyment as well as dozens of photographs of the countryside I over-flew.

On lovely sunny still days, summer and winter, I would cruise over the villages, fields and fells of the north-east. While the kite's engine chuttered above me and the countryside slipped away below, a great contentment satisfied my soul, for deep within me was a connection with my childhood. The micro-light fulfilled my dream born that July day in 1935 in my uncle's hayfield when I saw the biplane come over. Now I knew what that pilot had experienced. The wind blowing in my face, the thermals playing on the controls, the sheer exhilaration from the closeness of the air and the freedom of a bird; even flying in a Lancaster bomber had not been able to give me these sensations.

I stayed with the Birmingham firm until my 65th birthday, although my final day at work was actually the previous Friday. Like so many people, it was with mixed feelings that I walked away from work and entered the world of retirement. I had thoroughly enjoyed my working life, which had taken me far and wide and shown me many sights, but now there would be time for Enid and me to do all the things we had talked about. It was not to be. In February, Enid developed an unexpected health problem and died in April. It was not a good start to my retirement.

After Enid's death, life became rather more stressful and demanding. I sold my micro-light. Then about two years later, the Fishburn Aero Club was formed. The aerodrome is only about two miles from my home and I quickly joined; I am still a member today, visiting as often as I can. Failing eyesight forced me to give up driving around the time I turned ninety, but although I no longer have a car, I take a taxi to the club or else Julie and David take me whenever they can so that I can keep in touch with my friends there.

In the summer after I retired I began to develop an insidious health problem which traced back to my time on operations. St. Valentine's Day, which was also Ash Wednesday in 1945, had brought the night-time mission to Rositz when the ditching escape hatch on the top of the cockpit had been left loose by a careless ground crew fitter and had ripped off just after we left East Kirkby. As a result, not only did we have a miserable mission that night but now in later life it had come back to haunt both Jerry and me. Jerry had developed asthma and moved to the warmer climate of Spain. After a few years, his fingers gradually became numb and the hospital recommended that they should be amputated, together with both thumbs. In the end, he lost the top half-inch from each digit. In Jerry's case, it was the result of gripping the Lancaster column so tightly with frozen hands throughout the mission.

After my demob in 1947, I had realised that I could have trouble with my knees and feet later in life but was sure that keeping fit would help me to stave off any serious effects. When I was in the scouts I had enjoyed gymnastics and so I joined the North East Amateur Gymnastics Association. Additionally, every Friday night after work, I would go for a swim at the local baths before going home. I really enjoyed the gymnastics but unfortunately developed a cartilage problem in my left knee and, after some basic hospital treatment, had to give it up.

As I got older, and especially after my retirement, the condition of my 'undercarriage' continued to worsen, so much so that in 1998 my GP referred me to the local hospital where I was told that the cause of the problem was not my mission to Rositz after all. The diagnosis was confidently made as Reynaud's disease, for which I was given medication and an appointment to return in a month.

Five appointments later and with no sign of any improvement, the consultant had another go and decided that it must be Restless Leg Syndrome. More medication and another five appointments brought no hint of any change. At this point, the consultant ran out of ideas, gave up and discharged me with advice to revisit my GP, who would add to my already useless list of medication.

In early 2000, I was awarded a second war pension. The first had been for loss of hearing, known in the trade as Lancaster ear, a condition which affected some aircrew from long hours of exposure to the constant roar of the four great Merlin engines fitted to the Lancasters. This second pension was for the condition that my feet and legs were in, with a recommendation that I should see a vascular surgeon again. This turned out to be the shortest consultation ever. In the space of a few seconds, this consultant told me that I had the equivalent of Vibration White Finger Syndrome except it was in my legs and feet instead of my fingers, and no, my local hospital could not help me. Fifteen years later, North Tees Hospital, which is some twenty miles from Durham, diagnosed nerve damage and prescribed more tablets for me.

After the war I received four medals from the British government; the 1939-45 Star, the France Germany Star, the Defence Medal and the War Medal, often referred to as the Victory Medal. In 2016 I was appointed to the rank of *Chevalier* in the *Ordre national de la Légion d'honneur*, that is, a Knight of the French National Order of the Legion of Honour.

To this day, our own government has steadfastly refused to strike a medal exclusively for Bomber Command. Its failure to do so is not only an affront to the aircrew of the Command but also to the commitment, and on many occasions the great courage, of the ground crew men and women who served night and day throughout the war. Men often worked out in the open in appalling weather conditions to maintain our aircraft and at least two died from exposure whilst doing so at East Kirkby. WAAFs on all bomber stations fulfilled many roles and would often volunteer to wait up for returning aircrew and serve us tea and rum. They all ran the risk of death from intruder attacks on aerodromes, too many falling victim.

Despite having praised the Command so highly when the job lay ahead, Winston Churchill ignored us when the job lay behind us. The great advocate of area bombing, the authority behind overwhelming bomber production, didn't even mention us in his VE-Day speech, not worthy of his thanks on the day of deliverance. On 20th August 1940 he had addressed the House of Commons with a speech that everyone remembers, or at least that small part containing his memorable words, *"Never in the field of human conflict was so much owed by so many to so few."* Irrefutably and richly deserved though the praise for Fighter Command was, almost completely forgotten was the role of Bomber Command in the Battle of Britain.

The next sentence of the speech focused upon it, *"...but we must never forget that all the time, night after night, month after month our bomber squadrons travel far into Germany, find their targets in the dark by the highest navigational skill, aim their attacks, often under the heaviest of fire, often with serious loss, with deliberate, careful discrimination, and inflict shattering blows upon the whole of the technical and war making structure of the Nazi power. On no part of the Royal Air Force does the weight of the war fall more heavily than on the daylight bombers who will play an invaluable part in the case of invasion and whose unflinching zeal it has been necessary in the meanwhile on numerous occasions to restrain."*

Even allowing for his exaggeration on navigational skills, mission success and unflinching zeal, it reflects the tireless efforts of the Command which would continue to the very end of the war. Later, Churchill confidently stated, *"The Navy can lose us the war, but only the Air Force can win it. The fighters are our salvation, but the bombers alone provide the means of victory."* Yet when we had facilitated that victory, Churchill, the government, and a complicit public rejected us. The discrimination against the Command even extended to disqualifying crews who had flown operational missions against enemy invasion forces in and around the Channel ports from the Battle of Britain clasp. At best Bomber Command was damned by faint praise, at worst it was subjected to institutional character assassination.

We sustained the greatest percentage losses of any Allied force, and of the enemy only the Kriegsmarine Unterseeboote crews and the Luftwaffe fighter pilots shared our attrition rates. The army deservedly received four campaign medals. Bomber Command fought well over a thousand major battles during the war. It flew its first mission against Germany at 12.01 on 3rd September 1939 and its last on the night of 2nd/3rd May 1945. We got nothing. Harris, who had built up a good bomber force and was respected by his crews, was passed over too, and whilst he was eventually knighted, his contemporaries were granted peerages.

More than any other innovation, it was aviation which had changed the face of warfare. In addition to bombers and fighters, the RAF which Lord Trenchard had saved and nurtured now had flying boats to hunt for submarines, transport aircraft from which to launch airborne landings, and even specialist squadrons engaged in electronic jamming missions and clandestine operations. Of the latter, No.161 Squadron operated several types, including the Halifax and the versatile little Westland Lysander, which could slip into occupied Europe under the cover of darkness and land to drop off and pick up SOE agents such as Noor Inayat Khan and Eileen Nearne.

George Parker, whose brother Howard had been in the flooded cellar, had been a scout before the war, and at the outbreak had volunteered as a dispatch rider for the AFS. When the Home Guard was formed, he lied about his age and joined, was promoted to lance-corporal and then discharged when found to be still only sixteen. He joined the ATC, quickly becoming the first F/Sgt of No.481 Squadron at West Bromwich and, already an accomplished musician, when the squadron had a band, taught the buglers while Howard taught the drummers.

Although in a reserved occupation, George volunteered for aircrew, saying, "Any position will do, I just want to serve in the RAF." He trained as an air gunner and after several postings was selected for No.161 (Special Duties) Squadron based at RAF Tempsford in Bedfordshire as part of a Halifax crew. The job of these men was to fly unaccompanied covert missions over occupied France, there to drop agents, supplies, weapons, radios, messages and anything else that was needed, by parachute to the waiting resistance fighters.

Security around this squadron and its sister, No.138 was so tight that even the ground crews who serviced their aircraft didn't know the true purpose of the work. These were perilous missions which often involved low-level flying across the sea and then at little more than tree top height over the French countryside to avoid radar detection. Approaching the drop zone, the pilot would climb to the minimum altitude required for the parachutes to open, seek out the identification letters of the day flashed from a torch on the ground and then unload their cargo of supplies and agents with all haste. Amongst those who left Tempsford to parachute into France were Phyllis Latour, Nancy Wake, Violette Szabo, and Jacqueline Nearne, Eileen's elder sister.

The life expectancy of these crews was as short was that of the agents they dropped. For George Parker and his crew, the end came on the night of 10th/11th April 1944. Their Halifax V LK738 MA-T came under heavy fire from flak batteries and crashed in flames near the little village of St. Hilaire-sur-Rille, where the eight crew on board that night are buried. To her dying day, Lily Parker refused to accept that her son was dead. Howard had come back to her after she was told he had been killed, and she believed that George would do so too.

Although we grew up 200 miles apart, there was so much in George Parker's short life that reflected my own: scouting, Civil Defence, ATC, a reserved occupation, a burning desire to fly and serve in the RAF. There were many times when I didn't think that I would see my twentieth birthday. As a crew we were lucky, of that there is no doubt. More than anything, that is why we survived, but it could so easily have ended very differently.

The iniquity of our own government's decision not to honour Bomber Command has over time been compounded by the generosity of others. In recognition of my active service in Bomber Command, I received from other European governments various medals, including two from the Polish government in recognition of my five sorties over the Baltic Sea, the Netherlands Liberation Medal, the European Cross, which was a collective initiative following the formation of the European Economic Community, as the EU was then known, and which included Germany, a General Service Medal for active participation in the war, the

Normandy Association Medal for service with SHAEF and the invasion forces, and the unofficial Bomber Command Medal which was struck with the full support of Sir Arthur Harris, though not the British government.

My Warrant and medals

I have been very lucky. I have a wonderful loving, caring family who keep a watchful eye over me whilst I continue to enjoy life, a life which not all my friends managed to have. I came through the war physically unscathed. I could have been seriously injured as Len was, or shot down and taken prisoner. Seventy-six percent of Bomber Command aircrew ended their flying days prematurely. Between 3rd September 1939 and 8th May 1945 around 125,000 young men volunteered for Bomber Command aircrew: 55,573 didn't live to see peace return.

My family: L-R sitting, Julie [holding Tia], me, Stewart
L-R standing, James, David, Stephanie [holding Mucka]

Was it all worth it? When I look around, I sometimes wonder. Could we do it again if we had to? I hope so, although I rather doubt it. I did not go to war as a career choice, I went because I believed it was the right and patriotic thing to do when our way of life was under threat. Britain is very different now and I am not convinced that there is that same commonality of purpose within the population any more. There is no doubt that this country still produces some outstandingly fine young people from a variety of backgrounds, but unfortunately there seem too few who ask what they can do for their country and too many who ask what their country can do for them.

Chilling out with some friends at the Fishburn Aero Club